Sexual Minorities
and Politics

Sexual Minorities and Politics

An Introduction

Jason Pierceson

ROWMAN & LITTLEFIELD
Lanham • Boulder • New York • London

Published by Rowman & Littlefield
A wholly owned subsidiary of The Rowman & Littlefield Publishing Group, Inc.
4501 Forbes Boulevard, Suite 200, Lanham, Maryland 20706
www.rowman.com

Unit A, Whitacre Mews, 26-34 Stannary Street, London SE11 4AB

British Library Cataloguing in Publication Information Available

Library of Congress Cataloging-in-Publication Data

Pierceson, Jason, 1972–
Sexual minorities and politics : an introduction / Jason Pierceson.
    pages cm
Includes bibliographical references and index.
ISBN 978-1-4422-2768-2 (cloth : alk. paper) — ISBN 978-1-4422-2769-9
(pbk. : alk. paper) — ISBN 978-1-4422-2770-5 (electronic) 1. Gay rights movement—
United States—History. 2. Gay liberation movement—United States—History.
3. Sexual minorities—Political activity—United States—History. 4. Gay rights
movement—History. 5. Gay liberation movement—History. 6. Sexual minorities—
Political activity—History. I. Title.
HQ76.8.U5P54 2015
323.3'2640973—dc23   2015025498

Printed in the United States of America

For Dylan

Contents

Chapter 1

Introduction

What does politics look like for, until very recently, a thoroughly despised, and relatively small, minority? How do they begin to create political power and engage with political and legal systems with the goals of social transformation and policy change, particularly in the face of strong resistance in government and in society? These are the central questions of this book. The book explores the history of the LGBT rights movement, chronicles the building of political and legal movements and how political actors and institutions have dealt with the movement, examines philosophical debates within and about the movement, and assesses the current state of the politics and policies relating to sexual minorities. The book synthesizes scholarly work of political scientists, political theorists, and historians in an attempt to describe the politics of sexual and gender minorities in an accessible and useful manner, especially for students and interested citizens. The book is organized around significant subfields of political science: political history and development, political theory, American politics (public opinion, voting, and elections), comparative politics, public policy, and public law, or the study of courts and politics. Along with a distinct treatment of transgender politics, each approach is used to gain a fuller understanding of historical and contemporary politics of sexual and gender minorities.

While the book is mostly about the movement in the United States, attention is paid to global developments and issues. The book also examines the LGBT rights movement in comparison to other similar rights movements, such as the movements for racial equality and the women's movement. Part of the goal is to highlight the distinct features of the LGBT rights movement and its similarities to other movements. For instance, the LGBT rights movement developed later than other movements, and without some of the supporting elements of these movements, but it also adopted many of the techniques and approaches of other movements, such as grassroots mobilization, electoral strategies, and litigation. For instance, while religion and religious institutions were crucial to the advances of the African American civil rights movement (Indeed, the leader of the twentieth-century movement, Dr. Martin Luther King, Jr., was a Baptist minister.), religion, especially the way that mainstream religion has historically treated nonheterosexuality, has mostly been a constraining force on the political and legal advancement of sexual minorities. While religion was a similar constraint for the women's movement, the sheer number of women in society helped to propel that movement, while the much smaller number of sexual minorities has constrained the movement. In a democracy, numbers matter.

The political landscape for sexual minorities has been shaped significantly in the past several decades by the rise of the Religious Right as a potent force in U.S. politics. Particularly compared to democracies in Canada and Western Europe, religious conservatives impart significant, and disproportionate, clout on the system, particularly through a strong alignment with the Republican Party and committed activists. While estimates place this group between 20 and 30 percent of the U.S. population, their influence has been significant, although it may be waning.[1] While the mixing of religion and politics is nothing new, this particular relationship dates to the 1970s. This movement seeks to impart a particular, and often very selective, literal Christian Biblical interpretation on sexuality and gender roles. Indeed the movement emerged partially in opposition to the feminist movement of the 1960s and 1970s, in particular in opposition to reproductive rights and the failed Equal Rights Amendment (ERA). It also set its sights on the parallel lesbian and gay liberation/rights movement as sexual minorities made more claims in the political arena in the 1970s. While many religious denominations support rights for sexual minorities out of theological perspectives and interpretations that do not condemn but embrace LGBT individuals, the conservative religious mobilization has, to date, outweighed the more progressive religious movement.

More broadly, opposition to rights and equality for sexual and gender minorities reflects what political philosopher Martha Nussbaum calls the "politics of disgust." This politics is grounded in repulsion to some aspect of the human body, according to Nussbaum, and it has historically been targeted at racial minorities, women, and Jews. In contemporary politics, it is primarily directed at sexual and gender minorities. Its purpose is to degrade the object of repulsion, or, as she states, it is "a fundamental refusal of another person's humanity."[2] It is quite common for opponents of LGBT rights to cite false statistics about high rates of disease and death in the community and to reduce individuals in the community to sex acts, rather than recognizing their full humanity. During the debate on same-sex marriage in North Carolina in

2012, pastor Charles Worley of the Providence Road Baptist Church called for gays and lesbians to be put into an electrified pen where they would eventually all die.[3] The 2010 Texas Republican Party Platform declared: "We believe that the practice of homosexuality tears at the fabric of society, contributes to the breakdown of the family unit, and leads to the spread of dangerous, communicable diseases."[4] During the 2013 debate over marriage equality in Hawaii, citizen opponents gave hours of testimony, much of it repeating the same disgust-related testimony. As political scientist Gary Mucciaroni puts it, "Many people find displays of intimacy between two men and two women repellant. . . . The 'ick factor' reflects the taboo of gay sex, much of it fed by centuries of religious injunctions against sexual conduct between same-sex partners."[5]

Another unique aspect of politics of sexual minorities is the fact that sexual minority communities form in ways different from other marginalized groups. For sexual minorities, there is generally not the same level of early socialization and community identity formation. As political scientist Ken Sherrill has noted, "In the United States, as in most of the world, lesbians, gay men, and bisexuals are outnumbered and despised. Unlike most other potentially political groups, gay people are further disempowered by virtue of being born as if into a diaspora—probably randomly distributed about the population at birth." Most LGBT individuals are raised in heterosexual families, and as Sherrill also notes, sexual minorities "are unique by virtue of going through childhood socialization experience designed to make them the opposite of what they are."[6] From the start, they are defined in opposition to the family norm, to the extent that they recognize their sexual diversity. This can result in tremendous stress and alienation. At the very least, there is very little education about the politics and history of the family's identity, as there would be in, for instance, Jewish or African American families. While this dynamic is changing a bit as more out LGBT individuals and couples raise children (some of whom may be LBGT), historically sexual minorities have had to leave the family and find social and political communities that can become the basis for political awareness, action, and mobilization. More recently, the Internet and social media has lessened this effect, at least for some. As an example, one of the reasons for the relatively low levels of sexual minority mobilization in Latin America stems from the fact that young people live at home longer than in the United States. This has resulted in less formation of LGBT political identity, although this is changing in many Latin American countries.[7] It is also no surprise, then, that the politics of sexual minorities in the United States has largely occurred in urban areas, where LGBT individuals first formed social, then political, communities and where diversity is generally more valued and appreciated, or at least tolerated. Indeed, cities like New York, San Francisco, Los Angeles, Washington, D.C.,

Chicago, and Philadelphia, as well as progressive college towns, were the sites of early political activism by sexual minorities in the twentieth century. As the movement has matured, smaller cities and rural areas have been the sites of increased sexual minority politics, but the constraints here are still quite powerful. Interestingly, there is evidence that a more progressive and cosmopolitan family background can increase the formation of lesbian and gay identity in persons who exhibit same-sex attraction.[8]

In Focus: Coming Out

Creating identity for sexual and gender minorities often involves the coming out process, where individuals are said to come out of the closet. In the closet, individuals hide their true identity by "passing" as straight, cisgender, or not intersex. This often involves a lot of deception and physical and emotional stress, but it is seen as necessary out of the fear of rejection of family, friends, and colleagues, even violence. Life in the closet can be deeply alienating and isolating, with little support from family and friends. There is not the same socialization into identity issues and pride in identity as with other marginalized groups, such as racial and ethnic minorities. The decision to come out can be a long and complicated one, as individuals weigh the costs and benefits of doing so. Activist Harvey Milk defined coming out as a political act, as it forces others to think about LGBT people and their plight, especially in the context of a personal connection. According to some estimates, up to half of the LGBT community is still closeted, thus limiting the full potential of the movement. Even as the culture has become more welcoming for gender and sexual minorities, the possibility of rejection and violence remains real.

In addition to identity politics, morality politics affects the politics of sexual minorities. Both identity politics and morality politics are "new" forms of politics identified by political scientists. The primary behavioralist understanding of politics by political scientists is that of individuals rationally pursing their economic self-interest. Thus, in this understanding, politics is mostly about who gets what, and how much. They are not interested in what identity group they belong to, only how government policy will affect their financial situation. This type of politics promotes compromise, given that it is relatively easy to bargain for, and compromise on, tax rates, subsidies, regulations, etc. Morality politics, however, is grounded in values, not interests. This form of politics is more conflict-driven, highly visible, and less open to compromise. According to political scientist Christopher Z. Mooney, the form of politics involves "conflicts of first principle, technically simple policy, potential for high salience, and high levels of citizen participation."[9] Opponents of rights for sexual and gender minorities have effectively used citizen participation by utilizing the political institution of the citizen initiative and referendum. From overturning local antidiscrimination protections, to outlawing lesbian and gay teachers, to banning all forms of relationship equality, opponents have painted sexual minorities as immoral and/or as threats to children and civilization itself, and more recently to religious freedom, in their campaigns to enact anti-LGBT policies. Thus, morality politics, combined with popular policymaking, has been a potent element of opposition to rights and equality for sexual minorities. As political scientists Donald Haider-Markel and Kenneth Meier found, LGBT policies are more successful when enacted by elites, like legislators and judges. These elites can often shield the policies from excessive opposition. Direct democracy prevents this protection from elites, exposing policies to morality politics and unsupportive public opinion. They refer to this as "expanding the scope of the conflict."[10] This is true for other marginalized groups, as well. When minority rights are put to a popular vote, they almost always fail.[11] Put another way by political scientist Amy Stone, "The Religious Right is far more successful at the ballot box, where it can rely on voters' homophobia, than in the legislative or judicial arenas."[12]

Adding to this problem, until recently, the federal government was not an ally in combating local and state hostility to sexual minorities, as it was for other identity-based groups. There were no national civil rights laws and aggressive enforcement of these laws from the Justice Department. The federal courts have also been reluctant to provide leadership on the issue. To this day, sexual orientation discrimination is reviewed much less critically in federal jurisprudence than discrimination on the basis of race and sex/gender. Things appear to be changing on this front, especially the strong support for LGBT rights from the administration of President Barack Obama and recent changes in federal jurisprudence outlined in chapter 5. But for most of the history of the organized movement for LGBT rights, many powerful elements in the political system were constraining the movement, and the usual allies of marginalized groups were absent.

Thus, for most LGBT policies, states and localities have been the front lines of the movement for rights and equality to a degree generally unmatched in other countries. This reflects U.S. constitutional structure and political practice. States possess broad authority to legislate under what is traditionally referred to as the police power (the power to legislate to promote the health, safety, and morality of citizens), unless the national government is explicitly authorized by the Constitution to act. In areas of law and policy directly relevant to sexual minorities, states have traditionally exercised significant authority: criminal law, health and safety laws and regulations, family law and marriage, and educational policy. Thus, in the pages that follow, state and local governments loom large in the discussion. This strong element of federalism, or a strong policy role for state and local government, has provided both opportunities and constraints for sexual minorities. On the one hand, it has allowed for policy innovation in more progressive political and legal jurisdictions, but it has also empowered opponents in less progressive jurisdictions, including expanding the scope of the conflict by trumping a positive legislative or judicial enactment with a popular repeal of the LGBT-positive policy.

Party politics has also played a strong role in LGBT politics. Despite the fact that many individual Republicans at the state and federal levels have supported LGBT-supportive policies, the Republican Party has opposed, and continues to oppose, these policies, largely through its strong alliance with the Religious Right. Almost all policies have been enacted when Democrats controlled the levers of power (legislatures and executive branches).[13] In addition, policy momentum often stalls when Republicans gain control of all or part of the governing apparatus. This will change when we see Republican-controlled governments at the state and federal levels enact explicitly LGBT-supportive and protective policies, such as hate crime laws, antidiscrimination laws, marriage equality, etc. While the Democratic Party has been reluctant to embrace sexual minorities in the past, the party currently supports a range of policies and is generally more responsive to activists in the LGBT rights movement.

WHAT IS POLITICS?

Politics is potentially a broad concept. A more traditional view is that politics is that which deals directly with governmental policy and law—elections, lobbying, litigation, etc. Undergirding this traditional view is the distinction in liberal political philosophy between that which is public and that which is private. Politics is the realm of the public but not the private arena. Indeed, under classical liberalism, it is unjust for politics to intrude into the private sphere, the realm of personal choice—family, religion, property, etc. Implicit in this view is the notion that power only exists in the public sphere through government and that one of the purposes of politics is to keep this power out of the private realm.

However, feminist and postmodern critiques of liberalism have noted the power dynamics that exist in the private sphere and have largely rejected the public/private distinction. The feminist slogan from the 1960s, "the personal is political," reflects this approach, as does the postmodern philosopher Michel

Foucault's assertion that "power is everywhere." Nearly one hundred years before these statements were made, the philosopher John Stuart Mill noted the coercive power of social norms and mores in his famous essay, *On Liberty*. Mill argued that the constraint of social pressure was equally a threat to individual liberty as was governmental constraint through formal laws. These perspectives point to a broader conception of politics, one that pays attention to the power of social norms both as they are attached to law and policy and for their independent power to shame and coerce. For example, the gay rights activist Harvey Milk emphasized the importance of lesbians and gays coming out of the closet to their family and friends and living openly with their sexuality as a political act. It is harder to shame someone known as a friend or family member. Indeed, public opinion research shows that support for LGBT rights increases with a personal connection to a person who is out. This is called contact theory.[14] But coming out still is difficult for many, given continuing social stigma. Being out is also the first step to political activism and mobilization, and the persistence of the power of the closet continues to restrict political activism and mobilization. Even before this kind of political activity, however, politics can exist simply by defying the social conventions, often reflected in law and policy designed to restrict the liberty and equality of sexual minorities. For instance, before widespread political mobilization by sexual minorities starting in the 1970s, the creation of lesbian and gay social spaces, usually bars, was a political act. It was a way to exit from the social stigma of most social spheres, but even these attempts at "private" organizing were met with legal resistance, as locales created laws to prevent lesbian and gay bars from operating. Thus, merely creating a social space was a form of political resistance. Indeed, patrons of these establishments often challenged invasive policing of their spaces with litigation, riots, and other forms of resistance, culminating in the most famous of these events, the riot at the Stonewall Inn in New York in 1969.

This book attempts to distinguish politics from other cultural expression of cultural identity, such as music, film, and literature. Indeed, much of work in LGBT studies has been focused in the humanities. Systematic attention to politics has come more recently in the study of sexual minorities. Indeed, as the historian Marc Stein notes, political activism has often taken a back seat to cultural expression and activism in sexuality studies.[15] I agree with Stein that both forms of activism are important, but share his desire to focus more directly on political activism. While a broad definition of politics will be kept in mind, much of this book focuses on political and legal activity explicitly and directly intended to achieve changes in law and policy, with an understanding that the classical liberal line between public and private, and the traditional conception of power, is not sufficient to understand power in the context of sexual minorities.

TERMS AND CONCEPTS IN SEXUALITY STUDIES

A discussion of important terms and concepts relating to the politics of sexuality is necessary. The acronym LGBTQIA stands for distinct, yet connected, sexual and gender identities. But first it should be understood that sexuality or sexual orientation refers to one's sexual attractions. Gender identity refers to how one identifies oneself in terms of the cultural definition of masculinity and femininity. A lesbian (L) is a female who is primarily attracted to other females. A gay man (G) is a male who is primarily attracted to other males. A bisexual person (B) is someone who is attracted to both males and females. A transgender, or trans, person (T) is someone who possesses a gender identity not fully consistent with society's expectation of their biological sex. The term cisgender, the companion term to transgender, refers to a person whose gender identity and expression is consistent with their biological sex. Queer (Q) is a blanket term often used by individuals wishing to identify as someone who challenges conventional sexuality and/or gender-based norms. Someone who identifies as queer takes pride in an identity that challenges conventional norms and embraces a term that has historically been used as a derisive term. Intersex (I) refers to someone born with both male and female, or indeterminate, genitalia and reproductive organs. As a reflection of the power of the male/female binary in our culture, surgery has been used to "make" someone one sex or the other in these circumstances. Today, this is increasingly seen as interfering with the individual's personal integrity and right of self-determination. Asexual (A) is an identity of someone who does not exhibit a sexuality. The "A" also refers to "allies," non-LGBTQI individuals who are sympathetic to the cause of sexual minorities. For the most part, this book deals with the politics of LG and T. Most political activity has taken place around these identities. For instance, bisexuals have been slower and more reluctant to organize and politically and legally mobilize, partially because they are often critical of the distinct categories of sexuality that undergird the contemporary movement. Legally, bisexuality is potentially covered by protections for sexual orientation. Thus, many laws and policies protecting lesbians and gay men also protect bisexual persons. Related to bisexuality, pansexuality refers to physical attractions to all gender identities. The word "homosexual" is generally not used to describe individuals in contemporary discourse. It is more of a scientific term used in juxtaposition with the term heterosexual. It is preferable to use gay or lesbian rather than homosexual, for instance, "the lesbian and gay community" rather than "the homosexual community." This book uses the term "sexual minorities" often as synonymous with the LGBT community. Technically speaking, the term used should be "sexual and gender minorities," but the shorter term is often used for stylistic reasons.

Homophobia/biphobia/transphobia describes hostility toward, and bias against, lesbians, gay men, bisexuals, and transpersons. It is not a perfect term, as "phobia" usually refers to a fear. Someone can have bias toward sexual minorities without fearing them, or at least consciously knowing that they fear. The terms are more generally used to describe bias against groups based on sexual orientation and gender identity. These terms also connect to another term often used in sexuality studies, heteronormativity. Political scientist Cathy Cohen's definition of the term is useful: "By 'heteronormativity' I mean both those localized practices and centralized institutions that legitimize and privilege heterosexuality and heterosexual relationships as fundamental and 'natural' within society."[16] We might also call this heterosexism. It is a pervasive assumption in governmental and nongovernmental institutions, and among individuals, that heterosexuality is the only acceptable form of intimate relationships. It is coercive to the extent that social sanctions and governmental laws and policies are used to preserve the privileged status of heterosexuality. Part of the challenge for sexual minority politics is the struggle to undo the profound heterosexism in culture, religion, politics, and law that has accrued over centuries of Western history.

As we will see, much of the opposition to the LGBT rights movement stems from the destabilization of traditional gender norms. For instance, opposition to marriage equality often expresses confusion about who will perform the male and females roles in a marriage without a male or a female. One of the questions asked by the media of male same-sex couples in the 1970s was who does most of the household duties traditionally associated with women in a marriage. More recently, this has persisted in gendered notions of child rearing, and the notion that children need distinctly male and female role models, and that men and women bring vastly different skills and approaches to child rearing, and both sets of attributes are needed. Indeed, the state of Utah made exactly this argument in its defense of its prohibition, enacted in 2006, of same-sex marriage after the ban was struck down by a federal judge in 2013.[17] Members of the transgender community challenge entrenched gender norms most directly, and they face the highest levels of violence and discrimination in the LGBT community, as will be more fully explored in chapter 7. Thus, there can be no effective discussion of the politics of sexuality without understanding the politics of gender.

ESSENTIALISM VS. SOCIAL CONSTRUCTION

Sexuality can be quite fluid. Indeed, the lines between gay, straight, and bisexual are not always clear, and often they shift for individuals over time. At the same time, most individuals have a sexuality that remains fixed over time. For the purposes of trying to understand the politics of sexual minorities, this book assumes that there are modern, relatively fixed sexual identities on which people take political action, and upon which society imposes judgments and regulation for those sexualities disfavored by the majority, or a powerful group in society. As political scientist Charles Anthony Smith states, "While sexuality collectively seems to present itself along a scale, it seems for individuals to become fixed at some point along that scale."[18]

In sexuality studies, there is a debate about the fluid versus fixed element of sexuality. Queer theorists emphasize that sexuality is socially constructed, or created, by society. Under this view, sexuality and gender identity are the products of cultural forces (economic, religious, political, etc.) constructing what is socially acceptable for sexual practices and expressions of gender. Indeed, the notion of an identity based upon sexuality is a relatively recent phenomenon, having formed primarily by the late nineteenth century. While nonheterosexuality existed prior to this, sex acts were seen (and mostly condemned) by society, not fuller identities. And where alternative sexualities were socially accepted, they took very different cultural forms. For instance, in ancient Greece, men formed emotional and sexual bonds, but this was mostly expressed through a mentoring relationship between older and younger men. While these relationships were celebrated and honored in Athenian culture and philosophy, it was not acceptable for men of the same age to form a similar relationship, and men also had wives at home. Women were relegated to the domestic sphere, and male same-sex relationships were the product of the all-male political sphere of the ancient polis, or city-state.

Essentialist perspectives emphasize that there has always been a biological variety in human sexuality, and individuals have lived, or tried to live, lives based upon nonheterosexual sexual identities. Given societal opprobrium, this has usually taken place in private settings, thus contributing to a lack of historical evidence. However, historians have begun to uncover evidence of gay men and lesbians living as couples with same-sex partners before the creation of the modern "homosexual," or seeking same-sex intimacy For instance, Molly Houses were eighteenth-century British meeting houses for mostly gay men. Boston marriage is a term used to describe women who lived together, essentially as married couples, before the rise of the twentieth-century LGBT rights movement.

Scientific evidence also points in the essentialist direction. While all human traits and characteristics are a complex mix of biological and social forces, many scientific studies point to a genetic and/or biological component of sexual orientation. Human sexuality is very complex, but the argument that physical and emotional attractions are exclusively culturally constructed appears difficult to maintain given the emerging scientific evidence. While no "gay gene" is likely, sexuality appears to be connected to biology on some level. However, scientific inquiry into sexuality has often been influenced by cultural norms and biases. In the twentieth century in particular, this was a bias toward heterosexual monogamy. Science and scientists are obviously susceptible to viewing their work through their own cultural socialization and thus reinforcing the power of these cultural biases, especially through the power of scientific expertise.

This book takes a middle position on this debate. Sexual identity is a biologically/genetically influenced factor that may transcend culture, but its manifestations are often heavily shaped by culture. There likely have always been lesbians, gay men, bisexuals, pansexuals, etc. Some have recognized and acted upon this identity, but this has been culturally constrained and shaped, with some individuals choosing to challenge cultural norms. Others have been profoundly shaped by culture and have not recognized their sexuality as an identity. Conversely, cultural norms and practices have encouraged same-sex sexual behavior in people who are primarily attracted to the opposite sex, or have channeled more fluid desires into more culturally acceptable avenues. However, the particular shape of the politics of sexual minorities in the United States formed with late-nineteenth-century urbanization and the rise of lesbian and gay communities in cities and the cultural, political, and legal reaction to it. This is the framework of a sexuality of politics used by this book: sexual minorities claiming rights and equal treatment in liberal democratic settings through public and private institutions. Ultimately, the choice of intimate partners should be a human right, regardless of the motivation of the choice—biological, cultural, or political. While this approach to understanding politics is open to legitimate and important critiques (more fully explored later in the book), it is the way in which contemporary politics is mostly organized, at least in the United States and similar countries.

HOW LARGE IS THE SEXUAL MINORITY COMMUNITY?

A common perception is that 10 percent of the population is LGBT. This figure is derived from Kinsey's finding that 10 percent of men had sexual relationships with men for a significant part of their lives. Over time, activists have used the number to demonstrate that a significant portion of the population is composed of sexual minorities. Interestingly, a recent survey indicated that the public estimates the number to be 25 percent. In reality, the numbers are much lower. In fact, Kinsey found four percent of men to be exclusively gay during their lifetimes. Recent estimates from demographer Gary Gates indicate that 3.8 percent of the population identifies as LGBT, with more still closeted. The largest portion is lesbian, gay, and bisexual, with a smaller percentage being transgender. Of course, higher levels of social stigma for trans individuals could dampen that number. According to Gates, if we measure a five-year time horizon, about 37 percent of LGBT people are closeted, but the number goes as high as 70 percent if you measure lifetime sexual activity. If you include the more conservative closeted measure, the overall number is about 5.5 percent. Similar to the finding that sexual identity is influenced by the more progressive background of parents, higher levels of identification occur in more progressive and urban jurisdictions. According to a 2013 Gallup study (also by Gates and Frank Newport), the ten states/ jurisdictions with the highest rates of LGBT identification were Washington, D.C. (10 percent), Hawaii (5.1 percent), Vermont (4.9 percent), Oregon (4.9 percent), Maine (4.8 percent), Rhode Island (4.5 percent), Massachusetts (4.4 percent), South Dakota (4.4 percent), Nevada (4.2 percent), and California (4 percent). The ten with the lowest were: Iowa (2.8 percent), Alabama (2.8 percent), Pennsylvania (2.7 percent), Nebraska (2.7 percent), Idaho (2.7 percent), Utah (2.7 percent), Tennessee (2.6 percent), Montana (2.6 percent), Mississippi (2.5 percent), and North Dakota (1.7 percent).[19]

Why does this matter? Beyond an empirical interest, advocates have an interest in showing relatively high numbers of sexual minorities, while opponents of sexual equality often emphasize that the sexual minority is small and not worthy of consideration or protection. Of course, the relatively small number of Jewish Americans in the population (about 2 percent) does not prevent political and legal protections being in place. In other words, the numbers are themselves political. The size of a group is not necessarily as important as the type of marginalization and discrimination that they face. For example, women are technically a majority of the population, but discrimination on the basis of sex and gender persists and affects the social, political, and legal status of women.

CONCLUSION

The pages that follow will explore the history of the sexual minority rights movement, philosophical perspectives on minority rights and sexual diversity, the role of law as a friend and foe of sexual minorities, the social movements for LGBT rights and equality, sexual minorities in the electoral process, public policies relating to sexual minorities, the transgender rights movement, and the global movement for sexual and gender minorities. The themes identified in this chapter (the role of religion, the politics of disgust, heterosexism, identity formation and solidarity, federalism, morality politics, etc.) will be further explored to assist in the understanding of the unique politics of sexual and gender minorities.

KEY TERMS AND CONCEPTS

Behavioralism
Cisgender
Contact theory
Diaspora
Essentialism
Expanding the scope of the conflict
Federalism
Gender identity
Heteronormativity
Homophobia/biphobia/transphobia
Identity politics
Intersex

Kinsey scale
LGBT population size estimates
Morality politics
Party politics and LGBT rights
Politics of disgust
Queer
Religious Right
Sexual orientation—lesbian, gay,
    bisexual, pansexual, asexual
Social construction
Transgender

QUESTIONS FOR DISCUSSION

1. How and why have group identities formed around sexual and gender identity? Why might these identities be potentially unstable?
2. How does heteronormativity help to create the politics of sexual and gender minorities?
3. In the United States, why are states such important realms for sexual and gender minority politics?

NOTES

1. Cynthia Burack, *Sin, Sex, and Democracy: Antigay Rhetoric and the Christian Right* (Albany: State University of New York Press, 2008), 137.

2. Martha Nussbaum, *From Disgust to Humanity: Sexual Orientation & Constitutional Law* (New York: Oxford University Press, 2010), xiii.

3. Isolde Raftery and James Eng, "Standing Ovation Greets Pastor Charles Worley, Who Made Anti-Gay Statements," NBCnews.com, May 27, 2012, http://usnews.nbcnews.com/_news/2012/05/27/11908278-standing-ovation-greets-pastor-charles-worley-who-made-anti-gay-statements?lite.

4. "2010 State Republican Party Platform," http://static.texastribune.org/media/documents/FINAL_2010_STATE_REPUBLICAN_PARTY_PLATFORM.pdf.

5. Gary Mucciaroni, *Same-Sex, Different Politics: Successes & Failures in the Struggles Over Gay Rights* (Chicago: University of Chicago Press, 2008), 23.

6. Kenneth Sherrill, "The Political Power of Lesbians, Gays, and Bisexuals," *PS Political Science and Politics*, 29:3 (September 1996), 469–73: 469.

7. Javier Corrales and Mario Pecheny, "The Comparative Politics of Sexuality in Latin America," in *The Politics of Sexuality in Latin America: A Reader on Lesbian,*

Gay, Bisexual, and Transgender Rights, Javier Corrales and Mario Pecheny, eds. (Pittsburgh: University of Pittsburg Press, 2010), 1–30.

8. Patrick J. Egan, "Group Cohesion without Group Mobilization: The Case of Lesbians, Gays, and Bisexuals," *British Journal of Political Science*, 42:3 (July 2012), 597–616.

9. Christopher Z. Mooney, "The Decline of Federalism and the Rise of Morality-Policy Politics in the United States," *Publius*, 30:1 (Winter 2000), 171–88: 174.

10. Donald Haider-Markel and Kenneth Meier, "The Politics of Gay and Lesbian Rights: Expanding the Scope of the Conflict," *Journal of Politics*, 58:2 (1996), 332–49.

11. See Donald P. Haider-Markel, Alana Querze, and Kara Lindman, "Lose, Win, or Draw? A Reexamination of Direct Democracy and Minority Rights," *Political Research Quarterly*, 60:2 (2007), 304–14.

12. Amy Stone, *Gay Rights at the Ballot Box* (Minneapolis: University of Minnesota Press, 2012), xv.

13. Jami Taylor, et al., "Content and Complexity in Policy Reinvention and Diffusion: Gay and Transgender-Inclusive Laws against Discrimination," *State Politics & Policy Quarterly*, 12:1 (2013), 75–98; Donald Haider-Markel, "Shopping for Favorable Venues in the States: Institutional Influences on Legislative Outcomes of Same-Sex Marriage Bills," *The American Review of Politics*, 22 (2001), 27–53.

14. L. Marvin Overby and Jay Barth, "Contact, Community Context, and Public Attitudes toward Gay Men and Lesbians," *Polity*, 34 (2002), 433–56.

15. Marc Stein, *Rethinking the Gay and Lesbian Movement* (New York: Routledge, 2012), 10.

16. Cathy J. Cohen, "Punks, Bulldaggers, and Welfare Queens: The Radical Potential of Queer Politics?," in *Sexual Identities Queer Politics*, Mark Blasius, ed. (Princeton: Princeton University Press, 2001), 203.

17. Brooke Adams, "Procreation Argument Dropped in Stay Application," *The Salt Lake Tribune*, January 2, 2014, http://www.sltrib.com/sltrib/blogscrime-courts/57340626-71/marriage-state-sex-court.html.csp.

18. Charles Anthony Smith, "Gay, Straight, or Questioning? Sexuality and Political Science," *PS: Political Science and Politics*, 44:1 (January 2011), 35–38: 35.

19. Gary J. Gates, "LGBT Identity: A Demographer's Perspective," *Loyola of Los Angeles Law Review*, 45 (Spring 2012), 693–714; Gary J. Gates and Frank Newport, "LGBT Percentage Highest in D.C., Lowest in North Dakota," Gallup.com, February 15, 2013, http://www.gallup.com/poll/160517/lgbt-percentage-highest-lowest-north-dakota.aspx.

BIBLIOGRAPHY AND FURTHER READING

Simon LeVay, *Gay, Straight, and the Reason Why: The Science of Sexual Orientation* (New York: Oxford University Press, 2011).

Steven Seidman, *The Social Construction of Sexuality*, 2nd ed. (New York: Norton, 2013).

Chapter 2

The Emergence of a Movement for Sexual Minorities and Its Opposition in the United States

The history of the sexual minority political and legal movement in the United States begins, for the most part, in the 1950s. It was not until the end of the nineteenth century that any conception about a class of people defined by nonheterosexuality began to form, and much of the activity took place outside of the United States, especially in Germany. However, the frame of sexual minority rights as being part of liberal democratic framework with legal and political movements striving for equal rights and equal treatment is a more recent one in world history, but it is the frame that has informed the politics relating to sexuality for over a century. At the same time, this frame has been resisted by a dominant Western, largely Christian, tradition of exalting only heterosexuality as a social, political, and legal identity, and framing alternative sexualities as sinful and threatening. This chapter on the history of the movement is meant to provide a broad overview of the evolution of the movement, rather than a detailed history, as historical material is also covered in later chapters.

EARLY THEORIZING AND MOVEMENT FORMATION

Modern identity based upon sexual diversity only began to form in the late nineteenth century. The term "homosexual" appeared for the first time in print in the 1860s. Previously, same-sex sexual activity was seen as deviant sexual behavior—not part of a larger identity that included an intimate life. Any nonprocreative sex (oral sex, anal sex, sex with animals, etc.) was considered to be sodomy, and these acts were punished severely, often by death. Societal opprobrium against such conduct was so severe that it was nearly inconceivable that individuals would organize politically around sexual diversity. For instance, in the late 1700s, the English philosopher and legal reformer Jeremy Bentham wrote that intimate sexual acts between consenting adults of the same-sex ought to be decriminalized, but he kept the writings private and unpublished, concerned about damage to his reputation. Gay subcultures existed, but they were largely out of sight until the law punished individual members, serving as a warning to others. The trial and conviction of author Oscar Wilde was a prominent example of this in late-nineteenth-century England.

The situation shifted a bit in the mid-to-late-nineteenth century with artists and thinkers beginning to write about sexual variation in a more open manner. For instance, Walt Whitman wrote about erotic relationships in his Calamus poems, first published in 1860. Indeed, many late-nineteenth-century men, especially in Europe, with same-sex attraction looked to Whitman for inspiration and validation. England and Germany were the sites of the most writing, discussion, and activism. German Karl Ulrichs published essays in the 1860s arguing for a more enlightened view of homosexuality. He famously claimed that a third sex existed—the urning (a term derived from Greek mythology)—someone who exhibited the gender traits of the opposite sex, and that this was an innate aspect of the urning's sexual identity, developed but not innate. According to Ulrichs, the urning was not deviant. Of course, his gender essentialism is problematic, but Ulrichs' writings laid the foundation for decades of thought, as others tried to find a more morally or scientifically neutral way of understanding variety in sexual attraction that could lay the foundation for political change and legal reform. England also saw limited activity through the theorizing and advocacy of Edward Carpenter and Havelock Ellis. From their writings came the view of sexual inversion, or the notion that gay men were effeminate males and that lesbians were masculine females. This "inversion" was innate, according to this view. Again, we see strong gender essentialism, but the theory shaped the thinking of many in England and the United States in the early decades of the twentieth century. Indeed, many activists referred to themselves as "inverts."

Given that much of the early thinking about sexual diversity came from scientists, doctors, and psychiatrists and therapists, the study and discussion of sexual diversity was long-influenced by medicalization and the corresponding sense that nonheterosexual forms of sexual activity and expression were deviant and needed to be cured through medical treatments or therapy. Even the most enlightened thinkers on the topic, such as Sigmund Freud, generally viewed homosexuality and bisexuality as less ideal than heterosexuality, especially to the extent that their patients challenged conventional gender norms. This resulted in generations of sexual and gender minorities being subjected to dangerous and damaging therapies, such as electric shock therapy, chemical castration, frontal lobotomies, and forced institutionalization.

It also allowed political and cultural opponents of sexual diversity to use the authority of science and medicine to bolster their agendas of discrimination, marginalization, and violence.

In Focus: Sigmund Freud

Few figures had as much impact on the politics of sexual minorities in the twentieth century as Sigmund Freud, largely through a misinterpretation and misapplication of his theories about sexuality. In contrasts to the leading sexologists of the late-nineteenth and early-twentieth centuries, Freud rejected the idea that homosexuality was an inborn trait in a subset of the population. Rather, he argued that everyone was born bisexual but that heterosexuality was the end result of normal sexual maturation. He viewed persons with same-sex attraction as in a situation of arrested development—not fully formed heterosexuals. As he wrote to the mother of a gay son, "Homosexuality is assuredly no advantage, but it is nothing to be ashamed of, no vice, no degradation; it cannot be classified as an illness; we consider it to be a variation of the sexual function, produced by a certain arrest of sexual development. Many highly respectable individuals of ancient and modern times have been homosexuals, several of the greatest men among them."[1]

While he did not think that persons with same-sex attraction should be socially ostracized, his approach that left them as "less than" heterosexuals had the effect of, in the hands of psychotherapists following his teachings, entrenching the view that homosexuality was a mental illness to be treated. Eventually Freudian psychoanalysts took the view, as described by historian Nicholas Edsall: "The adult homosexual . . . was deeply troubled and functionally impaired."[2]

The first known attempt to create a sustained political movement for sexual minorities began in Germany in 1897, led by sex researcher and reformer Magnus Hirschfeld, with the creation of the Scientific Humanitarian Committee (WHK). The goal of the committee was to advocate tolerance of homosexuality in general and to repeal Germany's antisodomy law, Paragraph 175. According to historian Nicholas C. Edsall, "Hirschfeld lectured widely, and the WHK sponsored conferences and debates and distributed letters and copies of its petitions to priests and ministers, to newspapers, to local government officials, judges, and prosecutors, as well as to members of the Reichstag [the German national legislature] and the higher civil service."[3] Unfortunately, the campaign was not successful in repealing Paragraph 175. Hirschfeld's institute, and the reform movement along with it, was destroyed by the Nazis in 1937. Sexual minorities were victims of the Nazi concentration camps, under the authority of Paragraph 175. Their badge in the camps, a pink triangle (like the yellow Star of David for Jews), has become a symbol of the LGBT rights movement.

In the nineteenth and twentieth centuries, lesbians lived together in intimate relationships for long periods of time in what are commonly referred to as Boston marriages. Evidence exists for these relationships as early as the eighteenth century.[4] It was easier for these couples to hide the reality of their relationships, as lesbianism was not as threatening to society as male homosexuality. It was a bit less destabilizing to gender norms and roles. Men, too, lived as intimate couples, but this was often less visible. One of the more famous parties to a Boston marriage was the author of the poem-set-to-music, "America the Beautiful," Katherine Lee Bates. Bates lived for many years with her intimate partner, Katherine Comen, and both were professors at Wellesley College.[5]

While serving in Germany during World War 1, Henry Gerber, who was also born in Germany but emigrated to the United States, came into contact with the gay rights movement in Germany and was inspired to found an advocacy organization in the United States However, his Chicago-based Society for Human Rights (established in 1924 and was the first gay rights organization in the United States) never gained more than a handful of adherents, and soon came under the gaze of the antigay authorities when the wife of a member informed a social worker about the group, triggering a criminal inquiry. Ultimately, the case was dismissed, but the organization did not survive. The goals of the organization were quite limited—mostly convincing elites to remove criminal sanctions for homosexuality, just as the movement in Germany was centered around eliminating Paragraph 175. According to the organization's charter approved by the State of Illinois, its purpose was

> to promote and to protect the interest of people who by reason of mental and physical abnormalities are abused and hindered in the legal pursuit of happiness which is guaranteed them by the Declaration of Independence, and to combat the public prejudices against them by dissemination of facts according to modern science among intellectuals of mature age. The Society stands for law and order; it is in harmony with any and all general laws insofar as they protect the rights of others, and does in no manner recommend any acts in violation of present laws nor advocate any matter inimical to the public welfare.[6]

For Gerber, sexual minorities were "abnormal" individuals who needed to exercise "self-discipline," but he thought that criminalization was futile.[7] He thus internalized the largely negative view of the medical profession.

Given the overall climate of hostility, his minimal goals were appropriate, but even too demanding, for the time. Even though communities of lesbians and gay men had formed in cities by the early part of the twentieth century, the criminalization of sexual- and gender role variation was well established. But Gerber also harnessed the Declaration, and thereby attempted to tie the movement for legal reform for sexual minorities with fundamental values of the constitutional system. This, of course, was ahead of the times. The Supreme Court did not begin to constitutionally elevate sexual liberty until the 1960s, and then only for heterosexuals.

THE MATTACHINE SOCIETY AND
THE DAUGHTERS OF BILITIS

Two developments sparked the formation of the mid-twentieth-century lesbian and gay rights movement. First, the massive mobilization of men and women during World War II led to the creation of lesbian and gay social networks on an unprecedented scale. Through close living and working conditions, lesbians and gay men "found" each other. When the war was over, many of these individuals chose to stay in the port cities of Los Angeles, San Francisco, and New York, often the sites of their demobilization. In addition, the massive increase in federal jobs in Washington, D.C. during the New Deal and World War II led to many lesbians and gay men relocating to that city during the same period. These cities were the sites for some of the most fully developed political movements. As historian John D'Emilio describes it, World War II "created something of a national coming out experience."[8]

Second, Alfred Kinsey published *Sexual Behavior in the Human Male* in 1948, often referred to as the Kinsey Report. Kinsey, an Indiana University zoologist turned his attention to human sexuality after teaching a course on marriage. He eventually interviewed thousands of individuals about their sexual behavior. Homosexuality was only a part of his published study, but his findings about the high prevalence of same-sex sexual behavior caused a sensation and validated many who thought that their sexuality was natural and normal. Kinsey created a scale to reflect the fluidity of sexuality, with 0 on one end representing exclusive heterosexuality and 6 on the other end representing exclusive homosexuality. Further, he found that 37 percent of his subjects had engaged in same-sex sexual behavior and 50 percent had fantasized about it. Four percent of respondents were exclusively homosexual, while 10 percent of men had been exclusively homosexual for at least three years. Kinsey clearly viewed homosexuality as natural human sexuality, and he critiqued the social and legal stigma, largely fueled by religion, that had developed over centuries:

The enforcement of these fundamentally religious codes against the so-called sexual perversions has been accomplished, throughout the centuries, by attaching considerable emotional significance to them. This has been effected, in part, by synonymizing the terms clean, natural, normal, moral and right, and the terms unclean, unnatural, abnormal, immoral, and wrong. Modern philosophers have added concepts of mental degeneracy and psychosexual immaturity to the synonymy. The emotions evoked by these classifications have been responsible for some of the most sordid chapters in human history.[9]

Kinsey also published *Sexual Behavior in the Human Female* in 1953, but this work, in that it frankly addressed female sexuality, challenged societal assumptions even more directly and led to a great deal of condemnation of Kinsey and his work, even beyond his work on men. He eventually lost funding for his work and died in 1956. Kinsey never allied with the emerging movement, but his work had clear political implications. It both fueled the movement and led to more legal oppression, as many interpreted his findings to indicate more "enemies" in our midst.

Indeed, in the mid-twentieth century, it is difficult to separate the hysteria over homosexuality from the hysteria over communism. Historians refer to the hysteria against sexual minorities as the Lavender Scare that closely connects to the Red Scare. In both, political leaders saw secret and hidden threats from lesbians, gay men, and communists. Purges of suspected "sexual deviants" and communists from government employment were commonplace in the late 1940s and 1950s, as well as rhetoric from politicians and in the media about the threats to society stemming from these groups. The Red Scare is more commonly understood, but the Lavender Scare was no less damaging to individual lives and to the emerging movement for sexual minorities. And the two were often connected in the rhetoric and tactics of government officials and in the public mind, including the leader figures of these scares, Senator Joseph McCarthy. According to the historian David K. Johnson, "Both groups seemed to comprise hidden subcultures, with their own meeting places, literature, cultural codes, and bonds of loyalty."[10] In addition, American society was experiencing an obsession and fear of child molesters, most of whom were (incorrectly) thought to be gay men. As a sign of the cultural and governmental hostility toward sexual minorities, a U.S. Senate report from 1950 stated, "Sex perverts, like all other persons who by their overt acts violate moral codes and laws and the accepted standards of conduct, but be treated as transgressors and dealt with accordingly."[11] In 1953, President Eisenhower signed an Executive Order 10450. The order included "sexual perversion" as grounds for dismissal from federal employment, effectively banning federal employment by openly lesbian or gay individuals, or those suspected to be gay or lesbian, for decades.

However, an indication that things were changing slightly, in 1947 a woman using the pseudonym Lisa Ben (a play on lesbian) began publishing an anonymous newsletter, *Vice Versa*, in Los Angeles. The newsletter was mostly shared informally among lesbians. There was no attempt to create a mass circulation, largely out of the fear that the Post Office would seize it as obscene, despite its mild content of news and movie reviews (she was a secretary for a movie studio). The politics of the newsletter were forceful for the times. Ben wrote, "The third sex must be recognized as equally 'honorable' as those who are heterosexual."[12] She produced the newsletter for only nine months, but this was a sign that lesbians and gay men were starting to think of a world beyond isolation. It was an attempt to form an intellectual community out of which politics might eventually form. Indeed, lesbian and gay publications would play a central role in the emerging political movement. Additionally, a small social group, the Knights of the Clock, founded by African American gay man, Merton Bird, formed around this time in Los Angeles, but it was not very political. Another social organization, this one for gay veterans of World War II, was formed in New York in 1945, the Veterans Benevolent Association. Group conscious was forming.

Many individuals who became active in the lesbian and gay rights movements of the 1950s point to reading the book, *The Homosexual in America*, published in 1951 by Donald Webster Cory, a pseudonym for Edward Sagarin and a play on the title of the book defending homosexuality, *Corydon,* by French author André Gide. Sagarin was a sociologist who worked in the movement for several decades but eventually became more conservative and parted ways with the movement by the 1970s. The book was a defense for homosexuality and an argument for tolerance and decriminalization. It was one of the first long-form defenses of gay rights published in the United States. Cory's analysis was influenced by analysts of racial inequality, especially W. E. B. Du Bois, and he viewed gay men and lesbians as an oppressed minority, with more of a focus on the plight of gay men.

The U.S. lesbian and gay rights movement began in earnest in 1950/1951 with the creation of the Mattachine Society in Los Angeles. Harry Hay spearheaded the formation of the group. Hay was gay, a former communist, and very politically aware. He began to see a need for a liberation movement for sexual minorities. In fact, it was common for lesbian and gay activism to be linked with leftist politics in the early-to-mid-twentieth century. Marxism's language of oppression was applied to issues beyond economic class for many on the left. An offshoot of Marxism, Anarchism, was strongly connected to the gay rights movement in Germany. Anarchists applied Marxist analysis to all areas of life, including sexuality. They were advocates of "free love" as well as other freedoms, or as the Anarchist Emma Goldman stated, "Anarchism, then, really stands for the liberation of the human mind from

the dominion of religion; the liberation of the human body from the dominion of property; liberation from the shackles and restraint of government.
Anarchism stands for a social order based on the free grouping of individuals
for the purpose of producing real social wealth; an order that will guarantee
to every human being free access to the earth and full enjoyment of the neces-
sities of life, *according to individual desires, tastes, and inclinations* [italics
added]."[13] Sexual liberation without the constraint of religion, social norms,
and the law was thus central to the Anarchist's understanding of freedom.
This mode of thinking would animate many activists in the twentieth century,
but they needed to navigate the very real elements of restraint identified by
Goldman, especially the religion and the state, and the merging of the two.
It should be noted, however, that while the logic of Marxist thought could be
used to combat sexual repression, the Communist Party was generally hostile
to sexual diversity. Part of this resulted from the sexism in the movement and
the party (against which Goldman struggled), but addressing noneconomic
issues was seen as distracting from "true" (class-based) oppression. Indeed,
Hay left the party precisely for this reason.

Reflective of the communist background of many of the members, the
initial Mattachine Society combined intellectual assertiveness with secrecy.
It should be noted that most American communists were not agents of the
Soviet Union nor violent revolutionaries—they were attracted to Marxist
modes of thinking as a way to critique and deal with the economic and racial
injustice that they thought were real problems. They often worked within the
system, but with a distinctly socialist take on politics. For instance, Hay supported the presidential campaign of Henry Wallace in 1948 for the Progressive Party, the former Democratic vice president whose politics were to the
left of most Democrats at the time. Indeed, Hay discussed with others a group,
"Bachelors for Wallace," as a way to begin thinking about what a politics of
gay rights might look like. In 1950, Hay and his partner Rudi Gernreich asked
beachgoers to sign a petition opposing the Korean War. They also asked if
the beachgoers had heard about the Kinsey Report, and took the names and
addresses of those who expressed an interest. Out of these, and other, efforts
came the Mattachine Society. In other words, Hay and the other founders of
Mattachine with a communist background (Bob Hull, Dale Jennings, Rudi
Gernreich, and Chuck Rowland) were not plotting the overthrow of the country. They were engaging the most progressive elements of the political system
to begin to achieve change. The initial Marxist impulses were somewhat
muted by the involvement of James Gruber and Konrad Stevens in the initial
group. As John D'Emilio notes, "Their presence forced others to abandon
the jargon of the left and to frame their ideas in language accessible to non-
Marxists."[14] Mattachine members chose the word "homophile" (philia is a
Greek word for love) for their movement, not homosexual, to deemphasize

sexuality. The pre-Stonewall movement is generally referred to as the homophile movement. They chose the name Mattachine to reference a group of masked medieval court jesters who spoke controversial truths.

It was not violent overthrow that Mattachine envisioned, but education and persuasion to achieve substantial change, but while working within the system. The formal goals of the original organization were:

1. TO UNIFY:—While there are undoubtedly individual homosexuals who number many of their own people among their friends, thousands of homosexuals live out their lives bewildered, unhappy, alone,—isolated from their own kind and unable to adjust to the dominant culture. Even those who may have many homosexual friends are still cut off from the deep satisfactions man's gregarious nature can achieve *only* when he is consciously part of a larger unified whole. A major purpose of the Mattachine Society is to provide a concensus [sic] of principle around which all of our people can rally and from which they can derive a feeling of "belonging."
2. TO EDUCATE:—The total of information available on the subject of homosexuality is woefully meagre [sic] and utterly inconclusive. The Society organizes all available material, and conducts extensive researches itself—psychological, physiological, anthropological, and sociological—for the purpose of informing all interested homosexuals, and for the purpose of informing and enlightening the public at large.

   The Mattachine Society holds it possible and desirable that a highly ethical homosexual culture emerge[s], as a consequence of its work, paralleling the emerging cultures of our fellow minorities . . . the Negro, Mexican, and Jewish Peoples. The Society believes homosexuals can lead well-adjusted, wholesome, and socially productive lives once ignorance, and prejudice, against them is successfully combatted, and once homosexuals themselves feel they have a dignified and useful role to play in society. The Society, to these ends, is in the process of developing a homosexual ethic . . . disciplined, moral, and socially responsible.
3. TO LEAD:—It is not sufficient for an oppressed minority such as the homosexuals to be conscious of belonging to a minority collective when, as is the situation at the present time, that collective is neither socially organic nor objective in its directions and activities—although this minimum is in fact a great step forward. It is necessary that the more far-reaching and socially conscious homosexuals provide leadership to the whole mass of social deviants if the first two missions, (the unification and the education of the homosexual minority), are to be accomplished. Further, once unification and education have progressed, it becomes imperative (to consolidate these gains) for the Corporation to push forward into

the realm of political action to erase from our law books the discriminatory and oppressive legislation presently directed against the homosexual
minority.

The Society, founded on the highest ethical and social principles,
serves as an example for homosexuals to follow, and provides a dignified
standard upon which the rest of society may base a more intelligent and
accurate picture of the nature of homosexuality than currently exists in the
public mind. The Society provides the instrument necessary to work with
like-minded and socially valuable organizations, and supplies the means
for the assistance of our people who are victimized daily as a result of
our oppression. Only a Society, providing an enlightened leadership, can
rouse the homosexuals . . . one of the largest minorities today . . . to take
the actions necessary to elevate themselves from the social ostracism an
unsympathetic culture has perpetrated upon them.[15]

The focus on shared oppression, group consciousness, and a call for elite
leadership are elements common to Marxist thought, while the invoking of
other minority struggles reflects an attempt to place the struggle in the context of the American traditions of exclusion and rights claiming. The Society
initially used a communist leadership model of closed guilds that eventually
opened the organization to charges of secrecy and conspiracy. The emphasis on respectability indicates the internalization of society's stereotypes of
sexual minorities, as does the reference to "deviants." However, the document is remarkable for its frank assertiveness of the dignity of sexual minorities and the need for enlightenment and social and legal reform.

This approach would not last, however. After building a decent following,
especially through discussion groups that formed up and down the California
coast, in 1953 the original leadership was purged from the organization by
elements worried about the connections to communism, particularly during the height of the Red and Lavender Scares. These elements, led by Ken
Burns, also had a much more accommodationist and assimilationist approach
to the plight of sexual minorities. They did not wish to form a distinct culture;
rather, they emphasized how lesbians and gay men were just like everyone
else, except for the small matter of sexuality. They thought that if they could
just convince enough elites to understand this, the issue of homosexuality
would cease to be a dividing line in society, and sexual minorities would be
absorbed into the mainstream. Until such time, however, the organization
needed to keep a low profile. Particularly troubling to this group was the fact
that the first set of leaders sent a questionnaire from the society to political
candidates in Los Angeles. This explicitly political act was seen as dangerous
and unnecessary. The forces of reaction were probably correct in their assessment of the hostility to a political agenda for the times, but a more aggressive

organization might have built a movement earlier. The barriers to political action were strong. In fact, Dale Jennings was the victim of police entrapment. Mattachine successfully fought the charges, but this demonstrates the difficulty of creating a political movement in an era of criminalization and hysteria surrounding sexual diversity. Indeed, it would be another decade before the homophile movement would engage in politics on any sustained level. As a result, according to D'Emilio, the organization changed from "a radical, visionary gay organization into a conservative, closeted, and self-effacing one."[16]

Women were a part of the discussion groups of Mattachine, but they were not central to its leadership. In 1955, the Daughters of Bilitis was founded in San Francisco. Originally formed as a social organization, the Daughters eventually became more political. The name was inspired by erotic, lesbian-themed poems, "Songs of Bilitis," by Pierre Louys. The politics of its founders, including the couple Del Martin and Phyllis Lyon, were connected more to the politics of the New Deal, rather than communist politics. Martin and Lyon were admirers of Eleanor Roosevelt and her crusades for social justice. Martin and Lyon drove the move to more political activism, and Rose Bamberger, the initial organizer behind the group, eventually left because it became too political, in her estimation. A year after the original formation, a statement of purpose was created with four goals:

1. Education of the variant, with particular emphasis on the psychological, physiological and sociological aspects, to enable her to understand herself and make her adjustment to society in all its social, civil and economic implications—this is to be accomplished by establishing and maintaining as complete a library as possible of both fiction and non-fiction literature on the sex deviant theme; by sponsoring public on pertinent subjects to be conducted by leading members of the legal, psychiatric, religious and other professions; by advocating a mode of behavior and dress acceptable to society.
2. Education of the public at large through acceptance first of the individual, leading to an eventual breakdown of erroneous taboos and prejudices; through public discussion meetings aforementioned; through dissemination of educational literature on the homosexual theme.
3. Participation in research projects by duly authorized and responsible psychologists, sociologists and other such experts directed toward further knowledge of the homosexual.
4. Investigation of the penal code as it pertains to the homosexual, proposal of changes to provide an equitable handling of cases involving this minority group, and promotion of these changes through due process of law in the state legislatures.[17]

Here again we see a focus on elite outreach (especially in the medical community) combined with modest public education and legal reform efforts, all while behaving and dressing well. The power of the conformist mid-1950s is clearly seen in these statements.

Perhaps the most significant element to come out of this early organizing was the creation of lesbian and gay publications. The *Ladder* came out of the Daughters of Bilitis, and the *Mattachine Review* and *ONE* were extensions of the organizing around the Mattachine Society. In addition, to artistic and literary content, political content was a significant element. Stories about the ongoing legal regulation of sexual minorities were common, as were articles about political strategy, continuing to echo the original debate about difference versus assimilation, about militancy versus less visible and confrontational approaches. These publications and others were crucial to sustaining the movement during a time of intense social ostracism. However, under the legal regime of the time, these publications could be seized, and their publishers and authors prosecuted, under state and local obscenity laws. The mere mention of homosexuality, even in a cultural or political context, could trigger legal action. Fortunately, the Supreme Court began to view such a broad view of obscenity as violating First Amendment guarantees of free speech. In *Roth v. U.S.* (1957), the court narrowed considerably what could be properly deemed as obscene under the First Amendment, especially providing more protection for literary and political content. The Los Angeles postmaster seized copies of *ONE*, deeming them obscene. Relying on *Roth*, and overruling decisions from the lower courts, the Supreme Court found in favor of *ONE* in ONE *v. Olesen* (1958). This affirmation of the First Amendment–protected content of homophile magazines was critical to keeping the movement alive, especially intellectually, until a more open and militant set of activists took over the movement by the mid-1960s. *ONE* was especially important for maintaining a strong political ethic. As D'Emilio notes, "*ONE* strove to keep alive the militant spirit of the society's early years. . . . *ONE* adopted a stance of combative pride in being gay."[18]

THE MOVEMENT MATURES BUT STILL FACES OVERWHELMING CHALLENGES

By the end of the 1950s, the movement had not accomplished much, having gone mostly underground. On the West coast, San Francisco was a bright spot, with legal victories cutting down on police harassment of bars in the 1950s. José Sarria, a famous drag performer, ran for the Board of Supervisors in 1961, representing the first campaign for public office by an openly gay candidate. While he lost, his race was a signal that a gay voting bloc was forming in the city. San Francisco was also a central site of the emerging counterculture movement—a movement, reflected in the Beat poets like gay Allen Ginsberg, that began to chip away at 1950s' conformity. By the 1960s, a new advocacy group, the Society for Individual Rights, formed in the city.

Inspired by Dr. Martin Luther King's movement, a more open and militant movement also began to form on the East coast by the mid-1960s through the Mattachine Societies of Washington, D.C. and New York and the New York chapter of the Daughters of Bilitis. Franklin (Frank) Kameny, Randolph (Randy) Wicker, and Barbara Gittings were some of the leading advocates of this era. A new organization was formed, East Coast Homophile Organizations (ECHO), with monthly meetings from members of the New York and DC groups and the Janus Society of Philadelphia. A national organization with annual conferences was also formed, The North American Conference of Homophile Organizations (NACHO). This obviously represented a maturation of the movement—a small group of people were planning and organizing a movement and an agenda to affect legal and political change. At the first national gathering in Kansas City in 1966, the activists held a press conference to announce their goals. In advance of the 1967 meeting in Washington, D.C., Kameny wrote to President Lyndon Johnson requesting a letter of welcome and a meeting with the president or members of the White House staff. Of course, neither happened, but the request reflects the seriousness and relative self-confidence of the movement, or at least its leaders such as Kameny.

In addition, a strategy of direct action quickly emerged. No longer would quietly convincing elites to change their views on homosexuality be the main goal of the movement. This alliance resulted in the first public demonstrations of the homophile movement in 1965, as activists picketed the White House, the State Department, the U.S. Civil Service Commission, the United Nations, and the Independence Hall in Philadelphia. The goal was to get political leaders and other citizens to realize that the legal regime facing sexual minorities ran counter to fundamental American values of liberty and equality. Slogans on the picket signs included the phrases: "Homosexuals Ask For the Right of the Pursuit of Happiness; Homosexual Americans Demand Their Civil Rights; First Class Citizenship for Homosexuals; Sexual Preference is Irrelevant to Federal Employment." Kameny, inspired by the slogan, "Black is Beautiful," coined the phrase "Gay is Good," as the rhetorical centerpiece of the movement. In fact, Kameny's activism and rhetorical advocacy during this period places him as the leading figure of the 1960s' homophile movement. He was spurred to activism after being dismissed, pursuant to Eisenhower's order, as an astronomer (he had a PhD from Harvard) from the Army Map Service in 1957. He took his case, unsuccessfully to the Supreme Court, and he was particularly focused on reversing the ban on federal employment. His self-authored appellate brief to the court is a remarkable statement of his political philosophy and framework for reform. While Kameny's political philosophy is more fully addressed in chapter 3, it is illuminating to compare the statement of purpose he drafted for the D.C. Mattachine Society with the previous statements:

1. It is the purpose of this organization to act by any lawful means:
   a. To secure for homosexuals the right to life, liberty, and the pursuit of happiness, as proclaimed for all men by the Declaration of Independence; and to secure for homosexuals the basic rights and liberties established by the word and the spirit of the Constitution of the United States;
   b. To equalize the status and position of the homosexual with those of the heterosexual by achieving equality under law, equality of opportunity, equality in the society of his fellow men, and by eliminating adverse prejudice, both private and official;
   c. To secure for the homosexual the right, as a human being, to develop and achieve his full potential and dignity, and the right, as a citizen, to make his maximum contribution to the society in which he lives;
   d. To inform and enlighten the public about homosexuals and homosexuality;
   e. To assist, protect, and counsel the homosexual in need.
2. It is not the purpose of this organization to act as a social group, or as an agency for personal introductions.
3. This organization will cooperate with other minority rights organizations which are striving for the realization of full civil rights and liberties for all.[19]

This statement reflects a clear departure from the 1950s' statements. There is no discussion of "deviants" or "inverts"; rather, homosexuals and heterosexuals are put on the same footing. Also, the language used is drawn from the American constitutional tradition (not Marxism), and there is a clear attempt to create a political group, not a social group with some political tendencies.

Realizing that the stigma from the entrenched "homosexuality is an illness" narrative in the medical profession and in society was the largest barrier to the movement for sexual minorities, Kameny and Gittings focused much of their activism on persuading the American Psychiatric Association to delist homosexuality as a mental illness from its Diagnostics and Statistical Manual of Mental Disorders (DSM), which it eventually did in 1973. Kameny and Gittings were aided by a cadre of medical and psychiatric professionals led by Dr. Evelyn Hooker, whose research challenged and undermined the negative medical narrative, but they took their fight to the organization directly, lobbying and staging protests at conventions.

STONEWALL AND ITS AFTERMATH

The movement fundamentally changed in June of 1969 with the rebellion at the Stonewall Inn in Greenwich Village in New York City. Patrons of lesbian and gay bars had challenged police harassment through direct confrontation and resistance to arrest in other cities, but the resistance at Stonewall became the defining instance of this resistance, largely because of the significant media coverage that, of course, was mostly negative. The headline in the *New York Daily News* was "Homo Nest Raided, Queen Bees Stinging Mad." For several nights, bar patrons and their supporters violently confronted police on the streets surrounding the Stonewall Inn, taking a stand to eradicate the coercive and oppressive regulation of sexuality that had been a part of the nation's practice for decades. Both for those who were directly involved and those who were inspired by their actions, the Stonewall rebellion created a more broad-based, radicalized political sensibility. The approach was also a reflection of the more aggressive tactics of other prominent movements of the time, particularly the antiwar and Black power movements. Riots and clashes with police were common in the politics of the left at this time. The notion was that working within the system was futile and that direct confrontation was required to end racial oppression and to end the war in Vietnam.

For the homophile movement leaders, this approach was disorienting, and many were not supportive of the radicalization. Kameny and other homophile leaders were quite dismissive of this new generation of activists. The new leaders attacked the tactics of the homophile movement, calling for a more decentralized, radical, "in-your-face" movement aimed at destabilizing gender norms and social and legal conventions about sex and sexuality. While the homophile movement did its best to avoid a discussion of sex, the new movement saw sexual liberation and sexual freedom as central to its efforts. Groups like the Gay Activists Alliance (GAA) and the Gay Liberation Front (GLF) set out to undermine the homophile movement and push the overall movement in a more liberationist direction through the very institutions that it created. In fact, the new cadre of activists essentially took over the 1970 NACHO convention, effectively ending that organization's efforts. Throughout the 1970s, the movement moved along two tracks: more radical, direct action groups such as GAA, GLF, and the lesbian-feminist group, Radicalesbians (lesbians were also active in the growing feminist movement), and the vestiges of the homophile movement who continued more traditional forms of political participation, such as lobbying elected officials and litigation. This dividing line was not impermeable, however. For instance the GAA, while emphasizing a more liberationist approach, engaged in more traditional forms of political activity. In fact, the GAA eventually became a traditional advocacy organization, The National Gay and Lesbian Task Force (NGLTF). Overall, the new approach post-Stonewall included a wider array of tactics for change, especially more large-scale protests and demonstrations, represented by pride parades that became increasingly common in urban areas. The more radical immediate post-Stonewall movement was relatively short lived, as more radical groups, like the GLF, disbanded or formed coalitions with the more reformist homophile organizations by the mid-1970s. However, this brand of politics would reappear during the AIDS crisis of the 1980s, discussed later. And the more radical approach pushed the movement to think more actively about diversity. The lesbian-feminist movement particularly brought women's perspectives to the table for the first time on an equal and sustained basis.

THE MOVEMENT IN THE 1970s: ENGAGING LOCALITIES, GOING TO COURT, AND BACKLASH FROM THE RELIGIOUS RIGHT

After Stonewall, the movement evolved more publicly, with social and political institutions and organizations forming, mostly at the local level. In the political realm, the main goals of the movement were the elimination of sodomy laws, the creation of nondiscrimination policies based on sexual orientation (and, in some cases, gender identity), and bringing legal protections to families through the strengthening of parenting rights and calls for marriage equality. Eventually, national institutions emerged, and activists turned toward electoral politics, with openly lesbian and gay candidates running for office (and sometimes winning), and LGBT activists working for recognition and policy change within the Democratic Party. However, by the latter part of the decade, the emergence of the Religious Right as a potent political force led to policy gains being overturned or strongly resisted.

In the middle decades of the twentieth century, evangelical (aggressively spreading the faith through public and private communication with others not of the faith) and fundamentalist (believing in the literal interpretation of the Bible) Christians were not very active in politics, at least to the extent that they are today. In the 1920s, fundamentalist leaders emphasized the need to withdraw from the public arena and focus on personal spiritual concerns, especially after the Scopes Trial in which their views of Biblical literalism were subjected to ridicule in the media. By the 1960s and 1970s, however, leaders began to question this nonengaged approach. Several political and legal issues led to this reevaluation: the invalidation of school prayer by the Supreme Court, the creation of the right to choose an abortion as a constitutional right, the court-mandated integration of public schools (many fundamental

Christians created private schools to avoid the mandate of racial integration), and the prospect of the Equal Rights Amendment (ERA) and the perceived threat to theologically mandated gender roles. Conservative evangelical leaders like Jerry Fallwell, Pat Robertson, and Phyllis Schlafley saw an opportunity to build a political movement to prevent law and policy from moving away from their religious values and to enshrine those values into a law and policy. For a time in the 1970s, it was not clear which movement would align itself with which political party. Indeed, Democratic President Jimmy Carter was a Southern, evangelical Christian. However, by the late 1970s, an alliance with the Republican Party was formed, as each side saw great opportunity in the emerging movement working with a Republican Party that was becoming more conservative and targeting white Southern voters. This "Southern Strategy," started under President Richard Nixon, was an attempt to persuade white Southern Democrats dissatisfied with the Democratic Party's embrace of African American civil rights to support the Republican Party. This strategy was highly successful, as most white southerners now vote Republican, and many of them still identify with the Religious Right.

The new movement set its sights on the emerging movement for sexual minorities by using the popular initiative process to repeal legislatively enacted policies protecting sexual minorities in urban areas and college towns, where the LGBT movement was strongest. The first successful repeal was that of Miami-Dade County's antidiscrimination law in 1977, led by singer-turned-activist Anita Bryant. This was soon followed by repeal of antidiscrimination laws in St. Paul, Minnesota, Eugene, Oregon, and Wichita, Kansas. These repeals were a powerful blow to the LGBT rights movement, signaling the continued public scorn for sexual minorities. It also was the first sign that the Religious Right would oppose every positive policy development for sexual minorities with its increasing clout, especially in the Republican Party. The Religious Right had effectively painted sexual minorities as deeply immoral and a threat to American values and culture—indeed a threat to the country itself. These particular arguments and tactics, little changed after these early political conflicts, are further explored in later chapters. The AIDS crisis of the 1980s would further embolden the Religious Right, derail some of the efforts of the LGBT rights movement, and also help the movement to build arguments, institutions, and other resources.

While the marriage equality movement has occupied much of the contemporary LGBT movement, it was not the most central focus of the movement of the 1970s. However, legal and political activism for same-sex marriage did occur, starting in the immediate wake of Stonewall and often connected to mobilization and advocacy surrounding the Equal Rights Amendment, an amendment that would have elevated the category of "sex" to the fullest protection from discrimination under the Fourteenth Amendment. Until the backlash to a broad range of lesbian and gay rights claims driven by the rise of the Religious Right in the late 1970s, many couples and activists engaged the political and legal systems asking that same-sex couples be recognized by the state and given the full range of rights and benefits granted to married heterosexual couples.

Within a year of Stonewall, activists (first in Minnesota, then Washington state, and Kentucky shortly thereafter) requested marriage licenses from local officials but were rejected. This resulted in unsuccessful litigation (examined more in depth in chapter 5) efforts. These activists were directly inspired by the new activism unleashed by Stonewall, and some felt that the movement for the ERA supported claims for marriage equality, as many states had gender-neutral marriage statutes or had enacted state constitutional provisions banning discrimination on the basis of sex, or "mini-ERAs," as was the case in Washington State. More broadly, many couples felt that the plethora of benefits given to married couples, not to mention the societal and governmental approval provided by legal marriage, was their right as citizens. Many of the early marriage activists were quite militant, as reflected in the 1971 "zap" of the New York City Marriage License Bureau by the GAA. Members of the GAA took over the office in order to perform same-sex marriages to highlight the discriminatory nature of the heterosexual definition of marriage. Zaps were common forms of protest in New Left politics at this time. In 1975, a reform of Washington, D.C.'s family law resulted in the drafting of a gender-neutral marriage bill that activists hoped (perhaps naively) would legalize same-sex marriage. Also in that year, a county clerk in Boulder, Colorado, Clela Rorex, began granting marriage licenses to same-sex couples before being enjoined from doing so by state officials. This activity led many state legislatures to revise their marriage statutes to make clear that marriage was only between one man and one woman. Prior to that, this had merely been assumed to be the case in many jurisdictions. In fact, so many same-sex couples were applying for marriage licenses in California that the legislature revised the state's marriage statute in 1977. During the debate, however, some legislators recognized that cohabiting same-sex couples lacked basic legal protections and opposed the revisions. This initial round of marriage equality activism ended by the late 1970s, victim to the general rise of social conservatives as a potent political force. Activists then shifted the focus to domestic partnership laws at the municipal level.

This chapter has outlined the early movement for sexual minority rights and equality. The movement arose within the context of deep hostility toward sexual and gender minorities, but it slowly evolved through both radical critiques and more conventional liberal, democratic tactics and arguments. Later chapters will explore the movement as it evolved and began to change policy and law, as well as the continued barriers to change.

KEY TERMS, PEOPLE, AND CONCEPTS

American Psychiatric Association
Anarchism/Marxism
Bamberger, Rose
Bentham, Jeremy
Boston marriages
Bryant, Anita
Cory, Donald Webster
Daughters of Bilitis
Diagnostics and Statistical Manual
  of Mental Disorders (DSM)
East Coast Homophile
  Organizations (ECHO)
Executive Order 10450
Freud, Sigmund
Gay Activists Alliance (GAA)
Gay Liberation Front (GLF)
Gerber, Henry
Gittings, Barbara
Goldman, Emma
Hay, Harry and Rudi Gernreich
Hirschfeld, Magnus
Homophile movement
The Homosexual in America and
  Donald Webster Cory
Hooker, Dr. Evelyn
Jennings, Dale
Kameny, Franklin (Frank)
Kinsey, Alfred/The Kinsey Reports
Knights of the Clock

Lavender Scare/Red Scare
Left political movements and early
  LGB organizing
Martin, Del and Phyllis Lyon
Mattachine Society
Medicalization
Miami-Dade repeal
Molly houses
Movement radicalization
National Gay and Lesbian Task Force
  (NGLTF)
North American Conference
  of Homophile Organizations
  (NACHO)
Paragraph 175
Publications: *Ladder, Mattachine
  Review, ONE*
Radicalesbians
Religious Right
Sarria, José
Society for Individual Rights
Stonewall Rebellion
Ulrichs, Karl
Urning
Vice Versa and Lisa Ben
Veterans Benevolent Association
Whitman, Walt
Wicker, Randolph (Randy)
World War II effects

QUESTIONS FOR DISCUSSION

1. What events and factors led to the creation of the Homophile movement?
   How did the political thought of the left affect this process? What were the
   political aims of the Homophile movement?
2. How did the Stonewall Rebellion change the sexual minority rights
   movement?
3. How did the rise of the Religious Right affect the movement in the 1970s?
   What was the role played by the politics of the Equal Rights Amendment?

4. Do you think the movement for sexual minority rights could have done more to anticipate and neutralize the backlash by the Religious Right, or was this backlash inevitable?

NOTES

1. Cavan Sieczkowski, "Unearthed Letter From Freud Reveals His Thoughts On Gay People," *Huffington Post*, February 18, 2015, http://www.huffingtonpost.com/2015/02/18/sigmund-freud-gay-cure-letter_n_6706006.html.

2. Nicholas C. Edsall, *Toward Stonewall: Homosexuality and Society in the Modern Western World* (Charlottesville: University of Virginia Press, 2003), 244.

3. Nicholas C. Edsall, *Toward Stonewall: Homosexuality and Society in the Modern Western World* (Charlottesville: University of Virginia Press, 2003), 93.

4. Rachel Hope Cleves, *Charity and Sylvia: A Same-Sex Marriage in Early America* (New York: Oxford University Press, 2014).

5. Peter Drier, "'American The Beautiful' Author is Rush Limbaugh's Favorite Lesbian Socialist," talkingpointsmemo.com, February 5, 2014, http://talkingpointsmemo.com/cafe/america-the-beautiful-author-is-rush-limbaugh-s-favorite-lesbian-socialist.

6. Jonathan Katz, *Gay American History: Lesbians and Gay Men in the U.S.A.* (New York: Thomas Y. Crowell Company, 1976), 385.

7. Katz, 389.

8. John D'Emilio, *Sexual Politics, Sexual Communities: The Making of a Homosexual Minority in the United States, 1940–1970* (Chicago: University of Chicago Press, 1983), 24.

9. Quoted in C. Todd White, *Pre-Gay LA: A Social History of the Movement for Homosexual Rights* (Chicago: University of Illinois Press, 2009), 3. The quote is from pages 16–17 in *Sexual Behavior in the Human Male*.

10. David K. Johnson, *The Lavender Scare: The Cold War Persecution of Gays and Lesbians in the Federal Government* (Chicago: The University of Chicago Press, 2004), 33.

11. United States Senate, Committee on Expenditures in the Executive Departments. Report from the Subcommittee on Investigations, by Mr. Hoey, 1950, in *We Are Everywhere: A Historical Sourcebook of Gay and Lesbian Politics*, Mark Blasius and Shane Phelan, eds. (New York: Routledge, 1997), 243.

12. Quoted in Lillian Faderman and Stuart Timmons, *Gay L.A.: A History of Sexual Outlaws, Power Politics, and Lipstick Lesbians* (New York: Basic Books, 2006), 107. The quotation is from *Vice Versa*, 1:4 (June 1947), 4–5.

13. Emma Goldman, "Anarchism: What it Really Stands For," published in 1917, archived at: http://ucblibrary3.berkeley.edu/goldman/Writings/Anarchism/anarchism.html.

14. John D'Emilio, *Making Trouble: Essays on Gay History, Politics, and the University* (New York: Routledge, 1992), 28.

15. Mark Blasius and Shane Phelan, *We Are Everywhere: A Historical Sourcebook of Gay and Lesbian Politics* (New York: Routledge, 1997), 283–84.

16. D'Emilio, *Making Trouble*, 40.
17. Blasius and Phelan, 328.
18. John D'Emilio, *Sexual Politics, Sexual Communities*, 87–88.
19. "Statement of Purpose," Mattachine Society of Washington, DC, Papers of Franklin J. Kameny, Collections of the Manuscript Division of the Library of Congress, n.d. Copy on file with the author.

BIBLIOGRAPHY AND FURTHER READING

Barry Adam, *The Rise of a Gay and Lesbian Movement*, rev. ed. (New York: Twayne Publishers, 1995).

Vern Bullough, *Before Stonewall: Activists for Gay and Lesbian Rights in Historical Context* (New York: Harrington Park Press, 2002).

John D'Emilio, *Sexual Politics, Sexual Communities: The Making of a Homosexual Minority in the United States, 1940–1970* (Chicago: University of Chicago Press, 1983).

Vicki L. Eaklor, *Queer America: A People's GLBT History of the United States* (New York: The New Press, 2008).

Nicholas C. Edsall, *Toward Stonewall: Homosexuality and Society in the Modern Western World* (Charlottesville: University of Virginia Press, 2003).

Lillian Faderman, *Odd Girls and Twilight Lovers: A History of Lesbian Life in Twentieth Century America* (New York: Penguin, 1991).

Marcia M. Gallo, *Different Daughters: A History of the Daughters of Bilitis and the Rise of the Lesbian Rights Movement* (New York: Carroll & Graf, 2006).

David K. Johnson, *The Lavender Scare: The Cold War Persecution of Gays and Lesbians in the Federal Government* (Chicago: The University of Chicago Press, 2004).

Jason Pierceson, "Same-Sex Marriage and the American Political Tradition," in *Moral Argument, Religion, and Same-Sex Marriage: Advancing the Public Good*, Gordon Babst, et al., eds. (Lanham, MD: Lexington Books, 2009).

Jason Pierceson, *Same-Sex Marriage in the United States: The Road to the Supreme Court* (Lanham, MD: Rowman & Littlefield, 2013).

James T. Sears, *Behind the Mask of Mattachine: The Hal Call Chronicles and the Early Movement for Homosexual Emancipation* (New York: Harrington Park Press, 2006).

Marc Stein, *Rethinking the Gay and Lesbian Movement* (New York: Routledge, 2012).

C. Todd White, *Pre-Gay LA: A Social History of the Movement for Homosexual Rights* (Chicago: University of Illinois Press, 2009).

Chapter 3

Political Theory

Portions of this chapter appeared in Jason Pierceson, "Same-Sex Marriage and the American Political Tradition," in *Moral Argument, Religion, and Same-Sex Marriage: Advancing the Public Good*, Gordon A. Babst, Emily R. Gill, and Jason Pierceson, eds. (Lanham, MD: Lexington Books, 2009), 119–34. Reprinted with permission.

The emergence of a political and legal movement for sexual and gender minorities in the twentieth century occurred within a liberal, democratic framework, with the support of more radical philosophical approaches. In particular, the concern for individual freedom and autonomy, a concern for majoritarian oppression of minority groups, an attempt to fence out religions from a direct influence on politics and law, and the notion that the power of the state should not always touch all areas of life, all deeply rooted in liberal political theory, slowly shook loose a centuries-long condemnation of same-sex sexual activity and relationships. This condemnation was aided by notions in democratic theory that democratic societies ought to be able to legislate in order to preserve the common good, broadly defined, including the regulation of sexual morality, as defined by the political majority, often connected to theological views. By the end of the twentieth century and into the twenty-first, particularly in the United States and other liberal, democratic nations, the power of liberal ideas appeared to be winning over majoritarian morality in the courts, legislative arenas, and (to a lesser extent) in the realm of direct democracy. At the same time, however, a challenge to liberal theory from feminism and queer theory began to question liberalism's ability to truly liberate sexual minorities. This chapter explores these philosophical approaches and connects them to the political and legal arguments and aims related to the movement and its opposition. Different political philosophies

37

create different politics, and much of the politics of sexual and gender minorities involves deep philosophical differences among citizens, activists, elected officials, and judges. Understanding the differences and the different politics they create is central to understanding the contemporary movement for sexual and gender minorities and opposition to the movement.

CLASSICAL POLITICAL PHILOSOPHY: THE CELEBRATION OF SAME-SEX INTIMACY AND THE FOUNDATION FOR CONTEMPORARY OPPOSITION TO LGBT RIGHTS AND EQUALITY

It is somewhat ironic that the philosophical foundation for opposition to LGBT rights and equality comes from ancient Athenian society in which male and female same-sex sexual activity was tolerated and even celebrated. Of course, as previously indicated, this cultural acceptance was quite different from the modern view of sexual orientation as an identity. While Athens was the birthplace of democracy, its leading philosophers Plato and Aristotle, both of whom defined Western political philosophy for nearly two millennia, were critics of many elements of democracy, and their views of justice were imbued with elitism and inegalitarianism. They also thought that justice required a strong state that would promote personal and public virtue. Individual rights and political and social equality were foreign to this framework. Knowing one's placing and sacrificing for the public good were the main elements of a good system of justice in classical political philosophy.

Aristotle most consistently reflected this approach to politics. For him, humans were naturally inclined to form political communities, with an instinct toward collectivity, not individualism. The foundation for this view was the heterosexual family. For Aristotle, as humans naturally form families, they eventually form governments. Government was merely an extension of the human impulse to form communities, to unite for survival, protection, and to live a good life. Families form villages, and villages form governments. As he states, "The family is the association established by nature for the supply of men's everyday wants. . . . Hence it is evident that the state is the creation of nature, and that man is by nature a political animal."[1] Thus, in the classical setting, same-sex sexuality generally was not an alternative to the heterosexual family. An assumption about the "naturalness" of heterosexual families was deeply embedded in classical political philosophy. However, the much more radical Plato argued for the deconstruction of the heterosexual nuclear family in an ideal state in *The Republic* (men and women were to raise children in common without knowing who were their genetic children—a proposal strongly opposed by Aristotle).

Philosophical reasoning in the classical world was teleological, or focused on finding a thing's purpose or essence. As the philosopher Michael Sandel describes this classical focus on naturalness, "In the ancient world, teleological thinking was more prevalent than it is today. Plato and Aristotle thought that fire rose because it was reaching for the sky, its natural home, and that stones fell because they were striving to get closer to the earth, where they belonged. Nature was seen to have a meaningful order."[2] As the heterosexual family was "natural" for human preservation, so a large group of families, a political community, was natural for human flourishing. But this political community was demanding, requiring active participation by citizens, and the law had a direct role in creating and maintaining virtue (generally defined as a concern for the general good) among the populace. For Plato and Aristotle, the law was a teacher and had a strong role to play in maintaining morality. Communitarianism, not individual liberty, was the dominant political ideal.

Elitism was also a fundamental aspect of classical political thought and practice. In democratic Athens, slaves and women could not be citizens. Only nonslave males were thought to have the capacity to be citizens, especially in a direct democracy. Aristotle defended slavery as a necessary (and natural) social institution. It reflected a natural division and hierarchy among human capacities, and it allowed citizens the leisure to spend time governing. Plato envisioned an ideal polity run by philosopher kings, or those who were capable of understanding philosophy and making wise political decisions. He was less gendered in his thinking about human capacity than Aristotle, arguing that women could be philosopher kings. In the context of sexuality, not everyone could handle sexual liberty without it descending into harmful sexual anarchy, in the classical worldview. Too much, or exclusive, same-sex sexuality was inconsistent with the classical belief in moderation. Particularly for those men who could handle it and put in its proper context of a mentoring relationship and the celebration of beauty, both male and female, some sex with younger men was appropriate.

Indeed, same-sex sexual practices and relationships were an accepted part of Athenian society during the time of Plato and Aristotle. Philosopher Martha Nussbaum describes the classical approach to sexuality in the following manner:

> In Greek culture and practices, the gender of the partner assumes far less importance than it does in our own society and is usually taken as less salient than many other facts about a sex act. Nor are people very often categorized socially in accordance with their orientation toward partners of a particular gender. It is assumed that abundant appetitive energy may find an outlet in intercourse with either gender, and the two possibilities are frequently treated as more or less

interchangeable for moral purposes, youths and women being couples together as likely pleasures for a man to pursue.[3]

"Youths" were college-aged men, to use a contemporary reference. Some- times, the sexual relationship was between men closer in age, but there was usually some form of power difference between the parties. While the heterosexual family was natural for human survival, a range of sexual expres- sion was natural as well. Unlike contemporary natural law theory (discussed below), the view of the "naturalness" of the family did not preclude a range of morally acceptable sexual practices and relationships. In terms of lesbian- ism, socially acceptable intimate and romantic relationships between women in the classical world were accepted, especially in Sparta and more generally as reflected in the poetry of Sappho, a female Greek poet from the island of Lesbos (from which the term lesbian is derived) whose poetry contained clear themes of erotic love between women.

The ancient Greek acceptance and celebration of sexual diversity did not survive the rise of Christianity and the fusion of the theology of the Catholic Church with classical political philosophy. The approach of Aristotle and Plato became fused to Christianity through the work of Middle Ages philoso- phers like Thomas Aquinas. In terms of sexuality, procreative heterosexual intercourse became the only acceptable and "natural" type of sexual practice. The approach of Aquinas would be adopted by the "new natural law theo- rists" of contemporary philosophical debates, discussed below.

THE RISE OF LIBERALISM: SECULARISM AND INDIVIDUAL RIGHTS

Starting in the 1600s, Western political philosophy witnessed a significant shift away from the assumptions and values of classical political thought. Thomas Hobbes and John Locke began to push political thinking in a more secular, individualistic, and egalitarian direction in their early liberal thought. Eventually, liberalism matured and began to contemplate personal freedoms, including the right to determine one's personal path in the world, including intimacy, especially in the political thought of Jeremy Bentham and John Stuart Mill. In fact, in private writings consistent with his utilitarian philoso- phy, Bentham called for the decriminalization of same-sex sex acts, but he was too afraid of the negative reaction that would occur if this sentiment were published. Unlike the classical philosophers, early liberal theory evolved in a time of intense hostility to sexual diversity, but the logic of emerging liberal- ism would create the political framework for an eventual discussion of sexual diversity.

Hobbes and Locke

Thomas Hobbes is most famous for his argument that the only way to permanently escape the state of nature, in which life was famously "solitary, poor, nasty, brutish, and short,"[4] was for individuals to agree to surrender all power to the Leviathan, or the ultimate sovereign authority, in exchange for peace and security. Before the surrendering of power, however, Hobbes viewed politics through the prism of individualism and held that politics was driven by selfish human desires, not communitarian impulses, as Aristotle argued. This analytical individualism would powerfully shape the evolution of liberalism. In addition, for the politics of sexuality, his call for the secularization of politics and the undoing of centuries of merging of church and state was profoundly important. Hobbes's views about political philosophy were significantly shaped by the violence and chaos of the English Civil War (1642–1651), much of which was driven by religious differences. Indeed, he ridiculed the notion that politics could be grounded in theology, because theology is manipulated by humans for desired political ends, leading to conflict. As he stated in defending absolute sovereign power from superior claims of a religious power, "There is no covenant with God but by mediation of somebody that represents God's person. . . . But this pretense of covenant with God is so evident a lie, even in the pretender's own consciences, that it is not only an act of an unjust, but also of a vile and unmanly disposition"[5] (Hobbes used gendered language, but he also, like Plato, viewed women as political equals). Hobbes advocated religious toleration, but he opposed the direct mixing of theology and politics. Only a worldly sovereign authority could maintain stability and allow for any form of personal enjoyment. Indeed, Hobbes's philosophy is also important for a focus on individual happiness and pleasure and a diversity of human impulses for pleasure. While, in the end, the Leviathan could potentially limit human freedom, the stability of the Leviathan was the only route to any potential for individual happiness. Finally, in sharp contrast to the classical thinkers, Hobbes argued that humans naturally were equal to one another as a result of the relative equal power to kill one another. While future liberals would reject Hobbes's Leviathan solution, most of all would assume individualism, diversity, and equality both as natural conditions of humankind and as elements to be preserved in a just regime.

John Locke was such a liberal. His desired solution for the problems of the state of nature was a limited government, not an all-powerful one. Locke argued that individuals leave a somewhat less bleak, but still inhospitable, state of nature to form a government with limited powers, in order to retain much of the freedom and autonomy that the state of nature offered, but with more security for persons and property. The state was to be kept in its place by procedural protections (such as requiring the legislature to do its business transparently, limiting legislative sessions, and requiring legislators to live by the laws they make), but the ultimate check on state power was the right of revolution, or the right of the people to dissolve the government and create a new one. However, Locke argued that this right was to be invoked only for extreme cases. For the purposes of our discussion, however, Locke carved out a realm for individual autonomy more extensive than Hobbes, and he held that most personal matters should be left to individual discretion and choice—quite the opposite from the classical view that morality was the province of the state.

Mill, Bentham, and Burke

For understanding the politics of sexual minorities in the United States, there is perhaps no more critical a political philosopher than John Stuart Mill. His essay, *On Liberty*, had a profound impact on U.S. politics and law. In that essay, Mill defended freedom of speech and the freedom to make personal choices unencumbered by the state, or by society, through shaming and ostracism. This latter point is crucial, given that liberals like Locke had been mostly concerned with threats to individualism stemming from the government, not the "private" realm. As Mill wrote about "social tyranny,"

> Society can and does execute its own mandates: and if it issues wrong mandates instead of right, or any mandates at all in things with which it ought not to meddle, it practises [sic] a social tyranny more formidable than many kinds of political oppression, since, though not usually upheld by such extreme penalties, it leaves fewer means of escape, penetrating much more deeply into the details of life, and enslaving the soul itself. Protection, therefore, against the tyranny of the magistrate is not enough: there needs protection also against the tyranny of the prevailing opinion and feeling; against the tendency of society to impose, by other means than civil penalties, its own ideas and practices as rules of conduct on those who dissent from them; to fetter the development, and, if possible, prevent the formation, of any individuality not in harmony with its ways, and compel all characters to fashion themselves upon the model of its own.[6]

For Mill, as long as one's actions do not infringe on the rights of others, an individual should be unconstrained by government or society. (The line between self-regarding and other-regarding acts is not always clear, critics of Mill would emphasize.) In terms of free speech, Mill argued that human reasoning was fallible, thus preventing anyone from actually knowing the truth about a matter. As a result, ideas ought to be expressed freely in an open marketplace, where Mill expected that the best, and most true, ideas would emerge over time. This "marketplace of ideas" approach strongly influenced U.S. Supreme Court jurisprudence on the First Amendment in the twentieth century. As was discussed, this had benefits for the emerging lesbian and gay rights movement. Mill also called for "experiments in living." While he did not think that everyone could or should arrange their lives in new ways, he expected that some would, allowing the rest to learn from positive innovations. Thus, all would eventually benefit from allowing diversity in people's personal lives, and human freedom would be maximized.

> As it is useful that while mankind are imperfect there should be different opinions, so is it that there should be different experiments of living; that free scope should be given to varieties of character, short of injury to others; and that the worth of different modes of life should be proved practically, when any one thinks fit to try them. It is desirable, in short, that in things which do not primarily concern others, individuality should assert itself. Where, not the person's own character, but the traditions of customs of other people are the rule of conduct, there is wanting one of the principal ingredients of human happiness, and quite the chief ingredient of individual and social progress.[7]

This was a radical sentiment for 1859. Mill was very likely influenced by his own life experience, especially his relationship with Harriet Taylor. They met while Harriet was married and began a close relationship as friends, philosophical collaborators, and eventually, spouses. Of course, in England at the time, the social stigma against adultery, or simply between close relationships between men and married women, would have loomed large in Mill's life. As we shall see, Mill's arguments would eventually lay much of the philosophical and legal foundation for the lesbian and gay rights movement that emerged in the 1950s and 1960s.

Mill never directly addressed homosexuality, but one of his teachers and mentors did—Jeremy Bentham. However, Bentham was too fearful of damage to his reputation and his overall philosophical project by public statements on the topic, and he never published these writings (written between 1774 and 1824) during his lifetime. Bentham's utilitarian philosophy led him to think seriously about legal reform, and he was one of the leading legal reformers of his era. His philosophical starting point was that humans naturally pursue pleasure and minimize pain. As a result, the goal of politics and law is to maximize pleasure and minimize pain for the largest number of individuals, or to try to achieve the "greatest good for the greatest number." He was critical of tradition and morality as guides for law and policy, preferring a focus on utility, or the best outcome for the greatest number. His focus on human pleasure was revolutionary in legal and political thinking. Since classical times, some form of suppression of human appetites was seen to be crucial to a sound political and legal order.

Bentham's approach to philosophy is clearly reflected in his writings on same-sex intimacy. His writings were a significant challenge to the near universal condemnation of homosexuality from European legal and political philosophers of the 1700s and early 1800s. Indeed, he is critical of thinkers such as Voltaire, Montesquieu, and William Blackstone, all of whom condemned same-sex sex acts. Speaking of same-sex intimacy, he wrote, "As to any primary mischief, it is evident that it produces no pain in anyone. On the contrary it produces pleasure. . . . [if] The partners are both willing."[8] Thus, consensual same-sex intimacy ought not be criminalized. Indeed, the harsh legal treatment of same-sex intimacy, especially in England, outraged Bentham, but he was far too afraid to make his outrage known publicly. As he vividly and painfully wrote, "A hundred times have I shuddered at the view of the perils I was exposing myself to in encountering the opinions that are in possession of men's minds on [this] subject. . . . I have trembled at the thought of the indignation that must be raised against the Apologist of a crime that has been looked upon by many . . . as one among the blackest under Heaven."[9] Bentham's general ideas about legal reform were better received on the continent of Europe than in England. Indeed, sodomy was decriminalized in France in 1791 during the French Revolution, and this remained part of the Napoleonic Code.[10] The criminalization of sodomy would remain an Anglo-American phenomenon, especially in the era of British colonization. Sodomy laws were a vestige of British rule, present in British colonies. In areas of the world colonized or influenced by continental European powers, for the most part these laws were eliminated or never put in place.

In contrast to the liberal reformist thought developed by Hobbes, Locke, Mill, and Bentham, Edmund Burke articulated a perspective on politics that became the foundation for modern classical conservatism. Today, Burke's thought undergirds much of the opposition to equality for sexual and gender minorities. Burke's essay, "Reflections on the Revolution in France," presents a vision for politics grounded in tradition and religion. He objected to the rational and scientific turn in political philosophy represented by the liberal thinkers. He bemoaned the loss of chivalry, or the medieval code of human conduct that was sharply ordered along gender lines. As he declared, "The age of chivalry is gone. That of sophisters, economists, and calculators [including Bentham] has succeeded; and the glory of Europe is extinguished forever."[11] For Burke, the only true rights and liberties were those ratified by tradition and religion. As he wrote, "When ancient opinions and rules of life are taken away, the loss cannot possibly be estimated. From that moment we have no compass to govern us; nor can we know distinctly to what port we steer."[12] Thus, sexual practices and gender norms and roles defined by tradition and religion should not be challenged, because in general, individuals critical of the political and legal status quo "should approach to the faults of the state as to the wounds of a father, with pious awe and trembling solicitude."[13] We see the relevance of this approach to contemporary sexuality and gender politics in an exchange between federal appellate judge Richard Posner and an attorney defending Wisconsin's ban on same-sex relationship recognition. During oral argument in the Seventh Circuit Court of Appeals in August of 2014, Posner asked the lawyer for the state of Wisconsin what was the basis for the state's discriminatory ban on same-sex marriage and similar arrangements. The lawyer, Timothy Samuelson, responded, "Well, we have, uh, the Burkean argument, that it's reasonable and rational to proceed slowly."[14] While Poser and the other judges on the court rejected the argument, opponents continue to invoke Burkeanism on a range of gender- and sexuality-based policy areas, as will be discussed later in the chapter.

THE EMERGENCE OF LESBIAN AND GAY POLITICAL THOUGHT IN THE MID-TWENTIETH CENTURY

The influence of Mill and Bentham, as well as the general liberal rights framework, can be seen in early attempts of those dissatisfied with the political and legal status of sexual minorities in the United States in the mid-twentieth century. Recall from chapter 2 that Marxism and its legacy influenced the creation of the Mattachine Society but that this approach was eclipsed by much more conservative approaches in the 1950s. Eventually, a more liberal framework emerged, first, as articulated by Donald Webster Cory, relying on a Millian, negative liberty framework, but then turning toward more militancy and a focus on positive liberty and the need for recognition of the dignity of lesbians and gay men, as reflected in the writings of activist Frank Kameny. Both Cory and Kameny drew from the movement for racial justice that dominated civil rights activism in the mid-twentieth century.

Recall from chapter 2 the importance of Cory's *The Homosexual In America*. Published in 1951, it inspired a generation of activists. Cory's goal was to normalize homosexuality and place sexual minorities squarely within the emerging minority rights and human rights paradigm, to confront what he referred to as America's "minority problem."[15] But Cory noted that sexual minorities were in a different situation from other minority groups, with a lack of full identity formation, nearly complete social marginalization, and lacking cultural and family support in the face of hostility. "The ethnic group can take refuge in the comfort and pride of their own, in the warmth of family and friends . . . But not the homosexuals. . . . Constantly and unceasingly we carry a mask, and without interruption we stand on our guard lest our secret, which is our very essence, be betrayed."[16] This was a potentially more restrictive version of African-American thinker W. E. B. Du Bois's "dual consciousness," and Cory noted the maddening implication of the metaphor of the mask: because of the shame and social marginalization, no one would dare challenge the status quo, but leaders who are willing to do exactly that were needed to change the status quo. As he noted, "One is a 'hero' if he espouses the cause of minorities, but is only a suspect if that minority is the homosexual group."[17] In fact, it appears that Cory viewed himself as a gay version of Du Bois, taking a similar personal, cultural, historical, and sociological approach to inequality. Although Cory only cites Du Bois once, his spirit pervades the text.

Even though he expressed internal discomfort with homosexuality, he clearly saw the problem not with the gay and lesbian community, but with the majority heterosexual community. Paraphrasing Gunnar Myrdal, Cory wrote, "There are no minority problems. There are only majority problems. There is no Negro problem except that created by whites. . . . To which I add: and no homosexual problem except that created by the heterosexual society."[18] The deconstruction of heterosexual privilege and hypocrisy was one Cory's primary goals—a difficult sell in the profoundly conformist early 1950s. However, Cory viewed this as a crucial starting point in the fight for progress.

Cory's frame of analysis was clearly a liberal, rights-based framework. His demands were largely libertarian—the freedom to be left alone, the freedom to express and discuss sexuality, and sexual freedom. Indeed, his language was distinctly Millian:

> What the homosexual wants is freedom—not only freedom of expression, but also sexual freedom. By sexual freedom is meant the right of any person to gratify his urges when and how he sees fit, without fear of social consequences, so long as he does not use the force of either violence, threat or superior age; so long as he does not inflict bodily harm or disease upon another person; so long as the other person is of sound mind and agrees to the activity.[19]

Although he saw the importance of intimacy for personhood, this was not necessarily part of his political platform. He did not call for the recognition of same-sex relationships, even though he thought they might be possible; he simply felt that through a libertarian approach to sexuality, society would come to see the value of all types of sexual arrangements.

Indeed, his view of marriage was largely defined through a heterosexual prism. A bit of self-hatred and internalized homophobia was present in Cory's discussion of gay relationships. He could not quite see them the same as marriage; in fact, he argued that many gay men could continue in heterosexual marriages. Two distinct chapters of *The Homosexual in America* were devoted to the examination of the factors leading to gay men marrying women and the reasons gay men chose not to enter heterosexual relationships. Strikingly, Cory appeared to endorse the idea of heterosexual marriage for gay men as a way to have a complete life. For him, an exclusively gay life was solitary and pathetic. As he wrote,

The married homosexuals I have known never for a moment regret the home, the family life, the mutual care and tenderness, the pursuit of common interests that have arisen from the union with a woman. They regret most of all the mask, the fact that it cannot be discarded even with the one with whom the burdens of life are being shared. But if these men could look into the inner selves of other husbands, would they not find that all people wear masks, even in the presence of their most intimate companions?[20]

Thus, sexuality was marginal to personhood for Cory. A full life could be achieved without a substantial gay relationship. Cory also dismissed "sham marriages" with lesbians, but not for the most obvious reasons, like the injustice of forcing people to live a lie. For him, the problem was that lesbians were too cold and not likely to be housewives and mothers. Gay men were seeking real nurturers, housekeepers, and mothers of their children.[21] Consequently, Cory justified the notion of compartmentalization—the idea that gay men should separate their married lives from their gay lives. He could not conceive of the notion of a fully actualized and fulfilled gay individual.

While certainly limited by the times, Cory's analysis broke through, although on a limited scale, the cultural, legal, and political hegemony of homosexuality as pure deviance. By framing the issue as a civil rights issue and connecting it to the broader political conversations concerning inequality, Cory delivered the political version of Alfred Kinsey's scientific approach of the same time. But it also shows how distant the idea of same-sex marriage was from early theorizing on gay rights.

The movement took a more political and assertive turn in the early to mid-1960s, largely as the result of the actions and rhetoric of Frank Kameny. Kameny's brand of politics mirrored the increasing militancy of the civil rights movement. In fact, Kameny saw this movement as a direct model. In a speech given to the Mattachine Society of New York in 1964, Kameny outlined his vision of where the sexual minority rights movement, or the homophile[22] movement as it was called, needed to go. In the speech, Kameny focused on problems within and outside the movement. From within, he was clearly battling the internalized homophobia of the movement reflected by aspects of Cory's thought and the timid and limited tactics of the movement. Indeed, one of his explicit goals was to turn the movement away from its sole focus on self-help toward a "civil liberties-social action" approach.[23]

He was highly critical of the lack of self-confidence of the movement, instead calling for a public strategy for change: "We should have a clear, explicit, consistent viewpoint and we should not be timid in presenting it."[24] Kameny was particularly critical of the tendency of the movement to give equal status to antigay arguments, particularly those that came from professionals. Like Cory, he felt that central to any gay rights strategy was the challenging of elite opinion, particularly from the medical and psychiatric community. Kameny, the scientist,[25] criticized the "so-called authorities" on sexuality who demonstrated "an appalling incidence of loose reasoning, of poor research, . . . of non-representative samplings, of conclusions being incorporated into initial assumptions, and vice versa, with consequent circular reasoning."[26] This empiricism was driven by the desire to eliminate the stigma of homosexuality which was central to the lack of political progress, both from within the movement and from external moralism and flawed science. As he clearly stated, "I look upon homosexuality as something in no way shameful or intrinsically undesirable."

This is clearly a big step beyond Cory's ambivalence. Indeed, Kameny was not advocating simply the right to be let alone—his framework reflected a fuller sense of individualism, one that included notions of positive freedom. Quoting from the D.C. Mattachine Society statement of purpose (which he most likely authored), Kameny asserted that the rights desired were "the right, as human beings, to develop our full potential and dignity, and the right, as citizens, to be allowed to make our maximum contribution to the society in which we live."[27]

Like Cory, Kameny viewed sexual minorities as completely equivalent to other minorities striving for equality at the time. In the speech, he emphasized the similarities to the status, treatment, and goals of African Americans and Jews. He particularly emphasized this connection while refuting the choice/ change arguments made in opposition to rights for sexual minorities. "Why we are Negroes, Jews, or homosexuals is totally irrelevant, and whether we can be changed to whites, Christians, or heterosexual is equally irrelevant," Kameny stated in a clear attempt at solidarity.[28]

Kameny viewed same-sex marriage as a natural extension of his liberal reformism. In fact, he thought it was a certainty that the D.C. city council would enact a same-sex marriage law in the mid-1970s. This occurred at the same time that many same-sex couples saw this as a logical next step in the gay rights movement, with some of them bringing lawsuits challenging the state denial of their marriage license applications.

Unlike the more repressive 1950s where marriage, as represented by Cory, was viewed as much more of an essentially heterosexual institution, some liberal reformist thinkers like Kameny conceived of legal recognition of same-sex marriage as a natural outgrowth of a liberal, rights-claiming, and equality seeking framework. They saw that intimate relationships were a part of personhood and desired not to simply be left alone by government; they wanted public affirmation and support. As Kameny described an attempt by two men to gain a marriage license in D.C. in 1972, "This is another of the efforts of homosexuals to place their relationships on par with those of heterosexuals, and to achieve full equality in society. All rights and benefits of government and law available to heterosexual citizens are, by right, available to homosexual citizens."[29] Kameny saw the opportunity created by the changing nature of heterosexual marriage, in particular the move away from procreation toward companionate marriage. In doing so, he applied liberal rationalism to the issue of same-sex marriage and anticipated the approach of judges decades later who would be equally skeptical of the "procreation justification" for heterosexual-only marriage. Abandoning tradition alone as basis for analysis, he stated, "With the growing use of contraception and sterilization, with an absence of any ban on marriages between people physiologically or chronologically incapable of reproduction . . . , denial of marriage to homosexuals . . . is clearly untenable."[30]

This approach, of course, was political and legally naïve, with courts and legislatures (including the D.C. city council) refusing to support same-sex marriage. In addition, marriage was not favored by the more radical gay liberationist and lesbian-feminist approaches to the movement in the early 1970s. Indeed, unlike the demise of more radical approaches in the 1950s, the gay rights movement split into distinct philosophical camps in the early 1970s with the rise of gay liberationist and lesbian-feminist thought.

LESBIAN FEMINISM AND GAY LIBERATION

By the late 1960s and 1970s, Second Wave Feminism was emerging as a powerful movement. This feminist movement was focused on critiquing the patriarchal, or male-dominated, institutions and cultural practices throughout society. Challenging and changing entrenched gender roles, especially in the family and the workplace, was central to the feminist critique. Reproductive rights emerged as a central focus of the movement, as feminists argued that women could not be fully liberated and free to control their lives without complete control of their reproductive futures. Feminists also critiqued liberalism's tendency to view power and authority only in the public, or governmental realm, and began to point to the ways that men dominated women in the more private realms of the home and workplace. Thus, issues such as domestic violence and sexual harassment emerged as central to the movement.

Many lesbians obviously agreed with the philosophical approach of the feminist movement, and many became actively involved in the movement. However, given still-dominant heterosexism, some feminist movement leaders viewed the presence of lesbians in the movement to be a threat to the movement's success. Most famously, Betty Friedan, whose book, *The Feminine Mystique*, helped to ignite Second Wave Feminism, referred to lesbians in the movement as the "lavender menace" and attempted to purge them from leadership roles in the movement. In addition, many lesbians also witnessed sexism and discrimination in the male-dominated gay liberation movement. Partially in response to these experiences and partly out of the logic of feminist analysis, some lesbians created a movement and body of feminist thought that placed lesbians at the center of the feminist movement: lesbian feminism. Groups such as Radicalesbians and The Furies Collective and publications such as *The Furies* formed to impart this perspective on society and beginning the process, in their view, of transformation required for true gender equality and women's liberation.

In this era of lesbian-feminist thought, female-only relationships were seen as the path to the liberation of women. Women needed to abandon men and patriarchal society to fully challenge and eliminate sexism—an approach often referred to as lesbian separatism. A member of The Furies, Charlotte Bunch, stated,

> Women-identified lesbianism is, then, more than a sexual preference; it is a political choice. It is political because relationships between men and women are essentially political: they involve power and dominance. Since the lesbian actively rejects that relationship and chooses women, she defies the established political system. . . . We offer the end of collective and individual male supremacy.[31]

While the separatist impulse waned as an ideal, especially as many feminists continued intimate relationships with men, the feminist core critiques of sexism, patriarchy, and (increasingly) heterosexism persisted in much activism of lesbians, and lesbians became more integrated in the broader women's movement.

The Stonewall Riots occurred during the high point of New Left ideology, and a strain of political thought that developed in the wake of Stonewall strongly reflects the elements of this ideology. New Left thought was the philosophical basis for the student movements of the 1960s, outlined in the 1963 "Port Huron Statement." The New Left was part of the Marxist tradition, but it is also critical of Marxism, particularly traditional Marxism's emphasis on economic class–based oppression, to the exclusion of race, gender, sexuality, and a wide range of forms of oppression. The philosophy of Herbert Marcuse was a strong influence on the movement. As Roy Macridis and Mark Hulliung, describe the movement, "It is far easier to know what the New Left was against than what it favored. The students . . . were antihierarchical, antibureaucratic, antimanagerial, anticonsumer society, antiwork ethic, antiwar, anti-Old Left."[32] They favored a politics of liberation from the constraints of modern, complex, capitalist society in favor of a politics of authenticity in which every individual was empowered to follow their own unique path. In this way, New Left thought is directly connected to the Marxist/Anarchist thought that inspired the formation of the Mattachine Society, discussed in the last chapter.

An essay by Carl Wittman, "A Gay Manifesto," demonstrates the influence of New Left thought on what came to be known as the gay liberation movement. Using the framework of oppression/liberation, Wittman focused his essay on the institutional and cultural constraints placed on sexual and gender expression, and these oppressions were part of a larger system of oppression in "Amerika":

> We are children of straight society. We still think straight: that is part of our oppression. One of the worst of concepts is inequality. Straight (also white, English, male, capitalist) thinking views things in terms of order and comparison. . . . This idea gets extended to male/female, on top/on bottom, spouse/not spouse, heterosexual/homosexual; boss/worker; white/black and rich/poor. Our social institutions cause and reflect this verbal hierarchy.

A path out of this oppression was to "define for ourselves a new pluralistic, role free structure for ourselves. . . . Liberation for gay people is defining for ourselves how and with whom we live, instead of measuring our relationship in comparison with straight ones, with straight values." For Wittman, marriage was not a path to liberation but was part of the larger system of straight oppression: "Traditional marriage is a rotten, oppressive institution." Central to Wittman's analysis of oppression based upon sexuality was the notion that sexuality was fluid and that bisexuality was an ideal form of sexual expression. As he stated, "Nature leaves undefined the object of sexual desire. The gender of that object is imposed socially." The lifting of sexual taboos and the full exploration of erotic desire, in the context of full consent and reciprocity between partners, was, of course, central to Wittman's version of liberation. He noted the coercive power of the designation of sexual perversion, even within the gay community, and argued for a broad range of sexual expression. He called for "democratic, mutual, reciprocal sex." Sexual freedom, from both laws and social norms, was the central element of gay liberation. Seeing strong linkages between forms of oppression, he called for a coalitional approach to the new politics, with alliances formed with women's and racial minority groups. Indeed, Wittman was troubled by attempts to "rank" oppression. As he stated, "Talk about the priority of black liberation or ending imperialism over and above gay liberation is just an anti-gay propaganda."[33] Thus, he clearly viewed politics through the prism of group identity and activism.

Activist politics based on gay liberation and lesbian-feminist thought waned as more conventional politics began to dominate the movement, with the early 1970s marking the fullest activism of the movements. But many of the themes and critiques of the movements would be used by later generations of activists and theorists, especially the larger movement for sexual minority rights would become too conservative, gradualist, and nondiverse.

QUEER THEORY

Both the lesbian-feminist and gay liberation movements were grounded in fixed and firm sex/gender- and sexuality-based identities, but new frameworks challenged these essentialist assumptions by the 1980s and 1990s. The philosopher most responsible for this approach is Michel Foucault. Foucault directly influenced the politics of sexuality by theorizing that modern sexual identity was created in the late-nineteenth and early-twentieth centuries by medical authorities. He also laid the foundation for the notion that identity is socially constructed by arguing that power is not merely something that a political sovereign exercises but is something that exists "everywhere," as he famously put it. In other words, cultural norms and practices, language, professional norms (such as those in the medical community), all constrain human action and shape how we think of ourselves and present ourselves to society. Consequently, to fully understand and create human freedom, we must account for this nongovernmental power. As described by philosopher Wendy Brown, "If power operates through norms, and not only through law and force, and if norms are borne by word, images, and the built environment, then popular discourse, market interpellations, and spatial organizations are as much a vehicle for power as are troops, bosses, prime ministers, or police."[34] Foucault argued that sexuality was an arena where this power dynamic was particularly present. Recall that Mill made a similar point about the coercive power of norms, but his analysis was still grounded in liberalism, while Foucault is a critic of liberalism and its desire to maintain a line between public and private realms.

Queer theory developed from Foucault and the writings and arguments of other philosophers like Judith Butler. Butler argues that gender is purely socially constructed; there is nothing natural or essential about masculinity or femininity. In reality, gender is quite fluid or malleable. What we think we see as gender in ourselves and others is, in reality, a performance. In other words, according to Butler, we are all always in drag. Butler refers to gender as being "performative," in that it both reflects our learned and created expressions of gender and reinforces/creates gender norms. As political scientist Susan Burgess describes this theory, "When it comes to sex and gender, everyone is in drag all the time. Queer theorists wish to reveal identity as performative rather than natural, through creative drag performances which reveal that there is no there there."[35] Queer theorists thus have a preference for individuals and groups who challenge sex and gender norms to demonstrate to the rest of us how arbitrary, and powerful are these norms (but potentially powerless if we are aware of their arbitrary nature): dissidents, outsiders, rebels, or "queer" people in general. Like Mill, queer theorist Michael Warner rejects the politics of shaming and ostracism and points to those who challenge norms and convention as the inspiration for a liberationist politics, not "the respectable leaders of the gay community."[36] Thus, queer politics rejects conventional methods of legal, electoral, and insider politics in favor of a politics of confrontation and direct action designed to provoke a response in those who value and enforce dominant norms. For queer theorists, only when the norms are destabilized can a more just politics begin to form, but this may need to be eventually challenged as normalization sets in. Consequently, many queer theorists are disdainful of the homophile movement, even in its more aggressive forms, while praising the Stonewall Riot participants for their more queer brand of politics. Like the gay liberation and lesbian-feminist activists, queer theorists are critical of the marriage equality movement and what they see as its normalizing tendencies and its outsized role in the broader LGBT rights movement. As Warner states, "Marriage, in short, would make for good gays—the kind who would not challenge the norms of straight culture, who would not flaunt sexuality, and who would not insist on living differently from ordinary folk."[37]

Tensions Between Feminism and the Transgender and Intersex Movements

The notion that gender, and also biological sex, as intersex theorists and advocates claim, is socially constructed has created tension between some feminist thinkers and activists and queer theorists and transgender/intersex theorists and activists. While some feminists incorporate insights about social construction into their feminist analysis, others take a more essentialist view of gender as something fixed and culturally powerful. They fear that moving away from viewing gender through the prism of men versus women will undermine the critique of male power in society. In particular, some feminists are critical of transgender women, because, it is argued, they have the "choice" to remain in a socially and politically power role as men, or can retreat to this role when necessary. Other feminists argue that gender is significantly socially constructed, but that male power remains a significant cultural and political force. They view transgender individuals as a path to the equalization, if not elimination, of rigid gender categories and the power dynamics that come with those categories. But the antitransgender element of some feminist critiques has had powerful effects. As Shannon Price Minter notes, "Janice Raymond and Mary Daly, among other lesbian feminist theorists, demonized transsexual women as the epitome of misogynist attempts to invade women's space and appropriate women's identity."[38]

This, of course, can create barriers to LGBT movement growth and com-
plicates policymaking connected to the movement. The controversy over the
Michigan Womyn's Musical Festival has become emblematic of the contemporary manifestation of this tension. The festival's organizers bill the event
as being for "womyn born womyn." This is seen by critics as purposeful discrimination against trans women, and some LGBT civil rights organizations
have boycotted or critiqued the event, in addition to a boycott by the high-
profile musical group, Indigo Girls. In terms of policy, as will be discussed in
chapter 7, many transgender and intersex activists call for the elimination of
gender markers on government documents as a way to prevent discrimination
against transgender and intersex individuals. Some feminists object to this
approach out of concern that not using gender as a category in public policy,
especially in government documents, will make it more difficult to recognize
and quantify discrimination against women.

MODERN BURKEANISM AND THE NEW NATURAL LAW

In opposition to both a liberal, rights-based approach and liberationist/
feminist/queer theory approaches to the politics of sexuality and gender,
opponents of rights and equality for sexual and gender minorities, beyond
purely theological arguments (the theological arguments are usually in the
background, however), have attempted to frame their position in more secular
terms by looking to philosophical traditions seemingly supportive of their
arguments. One frame is explicitly Burkean: law and policy should reflect
traditional societal norms about sexuality and gender, and changes to the
norms, laws, and policies should be made gradually, if at all. This approach
is reflected in a dissenting opinion by Supreme Court Justice Antonin Scalia
in *Romer v. Evans* (1996). The majority of the court held that Colorado's
Amendment 2, a voter-approved constitutional amendment banning sexual
orientation–protective antidiscrimination laws, was based on animus toward
sexual minorities, thus running afoul of the court's requirement that all laws
must reflect a rational public policy, as opposed to a traditional, purpose.
Scalia described the Colorado voters who approved the amendment as fair-
minded Burkeans. According to Scalia, Amendment 2 was "a modest attempt
by seemingly tolerant Coloradans to preserve traditional sexual mores against
the efforts of a politically powerful minority to revise those mores through
use of the laws."[39] Similarly, Scalia dissented from the court's invalidation
of sodomy laws in 2003 in *Lawrence v. Texas* by arguing that the state's
law "undeniably seeks to further the belief of its citizens that certain forms
of sexual behavior are 'immoral and unacceptable,'"[40] and that this was an
appropriate use of the law. He called the decision to deem sodomy laws
unconstitutional "a massive disruption of the current social order."[41]

The New Natural Law movement is a movement in law, philosophy, and theology that is closely connected to the teachings of the Catholic Church. These thinkers ground their analysis not in liberal or liberationist traditions but the classical political thought of Aristotle and the adaptor of Aristotelian thought to Catholic doctrine, Thomas Aquinas. Central to this approach is the notion that law and policy should only promote heterosexual procreative sex and a family structure that supports this. Strong critics of this approach, philosophers Nicholas C. Bamforth and David A. J. Richards, note the implications for sexual and gender politics. They describe an "astonishing list" (particularly in modern, liberal democracies) of potential laws and policies regulating intimacy under natural law theory, including the use of contraception and abortion, gender roles within the family, and sexual practices. As they describe the implications, "Our sexual and emotional lives must be controlled, restricted, and channeled. . . . Paternalism and the restriction of intimate personal choices would become a social (or legal) imperative."[42]

Princeton University political scientist Robert George, a leading advocate of the New Natural Law, has put theory into practice. George, a leading theorist of the modern movement against LGBT rights, was the chairman of the National Organization for Marriage, the leading antimarriage equality organization in the United States. He is also one of the authors of "The Manhattan Declaration: A Call of Christian Conscience," a 2009 document declaring opposition to abortion and LGBT rights, particularly same-sex marriage, that merges conservative Christian theology and new natural law principles. In typical new natural law form, the document describes marriage as an "objective reality" created "by the sexual complementarity of man and woman." Nonheterosexuals are described as sinners worthy of love, but their "sexual immorality" creates individuals who have "fallen short of God's intentions for our lives."[43] Beyond opposition to marriage equality, George supports the legal regulation of nonprocreative sexual activity.[44] In other words, George and many like-minded thinkers support sodomy laws. They are the anti-Benthamites.

While modern Burkeanism and New Natural Law theory have been largely abandoned by courts in contemporary jurisprudence, they still retain a significant foothold in the political arena, increasingly framed in arguments allowing for the legal protection of religious beliefs aligned with the philosophical camp. As the law has become more secularized and shorn of appeals to pure tradition, traditionalists have begun to argue for exemption from generally applicable law, a tactic explored in later chapters.

CONCLUSION

Thus, it is impossible to understand the rise of LGBT politics and its opposition without understanding the ideas that have shaped these politics. Rights-based liberalism provided an opening for activists, but later generations of activists and thinkers saw these politics as too limiting—true liberation would require something more radical and systematically critical. Opponents looked back to Burkeanism and natural law traditions (shorn of their acceptance of same-sex intimacy) to halt the societal recognition and validation of sexual and gender minorities. The broad parameters of this philosophical debate will likely frame theorizing about this politics for some time to come.

KEY TERMS, PEOPLE, AND CONCEPTS

Analytical individualism
Aquinas, Thomas
Aristotle
Bentham, Jeremy/Benthamite legal reforms
Bunch, Charlotte
Burke/Burkeanism, Edmund
Butler, Judith
Classical approach to sexuality
Communitarian
Cory, Donald Webster
Elitism
Feminism/Second Wave Feminism
Foucault, Michel
The Furies
Gay liberationist thought
George, Robert
Hobbes, Thomas
Kameny, Frank
Liberalism
Liberal democracy

Libertarian
Lesbian-feminist thought
Locke, John
Mill, John Stuart
Marketplace of ideas
Marxism
New Left
New natural law
Nongovernmental power
Patriarchal
Performative
Plato
Radicalesbians
Queer theory
Sappho
Scalia, Antonin
Secularism/ secularization of politics
Teleological reasoning
Utilitarianism
Wittman, Carl

QUESTIONS FOR DISCUSSION

1. Despite the presence of socially sanctioned homosexuality in parts of the classical world, why was classical politics not conducive to the creation of a sexual minority politics?
2. How did liberalism provide a philosophical framework for a politics of sexual minorities to emerge? What are the limitations of liberal politics for sexual and gender minorities?

3. How do the "new natural law" thinkers influence anti-LGBT politics? What is the lineage of their arguments?
4. Which is a better framework for the contemporary politics of sexual and gender minorities? Liberalism or Queer Theory?

NOTES

1. Aristotle, *Politics*, Book I, ch. 2, in *The Broadview Anthology of Social and Political Thought*, vol. 1, Andrew Bailey, et al., eds. (Buffalo: Broadview Press, 2008), 178.

2. Michael Sandel, *Justice: What's the Right Thing to Do?* (New York: Farrar, Straus, and Giroux, 2009), 189.

3. Martha C. Nussbaum, *Sex & Social Justice* (New York: Oxford University Press, 1999), 305.

4. Thomas Hobbes, *The Leviathan*, ch. 13, para. 9.

5. Hobbes, *The Leviathan*, ch. 18, para. 2.

6. John Stuart Mill, *On Liberty*, David Spitz, ed. (New York: W.W. Norton, 1975), 6.

7. Mill, *On Liberty*, 54.

8. Jeremy Bentham, "Offenses Against One's Self: Paederasty," in *the Broadview Anthology of Social and Political Thought*, vol. 1, Andrew Bailey, et al., eds. (Buffalo: Broadview Press, 2008), 885.

9. Louis Crompton, *Byron and Greek Love: Homophobia in 19th-Century England* (Berkeley: University of California Press, 1985), 30.

10. Crompton, *Byron and Greek Love*, 17–19.

11. Edmund Burke, "Reflections on the Revolution in France," in *the Broadview Anthology of Social and Political Thought*, 831.

12. Burke, 832.

13. Burke, 832.

14. David Lat, "Judge Posner's Blistering Benchslaps At The Same-Sex Marriage Arguments," *Above the Law*, August 27, 2014, http://abovethelaw.com/2014/08/judge-posners-blistering-benchslaps-at-the-same-sex-marriage-arguments/.

15. Donald Webster Cory, *The Homosexual in America: A Subjective Approach* (New York: Greenberg, 1951), 4.

16. Cory, 10.

17. Cory, 14.

18. Cory, 228.

19. Cory, 231–32.

20. Cory, 221. The gendered language used here points to the gay male emphasis of Cory's writing.

21. Cory, 212.

22. This term was used by Kameny and others to de-emphasize the sexual aspects of the movement. Therefore, homophile was preferred over homosexual.

23. Franklin E. Kameny, "Civil Liberties: A Progress Report," *New York Mattachine Newsletter*, 10:1 (July 1965), 7–22: 8.

24. Kameny, 11.

25. Kameny was a physicist by training.

26. Kameny, 13.

27. Kameny, 15.

28. Kameny, 15.

29. Frank Kameny, Draft press release, Mattachine Society of Washington, DC, June 30, 1972. Papers of Frank Kameny, Library of Congress. Copy on file with the author.

30. Frank Kameny, "Action on the Gay Legal Front," unpublished manuscript, ca. 1975, 26. Papers of Frank Kameny, Library of Congress, copy on file with the author.

31. Charlotte Bunch, "Lesbians in Revolt," in *We Are Everywhere: A Historical Sourcebook of Gay and Lesbian Politics*, Mark Blasuis and Shane Phelan, eds. (New York: Routledge, 1997), 421–22.

32. Roy C. Macridis and Mark Hulliung, *Contemporary Political Ideologies: Movements and Regimes*, 6th ed. (New York: Harper Collins, 1996), 283.

33. Quotations take from Carl Wittman, "A Gay Manifesto," in Blasuis and Phelan, eds. *We Are Everywhere*, 380–88.

34. Wendy Brown, "Power after Foucault," in *The Oxford Handbook of Political Theory*, John S. Dryzek, et al., eds. (New York: Oxford University Press, 2006), 66.

35. Susan Burgess, "Queer (Theory) Eye for the Straight (Legal) Guy: *Lawrence v. Texas*' Makeover of *Bowers v. Hardwick*," *Political Research Quarterly*, 59:3 (September 2006), 401–14: 403.

36. Michael Warner, *The Trouble with Normal: Sex, Politics, and the Ethics of Queer Life* (New York: The Free Press, 1999), 36.

37. Warner, *The Trouble with Normal*, 113.

38. Shannon Price Minter, "Do Transsexuals Dream of Gay Rights? Getting Real about Transgender Inclusion," in *Transgender Rights*, Paisley Currah, et al., eds. (Minneapolis: University of Minnesota Press, 2006), 141–70: 155.

39. Romer v. Evans, 517 U.S. 620 (1996), 636.

40. *Lawrence v. Texas*, 539 U.S. 558 (2003), 599.

41. Lawrence, 591.

42. Nicholas C. Bamforth and David A. J. Richards, *Patriarchal Religion, Sexuality, and Gender: A Critique of New Natural Law* (New York: Cambridge University Press, 2008), 338.

43. The text of the Declaration may be found at http://www.manhattandeclaration.org.

44. Bamforth and Richards, 23.

BIBLIOGRAPHY AND FURTHER READING

Gordon A. Babst, *Liberal Constitutionalism, Marriage, and Sexual Orientation: A Contemporary Case for Dis-Establishment* (New York: Peter Lang, 2002).

Gordon A. Babst, Emily R. Gill, and Jason Pierceson, *Moral Argument, Religion, and Same-Sex Marriage* (Lanham, MD: Lexington Books, 2009).

Carlos A. Ball, *The Morality of Gay Rights: An Exploration in Political Philosophy* (New York: Routledge, 2003).

Nicholas C. Bamforth and David A. J. Richards, *Patriarchal Religion, Sexuality, and Gender: A Critique of New Natural Law* (New York: Cambridge University Press, 2008).

Mark Blasius, *Gay and Lesbian Politics: Sexuality and the Emergence of a New Ethic* (Philadelphia: Temple University Press, 1994).

Mark Blasius, ed., *Sexual Identities, Queer Politics* (Princeton: Princeton University Press, 2001).

Judith Butler, *Gender Trouble: Feminism and the Subversion of Identity* (New York: Routledge, 1990).

Michel Foucault, *The History of Sexuality*, Volume 1: *An Introduction*, trans. Robert Hurley (New York: Pantheon, 1978).

Emily R. Gill, *Becoming Free: Autonomy and Diversity in the Liberal Polity* (Lawrence: University Press of Kansas, 2001).

Emily R. Gill, *An Argument for Same-Sex Marriage: Religious Freedom, Sexual Freedom, and Public Expressions of Civil Equality* (Washington, DC: Georgetown University Press, 2012).

Martha Nussbaum, *Sex and Social Justice* (New York: Oxford University Press, 1999).

Shane Phelan, *Sexual Strangers: Gays, Lesbians, and the Dilemmas of Citizenship* (Philadelphia: Temple University Press, 2001).

Jason Pierceson, *Courts, Liberalism, and Rights: Gay Law and Politics in the United States and Canada* (Philadelphia: Temple University Press, 2005).

David A. J. Richards, *Women, Gays, and the Constitution* (Chicago: University of Chicago Press, 1998).

Michael Warner, ed., *Fear of a Queer Planet: Queer Politics and Social Theory* (Minneapolis: University of Minnesota Press, 1993).

Michael Warner, *The Trouble with Normal: Sex, Politics, and the Ethics of Queer Life* (New York: The Free Press, 1999).

Chapter 4

Social Movements, Electoral Politics, and Public Opinion

This chapter explores sexual and gender minorities in their quest to achieve policy change through the electoral process, as well as their opponents' use of the same process. First, a social movement framework is used to understand how the movement and its opponents build and use grassroots activism and elite-based organizations to further their agendas. Next, the chapter examines a uniquely American, but highly relevant for LGBT politics, element of electoral politics: the ballot initiative. The chapter then explores attempts by openly LGBT individuals to run for elected office, hoping to create policy change. Finally, the role of public opinion on public policy is explored, especially shifts in opinion over time and continuing divisions in opinion based on demographics.

SOCIAL MOVEMENTS

Social movements are generally movements of socially marginalized groups, usually a numerical minority, who mobilize and engage the political system (and often the larger culture) to eliminate their marginalization through changes in law and policy. The African American Civil Rights Movement, the Suffrage and Women's Rights/Feminist Movements, and the Disability Right Movement are all prominent examples of social movements. They became more common as mass politics emerged, or movements involving large numbers of average citizens (rather than elected officials or elites), and became more common by the end of the nineteenth and early-to-mid-twentieth centuries. Social movements use a variety of tactics: direct-action protests to create awareness or place pressure on the government, such as marches and sit-ins/demonstrations; directly lobbying/pressuring government officials; litigation; and media campaigns.

Political scientist Craig Rimmerman defines a tension within most social movements, in terms of overall strategy and approach, and certainly within the LGBT rights movement. He describes the tension as stemming from the competing frameworks of assimilation and liberation, explored in chapter 3. As he states,

> The assimilationist approach typically embraces a rights-based perspective, works within the broader framework of pluralist democracy—one situated within classical liberalism—and fights for a seat at the table. . . . Assimilationists are more likely to accept that change will have to be incremental and to understand that slow, gradual progress is built into the very structure of the US framework of government. . . . [A liberationist approach] favors more radical cultural change, change that is more transformational in nature and often arises outside the formal structures of the US framework of government.[1]

Rimmerman maintains that both approaches are needed for any successful social movement, and that the approaches complement one another. The assimilationist approach typically utilizes elite-based strategies of insider lobbying, financial electoral influence, and litigation. Liberationist approaches tend to focus more on direct action aimed at consciousness raising and social transformation.

Direct Action

Direct action can be very effective in changing attitudes and applying pressure on government officials, but it is difficult to sustain in the long term. It takes a great deal of commitment and focus on the part of activists, but energy generally wanes over time, and divisions among activists can undermine the effort. In terms of citizen participation, the "free rider" problem undermines efforts to sustain direct citizen activism. Such participation has costs for individuals (time, money, etc.), and it is tempting to let others incur the costs while you enjoy the benefits. For example, if a demonstration or march is going to happen with or without our involvement, why do we need to go, if the message of the event will still be made? Often, the costs of direct action can be severe, such as an arrest record for direct action that involves civil disobedience.

Direct action in the lesbian and gay rights movement began in the Homophile Era with the pickets described in chapter 2. After Stonewall, pride parades in large cities became increasingly common as a show of movement solidarity, as well as personal affirmation. The GAA Zaps were also attempts to creatively engage in direct action, modeled after consciousness raising efforts of other New Left movements. The first lesbian and gay rights march in Washington took place in 1979, ten years after Stonewall, and organized marches have taken place in 1987, 1993, 2000, and 2009. ACT UP is perhaps the most effective and consequential direct-action organization. As chronicled in chapter 6, its direct-action efforts, along with insider strategies, achieved results from a political and medical system highly resistant to addressing the AIDS crisis. Direct-action protests continue to the present day, recently exemplified by demonstrations in Washington, D.C. over the ban on open service by sexual and gender minorities in the military. In one protest, Lt. Dan Choi (a service member discharged for his sexual orientation who became one of the public faces of the movement) handcuffed himself, as did other activists, to the fence in front of the White House on numerous occasions in 2010.

Institutions and Organizations of the LGBT Rights Movement

After the Homophile Era, organizations were replaced by more radical groups like the Gay Liberation Front (GLF) after Stonewall; the 1970s saw the creation of national lesbian and gay rights organizations, and this process accelerated in the 1980s. These were more insider, liberal, reformist groups, focusing on electoral politics and litigation. The Gay Activist Alliance (a less radical organization than the GLF) eventually became the National Gay Task Force in 1973, which became the National Gay and Lesbian Task Force (NGLTF) in the 1980s and is now the National LGBTQ Task Force. This organization and the litigation-based Lambda Legal Defense and Education Fund, also founded in 1973, were the main nationally organized advocacy groups. NGLTF coordinated activist efforts and trained activists throughout the country. It has always been focused significantly on local issues, and it has served as a centralized resource and clearinghouse for activists throughout the country. Another significant national group, the Human Rights Campaign (HRC) was formed and developed primarily as a fundraising and insider/D.C. lobbying organization. Critics within the movement often point to the fact that the organization is too focused on this insider approach at the expense of more grassroots efforts. More recently, it has begun to engage state and local issues.

Much of the current structure of national groups was formed in the 1980s. Sociologist Tina Fetner describes the significant growth in the decade in the following way:

> At the start of the decade, the movement consisted of stand-alone, grassroots organizations in bigger cities and on college campuses, along with a few national organizations that were so underfunded and understaffed that their

activism consisted mostly of publishing newsletters and advising local groups. Over the course of the decade . . . several umbrella organizations and national lobbying groups were developed and expanded. Unlike many earlier groups that experimented with cooperative organizational forms and rotating leadership positions, this generation of lesbian and gay movement groups was organized hierarchically. These groups set national agendas, developed tactical plans, and managed the bulk of lesbian and gay movement resources. . . . For the most part, these corporate-style non-profit groups were well-funded, staffed with professionals, and embedded in networks with each other and with local activists.[2]

By the 1990s and 2000s, more national groups formed, often with a specialized focus, such as Servicemembers Legal Defense Network with its focus on LGBT military and veterans' issues. Gay and Lesbian Alliance Against Defamation (GLAAD) focuses on the portraying of the LGBT community in the media, while Gay and Lesbian Advocates and Defenders (GLAD) is a highly effective litigation group based in New England. Other current activist- and litigation-based groups include the National Center for Lesbian Rights (NCLR), the American Civil Liberties Union (ACLU), and the National Center for Transgender Equality. State-level groups also grew during this time, but fundraising and maintaining a professional staff are a challenge, especially in less populous and rural states.

Party Politics

While the Religious Right has been an integral part of the Republican Party since the 1980s, the LGBT rights movement long-struggled to find a home in a potentially more sympathetic party, the Democrats. Not until the 1990s, and the candidacy and presidency of Bill Clinton and his campaign promise to end the ban on military service, did movement activists and organizations become more fully integrated in the party. Even then, Clinton and his party were hesitant to fully embrace the movement and its demands, most dramatically reflected in Clinton's (and most Congressional Democrats') support for the 1996 Defense of Marriage Act. In the 2000s, the party struggled with the issue of marriage equality, not explicitly endorsing it in its platform until 2012, after previously supporting recognition short of marriage, such as civil unions. The first official mention of lesbian and gay rights was in the party's 1980 platform that called for an end to discrimination based upon sexual orientation. Activists began to engage the party, with great resistance, at the 1972 Democratic Party Convention—the first post-Stonewall convention.[3] Today, the movement (and its activists and organizations) is significantly integrated into the party.

Groups such as the Log Cabin Republicans have tried to make inroads into that party on behalf of lesbian and gay rights, but the clout of social conservatives has made this difficult. Despite the fact that many individual Republican activists and elected officials are supportive of lesbian and gay rights, especially marriage equality, the national party and the vast majority of state party organizations officially oppose LGBT-supportive policies.

ELECTORAL POLITICS

While courts and other elite policymakers can protect sexual and gender minorities from attack and promote their interest in some contexts, in the realm of electoral politics, these marginalized groups are more exposed. However, long-term positive policy change requires an engagement with electoral politics, first defensively in fending off attacks by opponents, then affirmatively through running for office to affect policy change in the legislative setting and enacting policy through direct referenda. After decades of a rather bleak electoral setting, sexual and gender minorities are beginning to more successfully engage the electoral process, but significant barriers remain.

Ballot Measures

Ballot measures are historically not good vehicles for protecting the rights of minorities. After all, a mechanism that privileges majoritarianism lacks safeguards for minority rights, such as judicial review. Of course, courts can review policies made through ballot measures, but judges are often hesitant to second-guess the public, except in extreme cases. For instance, the Hawaii Supreme Court appeared poised to mandate marriage equality in that state after several years of legal wrangling in the 1990s, but when 70 percent of voters approved a constitutional amendment granting sole authority to define marriage to the legislature in 1998, the legal process stopped.[4] It would take over 15 years for marriage equality to arrive in one of the most progressive states in the country after that.

Sociologist Amy Stone calculated that LGBT rights have been denied by voters in 70 percent of ballot measures on the topic.[5] Starting with repeals of antidiscrimination laws in the 1970s, through attempts in the 1980s and 1990s to erase sexual minorities from public policy and public jobs, to the wave of antimarriage equality amendments in the 2000s, social and religious conservatives have effectively harnessed a tool not available in most countries with movements for sexual and gender minority rights: the popular initiative and referendum. Famous examples include the 1977 Miami-Dade County antidiscrimination law repeal led by Anita Bryant, California's 1978 Briggs Initiative (a failed attempt to ban lesbian or gay public school teachers), Colorado's Amendment 2 in 1992, Oregon's Ballot Measure 9 in 1992, and the 8 antimarriage equality amendments enacted in 2004. Some of these and others are discussed in other chapters in greater detail. According to Stone, religious and social conservatives have been relentless and sophisticated in their use of ballot measures:

> The tactics used by the Religious Right . . . included everything from the most virulently moralistic homophobic attacks to legalistic arguments about changing civil rights laws. Religious Right activist used several different types of direct democracy, from simple referendums that rescind a newly passed law to initiatives that twist legal language to restrict LGBT rights in both the present and the future. Similar to other social movements that use direct democracy to further their goals, the anti-gay Religious Right has used the referendum and initiative process both to further its own goals and to restrict another movement's gains.[6]

The Religious Right's strategy was aided by the fact that, in many states, it is relatively easy to get a measure before the voters—it is simply a matter of collecting a certain number of voter signatures.

On one level, this tool was devastating for the LGBT rights movement. In addition to enshrining anti-LGBT policies into law, often in state constitutions, the fight against these ballot measures put the movement on the defensive for decades and diverted resources from positive movement efforts. However, in response to these ballot measures, the movement built an infrastructure of elite and grassroots organizations, financial resources, and messaging (or a specific tailoring or focusing of the main campaign message) that was eventually shifted toward positive policy change efforts. This was the case in 2012 when several states legalized same-sex marriage in popular votes and defeated an antimarriage equality referendum in Minnesota.

Stone refers to this process as the creation of the "model campaign," or a consistently successful template for LGBT rights popular campaigns. This model includes "improved voter contact [such as door-to-door campaigning], the development of effective messaging, successful fundraising, and an increase in professional campaign staff."[7] Stone acknowledges that this privileges an insider and elite-based strategy and downplays more radical and queer approaches and arguments. Indeed, sometimes the most effective messaging is much more conservative and mainstream than many activists would like. For instance, a focus on love and (presumably monogamous) commitment was more effective as a message in campaigns for marriage equality than arguments about equal benefits and constitutionalism more broadly.

LGBT-elected Officials

An obvious way for the LGBT movement to enact supportive policies is to elect openly LGBT individuals to public office. Representation based upon identity, in which it is expected that persons of a certain identity will push to enact policies favorable to the identity group and generally represent the members of that group, is called descriptive representation. When results are actually achieved, this is referred to as substantive representation. Symbolic representation may occur when, in this case, openly LGBT-elected officials affect the views of constituents, for instance, more progressive views on the rights of sexual minorities. Thus, openly LGBT-elected officials can contribute greatly to the overall progress of the movement. Given social stigma, it took some time for LGBT-elected officials to become commonplace. A handful of officials were elected at the local level in the 1970s, expanding to the state and federal levels in the ensuing decades. Urban areas and college towns first sent LGBT individuals to elected office, and this has continued with a larger number of officials from these areas. Rural areas do not elect openly LGBT individuals, either due to their social conservatism or a calculation by LGBT individuals that they will not likely be elected from rural areas, or even more conservative urban and suburban areas. In fact, LGBT candidates are quite selective about the areas from which they run for office—nobody likes to lose an election, and it makes sense that they choose districts most favorable to winning. Most elected officials have been either gay or lesbian, with far fewer openly bisexual or transgender officeholders. In the context of LGBT rights and policy, LGBT representation has made a difference, with evidence that the presence of openly LGBT officials effects policy outcomes, but their presence may also induce a backlash in the form of anti-LGBT policy proposals from conservatives.[8]

As was discussed in chapter 2, José Sarria was the first openly gay candidate for public office when he lost a race for the San Francisco Board of Supervisors in 1961. Frank Kameny ran unsuccessfully for Congress in 1971, the first openly gay person to run for Congress. The year 1974 was important in terms of the evolution of LGBT-elected officials: after previous members of the council, Nancy Wechsler and Jerry DeGriek, had come out after their elections in 1972, Kathy Kozachenko was elected to the Ann Arbor, Michigan city council (Ann Arbor is home to the University of Michigan). Elaine Noble was elected to the Massachusetts legislature, and a Minnesota state legislator, state senator Allan Spear came out as a gay man while in office and was subsequently reelected. Spear represented a district in Minneapolis that included the University of Minnesota. Noble represented a district in Boston. During the post-Stonewall years, many more candidates tried, and failed, to get elected, mostly in large cities.[9]

The most famous openly gay-elected official from this era is Harvey Milk. Milk was a community and gay rights activist who ran for office several times (first running in 1973) before being elected to the San Francisco Board of Supervisors in 1977. Milk was a strong believer in the power of electoral politics as a way to advance the agenda of lesbian and gay community. He famously advocated a form of contact theory, urging closeted individuals to come out as a political strategy. Indeed, Milk framed his political agenda in opposition to the conservative backlash against the expansion of lesbian and gay rights in the 1970s. Arguing that it was not enough to have allies of sexual minorities in positions of power, he argued for people to come out of the closet and run for office. He stated in 1978 in a version of his famous "Hope Speech,"

> You see there is a major difference—and it remains a vital difference—between a friend and a gay person, a friend in office and a gay person in office. Gay people have been slandered nationwide. We've been tarred and we've been brushed with the picture of pornography. In Dade County, we were accused of child molestation. It's not enough anymore just to have friends represent us. No matter how good that friend may be. . . . A gay person in office can set a tone, can command respect not only from the larger community, but from the young people in our own community who need both examples and hope.[10]

Of course, Milk was assassinated, along with Mayor George Moscone, by fellow Supervisor Dan White in 1978. White had resigned from the Board, but then changed his mind and wanted Moscone to reappoint him. Moscone eventually decided to appoint someone else. He first shot Moscone at City Hall, then Milk. Milk was a close ally to Moscone, and Milk and the much more conservative White eventually became political rivals. White was convicted of the lesser charge of involuntary manslaughter, and a sentence of just under eight years, after his lawyers argued what came to be derided as the "Twinkie defense," or that White had started eating junk food before the murders—an attempt to establish the defense of "diminished capacity." A less-than-aggressive prosecution also likely led to the outcome. This led to the White Night Riots, a night of violent protests at City Hall followed by police attacks on gay bar patrons. White was a former police officer.

Milk's vision of openly lesbian- and gay-elected officials took some time to develop. As political scientist Donald P. Haider-Markel notes, "By 1987 the movement could only claim 20 openly gay or lesbian elected officials in the country. . . . But by 1990 there had been a total of 50 openly gay public officials. . . . By April of 1998 this number had jumped to 146 and spanned twenty-seven states and the District of Columbia. In 2002, the number had risen above 200, but this was still a small fraction of the more than 500,000 elective offices in the United States."[11] As of 2014, there were nearly 500 out LGBT public officials,[12] including six members of U.S. House of Representatives and a U.S. Senator, Democrat Tammy Baldwin of Wisconsin. Baldwin had previously served as a member of the Dane County Board and as a member of the U.S. House of Representatives. She was elected to the Senate in

2012 and was the first lesbian or gay person elected to the Senate. Current House Members are Democrat Mark Pocan of Wisconsin (who replaced Baldwin in the House), Democrat Jared Polis of Colorado, Democrat David Cicilline of Rhode Island, Democrat Sean Patrick Maloney of New York, Democrat Mark Takano of California, and Democrat Kyrsten Sinema of Arizona. All of these members of the House are from urban districts. Sinema is the first out bisexual person to be elected to Congress. Several gay Republicans (including Steve Gunderson of Wisconsin, Jim Kolbe of Arizona, and Mark Foley of Florida) have served in the House, but they came out while in office or after they left office. The first openly gay Democrats to serve in the House, Gerry Studds and Barney Frank of Massachusetts, were outed while in office but subsequently reelected. Thus, to date, not a single out Republican nonincumbent has been elected to the House, and all of the current (all Democratic) members of the House come from urban or suburban districts (some districts have rural areas but are dominated by the urban or suburban areas). In other words, being elected to Congress from either party from a rural area continues to be a challenge.

Cities continue to be the main source of LGBT-elected officials. Democrats Annise Parker of Houston and Ed Murray of Seattle are out major city mayors. Parker was the first LGBT person elected to the office in a major city in 2009. David Cicilline was mayor of Providence, Rhode Island before he was elected to Congress. In very progressive Seattle and Washington State (voters approved same-sex marriage in a referendum in 2012), Murray's sexuality has been relatively uncontroversial. However, Houston (the fourth largest city in the United States) has a history of lagging behind other large cities in support for LGBT rights, and Parker's time in office has been a flashpoint for religious conservatives in the Houston area and Texas more broadly. In particular, in 1985 voters in the city repealed sexual orientation–inclusive antidiscrimination and affirmative action ordinances by a margin of 80 percent to 20 percent. Polls had shown majority support for the antidiscrimination ordinance, but a brutal antigay campaign by a religious leader resulted in the lopsided defeat.[13] More recently, conservatives have tried to repeal, and remove its supporters from office, an LGBT-inclusive antidiscrimination ordinance supported by Parker and enacted by the city council in 2014, well after most other major cities. In other words, not all cities are the same, in terms of LGBT rights. Especially in the South, an urban setting is no guarantee of strong support for LGBT rights, largely because opponents are, and feel, empowered to openly and actively oppose positive policy change, especially under the banner of religious liberty. For instance, after the repeal effort failed, religious opponents of the ordinance sued the city, arguing that the city erred in finding that opponents of the ordinance lacked the required signatures to trigger a voter repeal effort. In response to the lawsuit, the city emboldened the opposition by subpoenaing sermons and other documents from religious leaders in order to ascertain political content (a potential violation of the terms of their tax-exempt status). Parker eventually withdrew the subpoenas, but the religious leaders framed them as a governmental attack on religious freedom.[14] This became a cause célèbre for religious conservatives around the country.

Many LGBT individuals serve as city council members, and as state legislators (over 100 but still only about 1.5 percent of state legislators) in thirty-five states.[15] More progressive states have several (more than three) legislators, states such as California, Colorado, Connecticut, Maryland, Massachusetts, Nevada, New Hampshire, New York, Vermont, and Washington. There have been no LGBT-elected governors (New Jersey Democrat James McGreevey assumed the office and came out when he later resigned in a scandal), but some out individuals have been elected to lower statewide offices, including bisexual Secretary of State Katherine Brown who became governor in 2015 after the resignation of John Kitzhaber. These numbers should climb in future years, but we can expect continued difficulty in electing out candidates from exclusively rural areas and less progressive states for statewide offices.

Overall, the American public is more hostile to openly LGBT candidates than other minority groups, with the most hostility coming from older, conservative, religious, less educated male, and Republican voters.[16] In a 2006 poll, only 7 percent of respondents said that the country was ready for an openly gay or lesbian candidate, compared to 61 percent for a woman candidate or 51 percent for an African American candidate.[17] Haider-Markel estimates that about 25 percent of voters would never vote for an openly gay or lesbian candidate.[18] However, given the strategic choices of lesbian and gay candidates, sexual orientation can be reduced as a negative factor, and it is sometimes a positive factor. As he states, "Potential LGBT state legislative candidates are strategic in their pursuit of office. They tend to have greater experience and resources than the average state legislative candidate, and they appear to typically run in districts where voters are less likely to oppose an openly gay candidate. Indeed . . . being openly LGBT can even be an electoral advantage, at least for those running as Democrats."[19]

The Gay and Lesbian Victory Fund (now simply Victory Fund) is an organization focused on electing openly LGBT individuals to office. The organization was founded in 1991, and has as its mission "to change the face and voice of America's politics and achieve equality for LGBT Americans by increasing the number of openly LGBT officials at all levels of government."[20] The organization trains, endorses, and finances candidates in an attempt to bolster their chances of winning and in order to build a "bench" of plausible candidates. The organization was inspired by EMILY's List, an organization focused on electing women to office, founded in 1985. In its first year, the organization endorsed two candidates; in 2010, it endorsed 164 candidates.[21] These organizations reflect the fact that candidates for political office do not appear out of nowhere but are supported and cultivated by political parties and activist organizations.

PUBLIC OPINION

In a democracy, public opinion plays an important, but not always definitive role, in public policy outcomes. Over the long term, policies tend to reflect public opinion, as measured through scientific polls, but institutional dynamics, such as party politics, federalism, separation of powers/gridlock, court decisions, agendas of powerful policymakers and interests, may also determine policy outcomes.[22] For instance, as is explored in chapter 6, strong public support exists for antidiscrimination laws based on sexual orientation and gender identity, but most states and the U.S. Congress have not enacted these laws. However, legal and policy progress for sexual and gender minorities has coincided broadly with a gradual shift in public opinion away from overwhelming hostility to these minorities, but resistance in some areas of public opinion remains. Writing in 2008, political scientists Nathaniel Persily, Jack Citrin, and Patrick Egan described the dynamic thus: "Over the past thirty years, American public opinion regarding gay people, gay rights, and gay sex has moved unambiguously toward acceptance and tolerance. However, Americans remain deeply more uncomfortable with gays than with other demographic groups, and their support for gay rights does not extend as strongly to the domains of sexuality and relationships."[23] Despite the general trend, opponents of LGBT rights are overrepresented in the policy process. As political scientists Jeffrey Lax and Justin Phillips state, "The preferences of religious conservatives are 'overrepresented'. . . . Powerful conservative religious interest groups strongly affect gay rights policy at the expense of majoritarian congruence."[24] This dynamic can be overcome by the presence of a large amount of Democrats in legislatures, according to the work of Ben Bishin and Charles Anthony Smith.[25] The relationship between public opinion and policy outcomes is discussed at points in other chapters, but the following section provides a fuller overview of these shifts and the demographic factors that are associated with support for, or opposition to, LGBT rights.

The depth of hostility toward sexual minorities can be seen in polling data on the morality of same-sex intimacy. Since 1973, the General Social Survey has been asking respondents whether sexual activity between persons of the same-sex was "always wrong" or "not wrong at all." In that year, 73 percent responded "always wrong." This percentage actually rose gradually throughout the 1970s and 1980s, reaching a peak of 77 percent in 1991. This number declined significantly during the 1990s and 2000s to 46 percent by 2013, with 44 percent responding "not wrong at all."[26] Thus, the overall climate has improved, but nearly half of the country views sexual minorities through a strong lens of moral disapproval. During the period of high moral disapproval, majorities also supported the criminalization of same-sex sexual activity, with an increase in support for criminalization coming in the wake of the U.S. Supreme Court decision in *Bowers v. Hardwick* in 1986, in which the court upheld the constitutionality of sodomy laws, and during the height of the AIDS crisis. In the wake of *Bowers*, only approximately one-third of the public supported decriminalization. As of 2013, only about one-third supported criminalization.[27]

The strongest support for rights for sexual minorities has always been in the realm of antidiscrimination policy. As is discussed in chapter 6, public opinion is nearly unanimous in its support (around 90 percent) for laws prohibiting discrimination based upon sexual orientation. Even a majority (56 percent) supported this as early as 1976. Support for marriage equality has been, and is, much lower. As of 2014, many national polls showed support for marriage equality in the mid-50 percent range, with polls showing majority support for the first time in 2011, after decades of much lower levels of support. A Gallup poll from 1996 found 27 percent support for same-sex marriage, for instance. In polling terms, this is a rather dramatic change in support in a relatively short period of time.[28]

Significantly undergirding this rise in support for lesbian and gay rights is the fact that larger numbers of Americans respond that they have a coworker, close friend or relative who is gay or lesbian, 75 percent in 2013 versus 23 percent in 1985—a reflection of the power of contact theory. More Americans also believe that individuals are born gay or lesbian, nearly half (47 percent) in 2013, compared to 13 percent in 1978.[29] Studies have demonstrated a direct relationship between belief in the genetic nature of sexual orientation and support for gay rights.[30]

However, there is significant demographic and geographic variation in support for the rights of sexual minorities. Women are slightly more supportive of LGBT rights than men. Higher levels of education correlate with stronger support for LGBT rights, while higher levels of religiosity (as measured by frequency of church attendance) correlate to lower levels of support. Belief in Biblical literalism is associated with a resistance to LGBT rights. Political ideology also matters, with liberals more supportive and conservatives more opposed. Finally, and perhaps most significantly, younger people are much more supportive of LGBT rights than older people. This can clearly be seen in polling concerning marriage equality. According to Gallup, "Adults between the ages of 18 and 29 are nearly twice as likely to support marriage equality as adults aged 65 and over." Indeed, much, but not all of the change in opinion on marriage equality is due to "cohort replacement," or the fact that more opposed older citizens are being replaced in the population by younger, more supportive citizens. This indicates that support for LGBT rights should continue to climb.[31]

After voters in California narrowly approved Proposition 8 (a ban on same-sex marriage) in 2008, much was made of the fact that an exit poll showed high levels of support among African American voters for the measure. This played into and reinforced a larger cultural narrative that people of color do not support LGBT rights. However, subsequent analysis proved that the results of that poll were significantly overstated. While it is true that some racial minority groups have shown lower levels of support for marriage equality in the past, support is increasing. And the lower levels of support are attributable not to race but to high levels of religiosity in many communities of color. Indeed, when LGBT rights are framed as a civil rights issue, such as protections from discrimination in jobs and public accommodations, African Americans show higher levels of support for sexual minorities than whites. As Claire Gecewicz and Michael Lipka of Pew Research state, this likely stems, at least in part, from "empathy among African Americans for the perceived discrimination that gays and lesbians face in society."[32]

Public opinion also varies by region of the country and from state to state within regions. Broadly speaking, the regions with the most support for LGBT rights are New England and the West coast, with the South least supportive. Political scientists Jeffrey Lax and Justin Phillips measured mean public opinion across a range of LGBT rights issues in a 2009 study. The following five states had the lowest mean support: Alabama (44 percent), Arkansas (44 percent), Mississippi (45 percent), Oklahoma (43 percent), and Utah (38 percent). The following five states had the highest support: Connecticut (65 percent), Massachusetts (68 percent), New York (66 percent), Rhode Island (66 percent), and Vermont (65 percent).[33] Given the role that states and localities have played in LGBT policy, this state-level variation is consequential.

Distinct polls about transgender rights are not as common as polls about lesbian and gay rights, and transgender rights are often lumped into larger polling efforts, despite distinct political and policy issues. In a 2011 poll, about 75 percent of respondents favored transgender inclusion in national employment–based antidiscrimination and hate crime laws. Less clear is the level of popular support for government and private health plan–sponsored gender confirmation surgery, changes to gender markers on government documents, and support for transgender youth and affirmative school policies. In terms of contact theory, the 2011 poll found that only 11 percent of respondents had a close friend or family member who is transgender, illustrating a continuing challenge to the transgender movement.[34] Indeed, the fact that transgender individuals present a more direct challenge to the gender binary leads to less support than for sexual minorities.[35]

CONCLUSION

The political setting for sexual, and to some degree, gender minorities has improved greatly in recent years resulting in more out elected officials, fewer successful anti-LGBT ballot measures, and positive policy change, but the fragmented political system still empowers opponents of LGBT in many state and local settings and in Congress. Given contact theory and cohort replacement, progress should continue, mitigated by focused and determined opposition. Overall, the rapid shift in opinion bodes well for the future of LGBT-supportive policies.

KEY TERMS, CONCEPTS, AND PEOPLE

Assimilation versus liberation
Baldwin, Tammy
Ballot measures/Ballot Measure 9
Cohort replacement
Direct action
Descriptive/substantive/symbolic
  representation
Demographics and public opinion
Frank, Barney
"Free rider" problem
Kameny, Frank
Kozachenko, Kathy
Insider/elite strategies versus grass-
  roots activism
Marches on Washington
Mass politics

Milk, Harvey/"Hope Speech"
Model campaign
National and state LGBT organizations
Noble, Elaine
Parker, Annise
Party politics
Religious Right ballot tactics
Sarria, José
Shifts in public opinion
Sinema, Kyrsten
Social movements
Spear, Allan
Studds, Gerry
Victory Fund
White Night Riots

QUESTIONS FOR DISCUSSION

1. What is the optimal mix of insider and outsider strategies?
2. How has public opinion evolved over the past several decades? What is the influence of public opinion on public policy?

3. What unique challenges have LGBT candidates faced? What are strategies for electoral success for LGBT candidates?
4. Will LGBT candidates be elected in all regions of the country in the coming decade, or will their election continue to be an urban/suburban versus rural story?

NOTES

1. Craig A. Rimmerman, *The Lesbian and Gay Movements: Assimilation or Liberation*, 2nd ed. (Boulder: Westview Press, 2015), 5–6.

2. Tina Fetner, *How the Religious Right Shaped Lesbian and Gay Activism* (Minneapolis: University of Minnesota Press, 2008), 44–45.

3. For a discussion of the 1972 convention dynamics, see Bruce Miroff, *The Liberals' Moment: The McGovern Insurgency and the Identity Crisis of the Democratic Party* (Lawrence: University Press of Kansas, 2007).

4. Jason Pierceson, *Courts, Liberalism, and Rights: Gay Law and Politics in the United States and Canada* (Philadelphia: Temple University Press, 2005), 125.

5. Amy L. Stone, *Gay Rights at the Ballot Box* (Minneapolis: University of Minnesota Press, 2012), 4.

6. Stone, *Gay Rights at the Ballot Box*, 1.

7. Stone, *Gay Rights at the Ballot Box*, 73.

8. Donald P. Haider-Markel, *Out and Running: Gay and Lesbian Candidates, Elections, and Policy Representation* (Washington, DC: Georgetown University Press, 2010).

9. Marc Stein, *Rethinking the Gay and Lesbian Movement* (New York: Routledge, 2012), 117.

10. Chris Bull, ed., *Come Out Fighting: A Century of Essential Writing on Gay & Lesbian Liberation* (New York: Nation Books, 2001), 165–66.

11. Haider-Markel, *Out and Running*, 24.

12. This figure is from the Gay and Lesbian Victory Fund.

13. Dale Carpenter, *Flagrant Conduct: The Story of* Lawrence v. Texas (New York: W.W. Norton, 2012), 30–35.

14. Katherine Driessen and Mike Morris, "Mayor's Decision to Drop Subpoenas Fails to Quell Criticism," *Houston Chronicle*, October 29, 2014, http://www.chron.com/news/politics/houston/article/Mayor-set-to-make-announcement-on-sermon-subpoenas-5855458.php.

15. According to National Conference of State Legislatures, there are 7383 state legislators, http://www.ncsl.org/research/about-state-legislatures/number-of-legislators-and-length-of-terms.aspx.

16. Haider-Markel, *Out and Running*, 64.

17. Haider-Markel, *Out and Running*, 38.

18. Haider-Markel, *Out and Running*, 64.

19. Haider-Markel, *Out and Running*, 64.

20. Mission Statement, Victory Fund, https://www.victoryfund.org/mission.

21. Sheryl Gay Stolberg, "For Aspiring Gay Candidates, a Workshop on Campaign Strategies," *New York Times*, June 10, 2011, http://www.nytimes.com/2011/06/11/us/11train.html; "Endorsement Seal," Gay and Lesbian Victory Fund, https://www.victoryfund.org/our-story/endorsement-seal.

22. For the influence of state-level public opinion on LGBT policy, see Jeffrey R. Lax and Justin H. Phillips, "Public Opinion and Policy Responsiveness," *American Political Science Review*, 103:3 (August 2009), 367–86. For a discussion of the influence of institutions, see Gary Mucciaroni, *Same-Sex, Different Politics: Success and Failure in the Struggles over Gay Rights* (Chicago: University of Chicago Press, 2008) and Arthur Lupia, et al., "Why State Constitutions Differ in their Treatment of Same-Sex Marriage," *The Journal of Politics*, 72 (2010), 1222–235.

23. Nathaniel Persily, Jack Citrin, and Patrick Egan, eds., *Public Opinion and Constitutional Controversy* (New York: Oxford University Press, 2008), 235.

24. Lax and Phillips, "Public Opinion and Policy Responsiveness," 383.

25. Benjamin G. Bishin and Charles Anthony Smith, "When do Legislators Defy Popular Sovereignty? Testing Theories of Minority Representation Using DOMA," *Political Research Quarterly*, 66:4 (December 2013), 794–803: 801.

26. Seth Motel, "On Stonewall Anniversary, A Reminder of How Much Public Opinion Has Changed," Pew Research Center, June 26, 2013, http://www.pewresearch.org/fact-tank/2013/06/26/on-stonewall-anniversary-a-reminder-of-how-much-public-opinion-has-changed/.

27. Jeffrey M. Jones, "More Americans See Gay, Lesbian Orientation as Birth Factor," Gallup, May 16, 2013, http://www.gallup.com/poll/162569/americans-gay-lesbian-orientation-birth-factor.aspx.

28. See the citations for this polling data in chapter 6.

29. Jones, "More Americans See Gay, Lesbian Orientation as Birth Factor."

30. Persily, Citrin, and Egan, eds., *Public Opinion and Constitutional Controversy*, 252.

31. Persily, Citrin, and Egan, eds., *Public Opinion and Constitutional Controversy*, 245–51; Justin McCarthy, "Same-Sex Marriage Support Reaches New High at 55%," Gallup, May 21, 2014, http://www.gallup.com/poll/169640/sex-marriage-support-reaches-new-high.aspx.

32. Claire Gecewicz and Michael Lipka, "Blacks are Lukewarm to Gay Marriage, But Most Say Businesses Must Provide Wedding Services to Gay Couples," Pew Research Center, October 7, 2014, http://www.pewresearch.org/fact-tank/2014/10/07/blacks-are-lukewarm-to-gay-marriage-but-most-say-businesses-must-provide-wedding-services-to-gay-couples/; Patrick J. Egan and Kenneth Sherrill, "California's Proposition 8: What Happened, and What Does the Future Hold?" National Gay and Lesbian Task Force Policy Institute, January 2009, http://www.thetaskforce.org/static_html/downloads/issues/egan_sherrill_prop8_1_6_09.pdf.

33. Michael Lipka, "Gay Marriage Arrives in the South, Where the Public is Less Enthused," Pew Research Center, October 15, 2014, http://www.pewresearch.org/fact-tank/2014/10/15/gay-marriage-arrives-in-the-south-where-the-public-is-less-enthused/; Lax and Phillips, "Public Opinion and Policy Responsiveness," 373.

34. "Strong Majorities of Americans Favor Rights and Legal Protections for Transgender People," Public Religion Research Institute, November 3, 2011, http://publicreligion.org/research/2011/11/american-attitudes-towards-transgender-people/.

35. Aaron T. Norton and Gregory M. Herek, "Heterosexuals' Attitudes Toward Transgender People: Findings from a National Probability Sample of Adults," *Sex Roles*, 68:11–12 (June 2013), 738–53.

BIBLIOGRAPHY AND FURTHER READING

Tina Fetner, *How the Religious Right Shaped Lesbian and Gay Activism* (Minneapolis: University of Minnesota Press, 2008).

Donald P. Haider-Markel, *Out and Running: Gay and Lesbian Candidates, Elections, and Policy Representation* (Washington, DC: Georgetown University Press, 2010).

Gary Mucciaroni, *Same-Sex, Different Politics: Success and Failure in the Struggles over Gay Rights* (Chicago: University of Chicago Press, 2008).

Craig A. Rimmerman, *The Lesbian and Gay Movements: Assimilation or Liberation*, 2nd ed. (Boulder: Westview Press, 2015).

Craig A. Rimmerman, Kenneth Wald, and Clyde Wilcox, *The Politics of Gay Rights* (Chicago: University of Chicago Press, 2000).

Marc Stein, *Rethinking the Gay and Lesbian Movement* (New York: Routledge, 2012).

Amy L. Stone, *Gay Rights at the Ballot Box* (Minneapolis: University of Minnesota Press, 2012).

Chapter 5

Courts and the LGBT Rights Movement

Beginning with the homophile movement in the 1950s, sexual minorities have utilized the courts to protect them from marginalization and discrimination, with mixed success, but, on the whole, courts have been important allies. Inspired by the success of the National Association for the Advancement of Colored People's (NAACP) litigation strategy to eliminate the legal framework of racial discrimination, and the seminal case of *Brown v. Board of Education* (1954), sexuality activists saw the judiciary as a potential ally from the pervasive animus facing sexual minorities in the culture and reflected in their legal regulation and discrimination. After all, in the popular imagination, courts exist to protect individuals from oppression from the majority. In reality, however, they do not always play this role, and they did not for sexual minorities. Indeed, for much of the history of the LGBT rights movement, courts were hostile or ambivalent toward the legal claims of sexual minorities. Courts, especially the U.S. Supreme Court, have become a more consistent ally of the movement only recently.

While politics and public opinion affect judges in ways different from legislators and other public officials, politics often constrains judges, both internally and externally. Internally, judges possess ideological bias. While there is a norm that judges ought to remain neutral, the reality is that bias plays a role in their decision making, according to political scientists who refer to this as the attitudinal model. Thus, if a judge's ideology or other personal views reflect opposition to rights and equality for sexual minorities, these litigants may have an uphill climb in court. This type of bias is quite apparent in the cases discussed below, with many judges even citing Biblical passages to justify ruling against sexual minorities. The strategic model describes external constraints on judges, either from the preferences and goals of other judges on their court or from the preferences and goals of other governmental officials and the public. According to this model, judges are reluctant to challenge the political status quo out of fear of criticism and backlash from other policymakers and the public. Judges fear threats to their status and legitimacy, or more direct threats from political actions intended to punish them, such as a decrease in funding from the legislature for court operations or changes to their jurisdiction to hear certain cases.

The implication of the strategic model is that judges seldom rule in a manner that is radically out of line with the prevailing political sentiment. Thus, courts are not seen as agents of social change; rather, they are defenders of the political status quo. They are, as political scientist Gerald Rosenberg claims, "the hollow hope" for activists expecting social transformation from the judiciary. Rosenberg argues that the Supreme Court only acts affirmatively on a controversial issue after public opinion has shifted in one direction, and the court follows that shift. Asking for change too soon risks a backlash that will hurt the progress of the movement. According to Rosenberg, the best course is to emphasize grassroots politics and avoid litigation.

However, in judging the law plays a role that it does not play in other political contexts. In the U.S. legal system, judges are expected to rule within the parameters of established precedents—or previously decided cases with a similar legal question, or the legal model. This may independently drive judicial decision making, although attitudinal theory asserts that judges use precedents selectively to justify a decision made on the basis of ideology. At the very least, it must be understood that judicial decision making is not identical to other political decisions. Generally the politics of judging is less "raw" than it is in the political arena, though judges are not immune from political and cultural forces. Also, if we view the law as sometimes independent from politics, courts can create on their own through litigation, and advocates are justified in using the courts to achieve their goals. Court victories can change political dynamics by giving activists the leverage and status they may be lacking in the political arena.

Early litigation was not planned by national or regional litigation organizations as is now often the case. It resulted from real problems faced by LGBT individuals, particularly those who developed "legal consciousness," or a sense of being wronged for which the legal system offers a remedy. Of course, most victims of poor treatment or discrimination do not access the legal system. They might see themselves at fault through internalized homophobia or heterosexism, or they feel that they lack the knowledge and resources (financial and time) to successfully litigate. Scholars call these people "one-shotters," as opposed to "repeat players" in litigation. One-shotters are correct in their assessment, as repeat players often have a significant advantage in litigation because of their resources advantages, superior knowledge of the system, and relationships with legal actors formed through repeated litigation.[1]

As a result, the LGBT rights movement began to form litigation organizations, or allied with established groups like the American Civil Liberties Union (ACLU) by the 1970s. Today, groups such as Lambda Legal Defense Fund, The National Center for Lesbian Rights (NCLR), and Gay and Lesbian Advocates and Defenders (GLAD) bring test cases in carefully constructed litigation strategies. Timing is everything. A case brought before judges are willing to rule favorably will create a negative precedent that will make change even more difficult over the long run. Thus, these groups often actively oppose "orphaned" litigation, or suits brought by individuals and their lawyers outside of the more formal plans of the national and regional groups. Sometimes, however, these suits result in unexpected partial or complete victories. Orphaned litigation led to the landmark case of *Baehr v. Lewin* in Hawaii in 1993, the case that began the legal momentum of the contemporary marriage equality movement.

EARLY LITIGATION: CHALLENGING THE REGULATION OF HOMOSEXUALITY AND GOVERNMENTAL DISCRIMINATION

In order for a movement to form, individuals in that movement needed to be relatively free from regulation and harassment by the government. However, as has been noted, the legal environment in the 1950s was overwhelmingly hostile to sexual minorities. As they came into contact with the sexuality-based regulatory regime, activists began to turn to lawyers and the courts for assistance. They were able to poke some holes in the system, but the law was limited in its effectiveness, given the larger social constraints. Most individuals who came in contact with the homophobic hand of the state simply went along with their treatment out of a sense of shame or powerlessness, or both.

The Mattachine Society soon encountered this dynamic when Dale Jennings was entrapped by police and charged with "lewd and dissolute behavior."[2] Jennings and others in the group decided to fight the charges. A lawyer was hired, and the charges were ultimately dropped after a jury deadlocked, with only one juror holding out for a guilty verdict. This resistance, stemming from the consciousness associated with forming a new political group, led to legal activism in the form of publicity surrounding the trial and a written guide developed by the society to assist others in their encounters with the police and prosecutors. A flyer, entitled "Victory" and distributed in locations frequented by gay men, stated, "You didn't see it in the papers, but it could—and did—happen in L.A.: In a unique victory for California, Dale Jennings defended himself against entrapment by the L.A. police and won."[3] Growth in the organization was spurred by the arrest and the publicity campaign, but most individuals were not as fortunate as Jennings. For decades to come, this would be the exception to the rule of police regulation of real or perceived sexual behavior.

In California, lesbian and gay bar owners also fought invasive regulation of their establishments by the police, acting on liquor commission regulations, in court. Regulations made it illegal to sell liquor to homosexuals or "sexual perverts," but bar owners pushed back, like the owner of the famous Black Cat bar in San Francisco, and won victories in the California Supreme Court in 1951 (*Stoumen v. Reilly*) and 1959 (*Vallerga v. Department of Alcoholic Beverage Control*). As legal scholar William Eskridge notes, "Owners of profitable gay bars could afford to pay off investigators or, failing that, to retain counsel to challenge regulatory action."[4] But no other state high court took this approach, leaving most bars open to harassment and closure and their patrons subject to arrest. These cases were not a ringing endorsement of lesbian and gay rights, just the notion that "members of the public of lawful age have a right to patronize a public restaurant and bar so long as they are acting properly and are not committing illegal or immoral acts."[5] Indeed, the court ruled in *Vallerga* that lesbians kissing could have been sufficient to offend public morality and thereby trigger legal regulation, but, for procedural reasons, this did not apply in the case.[6] However, this was the first instance in which a statute targeting sexual minorities (after the 1951 decision, the legislature gave more power to regulators to shut down gay bars) was invalidated by a court. The case reflects the approach of victories of this period: judges reluctantly applying legal principles that had the effect of protecting sexual minorities while not endorsing those minorities. As Eskridge states, "*Vallerga* was a compromise that established the closet on terms favorable to homosexuals: they had a theoretical right to congregate but not if they touched or kissed one another, as that would be offensive to the hypothetical heterosexual."[7] An appellate court in New York also took this approach, but it was overruled by the state's highest court.[8] Outside of California, the modest level of protection was not a reality. The right of public association failed to protect sexual minorities everywhere else. Merely congregating in a public place was seen to be criminal or immoral. The situation improved somewhat by the late 1960s due to court rulings and resistance to regulation by local activists, resulting in less harassment, especially in the wake of the Stonewall Rebellion.[9]

A more permanent and consequential early victory was the Supreme Court case of *ONE v. Olesen* (1958), and the First Amendment provided protection for sexual minorities. The case was the court's first direct foray into the issue of homosexuality. As was discussed in chapter 2, this case facilitated the distribution by mail of lesbian and gay-themed magazines like *ONE*, *The Ladder*, and *Mattachine Review*. Copies of *ONE* had been deemed obscene, and six hundred were seized by the Los Angeles postmaster. The editors of the magazine challenged this action in federal court as a violation of the free speech and press provision of the First Amendment to the U.S. Constitution. They utilized the service of a heterosexual recent law school graduate, Eric Julber, who provided free legal representation to the magazine, because, according to Julber, the editors "were so clearly right that I thought they deserved legal representation."[10] They lost at the lower levels of the federal system, but the Supreme Court applied a recent obscenity decision, *Roth v. U.S.* (1957), and ruled that *ONE* was not obscene and was entitled to First Amendment protection. The court in *Roth* ruled that material with sexual content is not automatically obscene under the principle that "all ideas having even the slightest redeeming social importance—unorthodox ideas, controversial ideas, even ideas hateful to the prevailing climate of opinion—have the full" protection of the First Amendment.[11] Clearly uncomfortable with the content of *ONE*, however, the justices simply issued a one-sentence opinion applying *Roth* to the case. But they were concerned enough about the violation of the First Amendment that they took the case when they could have easily let the lower court decision stand. During the 1950s, the Warren court was increasingly sensitive to majoritarian discrimination against minorities, and many justices on the court saw their role as defending individual rights in most cases. However, this approach (at least for a majority of justices) would generally not include sexual minorities—only in this case implicating the First Amendment, another realm of rights expansion of the Warren court.

In this early litigation, the primary civil liberties litigation group, the ACLU, was not supportive of lesbian and gay rights. Indeed, the ACLU rejected a request to assist with the *ONE* litigation, and the national organization affirmed its support for sodomy laws in 1957. This would eventually change, but litigants in the 1950s were generally on their own. Litigation was sporadic due to a lack of favorable jurisprudence, a lack of resources, and a lack of legal consciousness among sexual minorities. A more broad-based and coordinated litigation strategy would not develop until the 1970s.

Things were slowly changing in the legal profession, however. The American Law Institute (ALI), an organization of leading lawyers and judges focused on law reform, recommended that consensual sex acts between consenting adults be decriminalized, as a part of its Model Penal Code, in 1955. Most members of the organization were older and more conservative on issues of personal morality, but the staff of the ALI was composed of younger lawyers who had been strongly influenced by legal realism. The use of social science data was a central element of the legal realist movement, in addition to the core insight that judges make decisions on the basis of personal motivations, or "hunches," similar to the contemporary attitudinal model. A staff report advocating the decriminalization of sodomy was strongly inspired by the Kinsey reports, and it downplayed the threat posed by sexual minorities.

It noted that "substantial numbers of males and females find themselves drawn to members of their own sex."[12] However, the voting members were less enthusiastic about this particular legal reform. A substantial number of the members opposed the move out of a concern for public morality, and those who advocated decriminalization largely emphasized the difficulty in enforcing the laws—they did not make a case for sexual freedom for sexual minorities. A similar conversation took place in England at the same time through the Wolfenden Commission. That group's recommendations led to the decriminalization of sodomy in the United Kingdom in 1967 and in Canada in 1969, but the ALI's recommendations were less followed by U.S. policymakers. Only Illinois soon followed the ALI recommendations, eliminating its sodomy law 1961. The next legislative repeals came in the 1970s. By the mid-1980s, about half of states still had sodomy laws on the books. As will be discussed below, the Supreme Court affirmed the constitutionality of these laws in 1986, but the court eventually struck them down in 2003.

All states possessed felony sodomy laws in the 1950s, but these laws often criminalized sex acts regardless of the genders of the persons involved. However, these laws were mostly enforced against same-sex sexual behavior, and they stigmatized sexual minorities as criminals, serving as a significant constraint on the legal and political movement for equality. They were also often used to deny parents custody of their children in family law proceedings, if a parent came out as lesbian, bisexual, or gay in the process. Furthermore, in response to the rise of the LGBT rights movement and the visibility of sexual minorities, many states revised these laws to specifically apply to same-sex sexual activity. For instance, Texas changed its law in 1974 to only apply to "deviate sexual intercourse" involving persons of the same sex. Heterosexuals were now free from the potential of arrest and prosecution stemming from consensual sexual activity in private, but the state's gaze was still focused on lesbians, gay men, and bisexuals. This state of affairs was reaffirmed by the legislature in the 1990s, when a majority of legislators refused to repeal the law.

In addition to legislative repeal efforts, individuals brought sporadic challenges in state and federal court in the 1970s, with generally little success in eliminating sodomy laws. Courts across the nation, despite the recommendations of ALI and developments in the North and across the Atlantic, were still as hostile to the claims of sexual minorities as were legislators, perhaps more so. Biblical citations in legal opinions were not uncommon. The U.S. Supreme Court rebuffed a sodomy law challenge in *Doe v. Commonwealth's Attorney* (1976). Many legal commentators were surprised by the court's lack of interest in the issue, given that the Justice had been creating a robust right to privacy, protective of intimate choices, over the previous decade, starting with the landmark decision of *Griswold v. Connecticut* (1965). However, this right was enforced by the court for heterosexuals only.[13]

The Supreme Court's indifference or hostility toward sexual minorities was present in other cases. Frank Kameny challenged his firing from the federal government and was rejected by federal courts at all levels, including the Supreme Court in 1961 in *Kameny v. Brucker*. His remarkable self-authored brief (his lawyer ultimately abandoned the case after losses in the district and appellate courts) made the case for full equality for sexual minorities, the first argument for gay rights formally presented to the Supreme Court. He focused not on the mere procedural questions associated with his dismissal (where the judges kept it), but he allied his cause with that of other oppressed groups and directly challenged the moral condemnation of homosexuality that was deeply entrenched in law and policy, including the federal policy resulting in his termination. As he boldly asserted, "Petitioner [Kameny] asserts, flatly, unequivocally, and absolutely uncompromisingly, that homosexuality, whether by mere inclination or by overt act, is not only not immoral, but that for those choosing voluntarily to engage in homosexual acts, such acts are moral in a real positive sense, and are good, right and desirable, socially and personally."[14] The court unanimously rejected the appeal. For decades, the federal courts allowed discrimination against sexual minorities in federal employment, including the military. Ultimately, action by Congress and the executive branch was required to end this, with the military ban on service by openly lesbian, gay, or bisexual service members remaining in place until 2011, and it took until the 1990s under President Bill Clinton for discrimination against civilian employees of the federal government to be fully eliminated.

Kameny's early failure demonstrates the political reality of litigation. Legal arguments may have logic and make legal sense in the abstract, but they also potentially challenge entrenched cultural and political forces, like heteronormativity, that compete for the loyalty of legal actors. Often the culture and politics needs to change for legal actors to respond and change the law. However, the legal framing of causes can provide a potential new framework for conceiving of a new cultural and political reality. Given that no visible public political movement for sexual minorities yet existed, it is not surprising that the courts did not respond to explicit appeals for full equality. The same year of his rejection at the Supreme Court, Kameny formed the Mattachine Society of Washington, D.C., and his activism would always focus on both the political and legal realms. But the early lesson was that the courts alone would not protect sexual minorities.

In *Boutilier v. INS* (1967), the Supreme Court affirmed the federal government's policy of excluding sexual minorities for immigration purposes by deeming them to have a "psychopathic personality." Three justices dissented, including the noted civil libertarian William O. Douglas, but a majority of the justices felt that the discriminatory and demeaning policy was justified.

Douglas relied on Freud, Kinsey, and the Wolfenden Commission to argue for a more enlightened approach. As he stated, "To label a group so large 'excludable aliens' would be tantamount to saying that Sappho, Leonardo da Vinci, Michelangelo, Andre Gide, and perhaps even Shakespeare, were they to come to life again, would be deemed unfit to visit our shores. Indeed, so broad a definition might well comprise more than a few members of legislative bodies."[15] However, the majority sided with the position that sexual minorities were ill and a potential threat to society, but at least the uniform hostility to sexual minorities was starting to wane, as reflected by the dissents. Liberal justices would begin to argue for the affirmative application of constitutional protections to sexual minorities, but this would take decades to become the majority position of the court. As Joyce Murdoch and Deb Price describe the legacy of *Boutilier*, "The Supreme Court literally stopped listening to homosexual rights arguments. . . . With the ruling, the U.S. Supreme Court joined the government war against homosexuals."[16]

DISCRIMINATION AND EQUAL PROTECTION

The most potentially supportive part of the U.S. Constitution for sexual minorities is the Equal Protection Clause in the Fourteenth Amendment. It states, "No state shall . . . deny to persons within its jurisdiction the equal protection of the laws." The amendment was one of the post–Civil War amendments intended to reintegrate former slaves into the nation's legal and political systems. At first glance, the language appears to outlaw almost all forms of discrimination by states, but the Supreme Court has interpreted the clause much more narrowly. Reflecting the connection to the Civil War, the court has determined that classifications based upon race are most suspect constitutionally, triggering what is deemed "strict scrutiny," a level of review triggering the "compelling interest test." Under the test, a government must present a very compelling reason for discriminating, and the discriminatory must be narrowly tailored. Under this level of review, few laws and policies are deemed to be constitutional. The court has deemed sex/gender-based discrimination to trigger a somewhat less demanding level of review—"heightened (or intermediate) scrutiny." This level of review is slightly more deferential to governmental entities wishing to categorize on the basis of sex or gender, but it is still a powerful constitutional tool against discriminatory policies. The most deferential level of review, the rational basis test, generally allows for a discriminatory policy to stand if the government can establish a legitimate policy reason for the discrimination. Most types of discrimination, including sexual orientation, fall under the level of constitutional protection. Thus, as interpreted by the Supreme Court, sexual minorities are less protected from discrimination than are racial minorities and women.

The court's creation of these levels of review has been somewhat arbitrary but tied to politics and the court's willingness (or lack thereof) to assert its power. In other words, the more types of discrimination that fall under higher levels of review, the more often the courts will be required to challenge laws enacted through the legislative process, executive orders or rulemaking, or popular initiative. In an attempt to limit this possibility, the court has developed a test to determine whether something beyond the rational basis test ought to be applied. The trait in question must not be relevant to the group's ability to contribute to society, the trait must be immutable (or resistant to change), a group must exhibit a history of discriminatory treatment toward the group, and the group must be politically powerless. While some lower federal courts and some state supreme courts have found sexual minorities to meet all elements of this test, the Supreme Court has never done so.

In *Romer v. Evans* (1996), the Supreme Court struck down a voter-approved state constitutional amendment (Amendment 2) in Colorado that took away existing sexual orientation–based protection in local antidiscrimination laws and prohibited them at the local or state level in the future. Speaking for a six-member majority, Justice Anthony Kennedy found the amendment to be unconstitutional even under rational basis review, thus reaffirming the low level of protection for sexual minorities while also defining a nondeferential rational basis review. He asserted that moral disapproval of sexual minorities was the reason for the amendment, but that this was an insufficient purpose under the rational basis test. He declared, "It is not within our constitutional tradition to enact laws of this sort."[17] A dissent by Justice Antonin Scalia accused the majority of taking the side of elites in the culture war over sexual diversity and asserted that morality was sufficient to justify a law under rational basis review.

In two significant Supreme Court cases, concerns over the equal treatment of sexual minorities were trumped by the First Amendment freedoms of those wishing to discriminate against sexual minorities. In both cases, the Supreme Court was at odds with state high courts that more rigorously defended equality principles. In *Hurley v. Irish-American Gay, Lesbian, and Bisexual Group of Boston* (1995), a unanimous court sided with South Boston St. Patrick's Day Parade organizers who excluded the group from participation in the march. The state courts deemed this action to violate the state's antidiscrimination law, but the Supreme Court ruled that this law was trumped by the First Amendment and the right of parade organizers to have complete control of the message of the parade, without interference from the government. In *Boy Scouts of America v. Dale* (2000), a five-member majority sided with the right of the Boy Scouts to expel Eagle Scout James Dale, for publicly declaring his homosexuality, under the First Amendment right of association. The New Jersey courts sided with Dale, viewing the action as violating the state's antidiscrimination law. Again, the Supreme Court was an imperfect defender of LGBT rights, leaving these disputes to the political and social arenas. Sexual minorities were still trying to gain access to the South Boston Parade as late as 2014, and the Scouts finally lifted their ban on openly gay scouts in 2013, while keeping it for scout leaders, perpetuating the narrative that lesbian and gay adults are threats to children.

THE CONTINUED CAMPAIGN AGAINST SODOMY LAWS

Given the constraining role played by sodomy laws in essentially criminalizing sexual minorities, either directly or how they were enforced, both the political and legal movements for sexual minorities viewed the elimination of sodomy laws as a top priority in the 1980s and 1990s. However, a strategy to bring the issue again to the Supreme Court backfired in 1986 with the court's ruling in *Bowers v. Hardwick*. After this decision, activists turned to state courts and found more success. By the time that the Court reversed itself in 2003 in *Lawrence v. Texas*, many remaining sodomy laws had been eliminated through this state litigation, or through the legislative process in the previous decades. However, *Lawrence* was a significant victory for the movement, and, along with the victory in *Romer v. Evans* (1996), established the court as a more robust defender of the rights of sexual minorities.

Bowers and Its Legacy

By the mid-1980s, one half of state-level sodomy laws had been repealed by legislatures or struck down by courts, with the vast majority removed by legislatures. Activists viewed a federal constitutional challenge as the best, quickest, and least labor-intensive way to eliminate the remaining laws—one path versus twenty-five. The court also had clearly developed a jurisprudence about the right to privacy that appeared to provide a solid legal foundation for the litigation. The court had repeatedly ruled that decisions about intimate matters were protected by the Constitution from undue state interference and regulation, but most of those cases dealt with heterosexual intimacy decisions.

In the early 1980s, the ACLU took a case that activists hoped would be the vehicle to eliminate sodomy laws. Michael Hardwick was leaving his job as a bartender with a beer in hand, which he threw in a trashcan in front of Atlanta police officer, Keith Torrick. Torrick gave him a ticket for public drinking. Hardwick eventually went to court and paid a small fine, but Torrick mistakenly thought that Hardwick missed the date. Torrick got an arrest warrant, and went to arrest Hardwick. He entered the apartment and found Hardwick engaged in oral sex with another man. He arrested them for violating the state's sodomy law—a law that was gender-neutral. However, from this point forward, the issue would be framed largely as the legality of two men having consensual sex in the home. The ACLU contacted Hardwick, and he agreed to challenge his arrest as a test case.

Hardwick and the ACLU lost in federal district court, but they scored a victory in the Eleventh Circuit Court of Appeals. That court ruled that the privacy jurisprudence applied to Hardwick. By the time that the case reached the Supreme Court, Harvard law professor Lawrence Tribe became the lead lawyer in the case. Trying to eke out a narrow victory on a fairly conservative court, Tribe focused his arguments on privacy, hoping to get the vote of Justice Lewis Powell, along with four more liberal justices: William Brennan, Harry Blackmun, Thurgood Marshall, and John Paul Stevens. The strategy initially worked: Powell voted provisionally with the others to overturn the Georgia law on the grounds that the law violated the Eighth Amendment's prohibition on cruel and unusual punishment. However, lobbying by the conservative wing (especially Chief Justice Warren Burger) led him to change his vote, and the court ultimately upheld the statute. This reflects the fact that a great deal of bargaining occurs among the justices behind the scenes in the court—the internal strategic model. Years later, Powell regretted changing his vote and largely blamed his decision on the lack of direct personal knowledge of lesbians and gay men. Many of his clerks were closeted while they worked for him, including a clerk working for Powell during the *Bowers* term.

The majority opinion authored by Justice Byron White defined the right to privacy as fundamentally heterosexual in nature, of course ignoring the general applicability of the statute. For White, the case was not about a broad right to privacy but the narrow question concerning a "fundamental right to engage in homosexual sodomy."[18] Noting that fundamental rights jurisprudence (the broad area that includes the right to privacy) requires that a right deemed by the court to be fundamental requires a strong historical foundation, White instead (incorrectly) held that the criminalization of same-sex sex acts was grounded in history, not its protection as a right. In a concurring opinion, Burger cited an infamous description by the eighteenth-century English common law scholar William Blackstone of sodomy as a "malignity worse than rape."[19] Thus, for Burger, consensual sex between persons of the same sex was worse than violent, nonconsensual sex.

Justice Harry Blackmun's lead dissent took a sharply different view, and pointed in the direction that the court would eventually take; however, he did not have a fifth vote for this approach. He noted the majority's selective focus on gay men and argued that Hardwick was protected by the court's clear privacy jurisprudence. He argued that intimate choices, regardless of sexual orientation, were protected by the Constitution: "The fact that individuals define themselves in a significant way through their intimate sexual relationships with others suggests, in a Nation as diverse as ours, that there may be many 'right' ways of conducting those relationships, and that much of the richness of a relationship will come from the freedom an individual has to choose the form and nature of these intensely personal bonds."[20]

Bowers was a crushing defeat for lesbian and gay rights activists. Despite a more visible and active movement, the Supreme Court established itself yet again as a barrier to change, and sodomy laws would continue to play the symbolic and real constraining role on individuals and the movement. In a few years, however, activists changed tactics and shifted litigation to state courts. Many state constitutions provide more robust individual rights and equality protections, either through explicit provisions that go beyond the U.S. Constitution, or through interpretation by state court judges. For instance, many state constitutions contain textual protections for the right to privacy. The right in the federal constitution was developed through interpretation, as the words, "right to privacy" or anything similar, do not appear in the U.S. Constitution.

As a result, in 1992 Kentucky was the first state to see its sodomy law struck down by a state high court after *Bowers*. This was soon followed by judicial invalidation in Tennessee (1996), Montana (1997), Georgia (1998), and Arkansas (2002). These courts all invoked the right to privacy in their states' laws, while some also invoked equal protection concerns, especially in states where same-sex intimacy was specifically targeted. Not all of the litigation was successful, as some state high courts upheld sodomy laws (most notably in Texas and Louisiana), but the general trend was toward judicial elimination of sodomy laws, thus setting the stage for intervention by the Supreme Court in 2003.

Lawrence v. Texas

Given this trend and general cultural and political change, activists were eager to get back to the Supreme Court to overturn *Bowers*. In 1998, John Lawrence and Tyron Garner were arrested under Texas' sodomy statute, after Garner's intoxicated boyfriend called 911 with a false report about a man with a gun in Lawrence's apartment. Lawrence and Garner denied that they were having sex, but the police officers on the scene claimed that they were. After the arrest, local activists contacted Lambda Legal, and it was decided that this would be a good vehicle to challenge *Bowers*. Reflecting the conservative politics of the state (judges are elected in Texas, and most of them were Republicans), most Texas judges voted to uphold the statute.

Indeed, two Republican judges who temporarily overturned the statute faced significant backlash from the state party.

The background of the case illuminates the unique role played by cause lawyers, or lawyers who litigate on behalf of a political movement. For most lawyers, the goal would have been to get the charges dropped, but this would eliminate the possibility of a test case. With the permission of Lawrence and Garner, the lawyers kept the criminal process going, in order to have a real controversy. Typically, the Supreme Court will not hear cases that are moot, or cases that have been resolved through settlement or the dropping of charges. They also would have lacked standing, or the legal right to bring a case to court, because they faced no charges. Doctrines like standing and mootness potentially limit the power of courts by preventing them from randomly addressing controversies. Had they lost, Lawrence and Garner would have had criminal records related to the events of that night, but they, too, wanted to make a political point and were willing to take a risk.[21]

Seldom does the Supreme Court repudiate a recent decision in such the sweeping manner as did the court in *Lawrence v. Texas*. Generally, the court is respectful of precedent, under the doctrine of *stare decisis*, or the Anglo-American legal tradition of following previous decisions. The idea behind this doctrine is to bring stability and continuity to the law, as well as placing limits on the ability of judges to push the law in radically new directions. Justice Anthony Kennedy authored the 6 to 3 decision striking down the Texas law, and thereby all remaining laws. Kennedy first attacked the poor history in *Bowers* by noting that, historically, sodomy laws were gender-neutral and the laws had only recently targeted same-sex sexual practices. Kennedy was assisted in the argument by an influential *amicus curiae*, or friend of the court, brief from historians outlining the historical status of sodomy laws. These briefs can be the source of useful information for judges, adding greater context to litigation. This, along with the *Bowers* court's incorrect fencing of same-sex intimacy outside of the protection of the Constitution led Kennedy to declare: "*Bowers* was not correct when it was decided, and it is not correct today. It ought not to remain binding precedent. *Bowers v. Hardwick* should be and now is overruled."[22] Kennedy took a distinctly Millian approach to the issue of privacy, one that clearly rejected the limited and heterosexual right to privacy of the *Bowers* majority:

> Liberty protects the person from unwarranted government intrusions into a dwelling or other private places. In our tradition the State is not omnipresent in the home. And there are other spheres of our lives and existence, outside the home, where the State should not be a dominant presence. Freedom extends beyond spatial bounds. Liberty presumes an autonomy of self that includes freedom of thought, belief, expression, and certain intimate conduct.[23]

Kennedy's opinion was also notable for its equating same-sex intimacy with opposite-sex intimacy. All of the moral judgment of *Bowers* was gone, and the issue was fundamentally reframed by Kennedy.

In dissent, Justice Antonin Scalia accused Kennedy of judicial activism (overturning a decision made through the democratic process), and argued that the right to privacy as developed by the court did not prevent a majority in a state from enacting a law grounded in theological morality. As he stated, "Many Americans do not want persons who openly engage in homosexual conduct as partners in their business, as scoutmasters for their children, as teachers in their children's schools, or as boarders in their home. They view this as protecting themselves and their families from a lifestyle that they believe to be immoral and destructive."[24] He also noted that Kennedy's supportive language could open the door to a future ruling validating same-sex marriage. In fact, a few months later, Chief Justice Margaret Marshall would rely heavily on Kennedy's language in finding Massachusetts' ban on same-sex marriage unconstitutional in the groundbreaking case of *Goodridge v. Department of Public Health* (2003).

With Lawrence, the court was now on the side of protecting the rights of sexual minorities. Nearly fifty years after the ALI recommendation, and decades after decriminalization in Canada and the United Kingdom, sodomy laws were unconstitutional and unenforceable, and the court applied fundamental constitutional protections to a class of people previously viewed by a majority of the justices as threats or persons to be pitied.

MARRIAGE EQUALITY LITIGATION

Litigation has been central to the gains made by marriage equality activists. Outside of Canada and a few other countries, most policy change in the direction of marriage equality has occurred through the legislative process. Activists in the United States have always turned to the courts, either spontaneously or organized with national litigation groups, as a part of the strategy to legalize same-sex marriage. While the legislative and popular referenda processes also have been engaged by activists, litigation has been an imperfect, yet often effective, tool to achieve policy change. The litigation has centered around constitutional arguments that prohibitions against same-sex marriage violate the fundamental right to marriage or violate state and federal constitutional provisions against discrimination, either on the basis of gender or sexual orientation. Because marriage is traditionally the jurisdiction of U.S. states, litigation initially occurred in states, but the decision of the Supreme Court in *United States v. Windsor* (2013) dramatically shifted the litigation to federal courts.

Early Litigation

In the wake of the Stonewall Riots, same-sex couples requested marriage licenses, were denied, and some went to court. While many activists did not see marriage issues as central to the movement at that moment, some did. They felt that constitutional principles should allow them to be married. For instance, a couple in Washington State argued that the state's recently enacted equal rights amendment (an amendment that forbade discrimination on the basis of sex) authorized same-sex marriages. While the courts in Washington rejected this argument, it illustrates the strong connection in the 1970s between the marriage equality movement and the women's movement, especially activism surrounding the federal Equal Rights Amendment. Many saw the denial of same-sex marriage licenses as a form of sex discrimination, in that the denial of licenses to same-sex couples stemmed from the fact that one of them was the incorrect gender.

Others, like Jack Baker and Michael McConnell, saw the issue in terms of the emerging lesbian and gay liberation movements. Their case out of Minnesota, *Baker v. Nelson*, eventually made it to the U.S. Supreme Court in 1972, but the court saw no federal constitutional violations associated with Minnesota's ban on same-sex marriage. This negative precedent would haunt the movement for decades, as it was a clear barrier to further federal litigation. Thus, litigating too soon can lead to setbacks that hamper future progress. The court's dismissive approach to Baker and McConnell's claims was reflective of all judges who addressed the issue during the early 1970s. They ruled that marriage was fundamentally heterosexual; thus, no state or federal constitutional provisions allowed same-sex couples access to the myriad of rights and benefits associated with the institution. On the state level, these number in the hundreds and over one thousand in federal law and policy. Over time, policymakers have privileged marriage in law and policy, thus making access to the institution more than simply a religious exercise, as marriage is often framed by opponents of marriage equality. Marital status is intertwined with the contemporary legal system and social welfare state. The ability to pass property to a spouse without taxation, the right to not testify against a spouse in a criminal proceeding, the right to visit a spouse in the hospital and make medical decision, and Social Security survivor benefits are just a few of the myriad of rights and benefits that come with marital status.

The Courts are Reengaged

Several factors led to the reemergence of litigation as a tool to protect same-sex relationships by the 1980s. Child custody problems arose, related to the fact that lesbian couples were increasingly raising children. The AIDS crisis demonstrated the legal fragility of gay male relationships. Partners were routinely denied health care access and decision making by "legal" family members, and these family members often ignored surviving partners and seized property that had been held in common. Despite the early legal failures, same-sex couples continued to believe that the law was treating them unjustly, and some of them decided to sue for marriage equality. Connected to this reawakening of legal marriage equality activism, the highest court in New York ruled that same-sex partners were considered family under a New York City rent control law, in *Braschi v. Stahl Associates* (1989). As law professor Carlos Ball notes, the case is important, because "it provided considerable legitimacy to the movement's claim that LGBT people were as capable of forming loving and lasting familial ties as were straight people."[25] In Minnesota, a high-profile legal struggle about the guardianship of a lesbian severely injured in a car accident, Sharon Kowalski, between her partner and her immediate family also highlighted to the LGBT community the need for more formal legal protections for their relationships. An appeals court sided with the partner, thus again demonstrating the potential of the courts as allies in the movement for marriage equality, a clear shift from earlier years.

However, because of the previous losses and due to philosophical objections to pursuing marriage as a goal, largely because of the institution's oppression of women, national litigation groups discouraged litigation. Marriage was not a legitimate goal (and other issues were more pressing), nor was the time right, legally or politically, for these groups. One dissenting voice was Evan Wolfson who would become one of the leaders of the marriage equality movement, eventually founding the organization, Freedom to Marry. Despite these strong objections, in 1990 a gay male couple from Washington, D.C. filed a federal challenge to D.C.'s lack of recognition of same-sex marriage, aided by the law professor of one of the men, William Eskridge, Jr. Eskridge would become a leading scholar of the marriage equality movement. The lawsuit was dropped after losses in the district and appellate courts, but one appellate court judge saw potential merit in their claim for equal treatment. The couple went on national television to argue their case, but the media largely ignored their suit, given the rejection by the federal courts.

Litigation begun at about the same time in Hawaii turned out to be much more visible and consequential. Same-sex couples who were denied marriage licenses sued the state with the assistance of local attorney Dan Foley. After a loss in a lower court, the Supreme Court of Hawaii ruled in 1993 in *Baehr v. Lewin* that the lack of recognition of their relationships was unconstitutional under the state constitution. In particular, the court applied strict scrutiny, because the justices viewed the discrimination as a form of sex discrimination under the Constitution's amendment forbidding sex discrimination, or "mini-ERA." Viewing the case as one of sexual orientation discrimination would have triggered a much lower level of judicial scrutiny. Rather than rule directly, however, the court remanded the case to a trial court to allow the state to potentially establish a compelling interest that would justify the discriminatory practice.

The decision was revolutionary. For the first time, a court ruled in favor of marriage equality claims, and the decision would begin the process of other state high courts ruling in a similar manner. However, it also triggered a substantial national backlash, as it appeared likely that Hawaii would legalize same-sex marriage, thus allowing for couples to marry in the state but return home and request recognition of their marriage. Indeed, in 1996, Congress enacted the Defense of Marriage Act (DOMA). The law denied federal recognition to state-sanctioned same-sex marriages, and it gave authority to states that wished to refuse recognition.

In Hawaii, the decision sparked several years of political and legal wrangling. In support of the decision, a commission created by the legislature to study the issue recommended that the state enact same-sex marriage. After waiting for the commission to complete its work, Judge Kevin Chang held the trial requested by the Supreme Court. The state argued that an interest in heterosexual procreation and child rearing was its compelling interest, but Chang rejected this argument after hearing from experts during the trial. This would be the first of only three full same-sex marriage trials by 2014. Most litigation would avoid trials in favor of summary judgment motions, or rulings by a judge before a trial that the party bringing a suit has, or has not, made a sound legal case, thus making a trial unnecessary. The legislature also enacted a reciprocal beneficiaries law providing for a minimal set of rights for any two persons not already married, nor related by blood. This was a scaled-down version of more complete domestic partnership proposals intended for same-sex couples by legislators and activists who agreed with the spirit of the Supreme Court decision but who calculated that same-sex marriage was not politically possible.

Opponents of the decision placed pressure on the legislature to invalidate the decision through a constitutional amendment. The amendment eventually passed by the legislature and approved by voters in 1998 did not define marriage directly. It gave the legislature the sole authority to define marriage. Thus, it trumped judicial action, but it also allowed a future legislature to enact a same-sex marriage statute without amending the Constitution. Mobilization by churches, especially money from the Catholic and Mormon churches, helped to pass the amendment with 71 percent of the vote.

A local couple also sued over the denial of a marriage license in Alaska where, in 1998, a trial court found that the state's same-sex marriage prohibition was unconstitutional.[26] The courts in Alaska have a reputation for being activist, especially in enforcing a libertarian jurisprudence. Indeed, the judge found that the ban was a violation of the fundamental right to marriage and was a form of gender discrimination. Voters passed a direct ban on same-sex marriage the same year as the decision, thus quickly short-circuiting the judicial process. But yet another legal system had directly confronted the constitutionality of same-sex marriage bans and found constitutional problems.

The New England Strategy

After the events in Hawaii and Alaska, the resistance within the movement to marriage equality litigation subsided, and activist lawyers began to bring coordinated test cases in states with favorable judicial and political cultures and where state constitutions were difficult to amend, effectively taking power away from conservative opponents. Finding such favorable legal venues is called forum shopping. Many New England states fit this pattern, and Gay and Lesbian Advocates and Defenders (GLAD), led by Mary Bonauto, initiated litigation in Vermont and Massachusetts. In Vermont, Bonauto worked with local attorneys Beth Robinson and Susan Murray to begin a political movement to support the eventual litigation they filed. A trial court judge ruled against them, but they found great success with the Supreme Court of Vermont in *Baker v. State* (1999). A unanimous court found a constitutional violation, despite invoking only rational basis review under the state constitution's equal protection provision. According to Chief Justice Jeffrey Amestoy, same-sex couples were entitled to "legal protection and security for their avowed commitment to an intimate and lasting human relationship" and that recognizing these relationships was "a recognition of our common humanity."[27]

Unlike the Hawaii court, Amestoy and the other justices definitively ruled on the constitutional problem, but they gave the legislature two options to remedy the problem. They could enact same-sex marriage, or they could create statutory framework that mirrored the state's marriage laws, but called something else. This reflected the potential political resistance to same-sex marriage even in liberal Vermont. Wisely, the court retained jurisdiction and would have mandated same-sex marriage in the absence of a legislative response inconsistent with the court's decision. After a contentious political battle, the legislature passed, and Governor Howard Dean signed, a civil union bill that fulfilled the second option presented by the Supreme Court. This was the most advanced relationship equality policy in any state to that point. The litigators were disappointed in this "separate but equal" approach, but the litigation in Vermont represented yet another significant legal and policy advancement.

GLAD then turned to neighboring Massachusetts where Bonauto achieved an unqualified victory in *Goodridge v. Department of Public Health* (2003).

In that decision, Chief Justice Margaret Marshall of the Supreme Judicial Court used much the same approach of the Vermont court, such as the use of the rational basis test with strong and supportive language, but differed from that court in not allowing for a remedy other than full marriage equality in the state. The Massachusetts court was more divided, with three justices dissenting, arguing that the state had a legitimate interest in heterosexual procreation and that any change to marriage law in the state was the proper jurisdiction of the legislature. Same-sex marriage became legal in May of 2004, making Massachusetts the first state to authorize same-sex marriage. Efforts to overturn the decision through a constitutional amendment were thwarted by legislative leaders over a period of several years, but eventually opposition waned as public opinion in the state increasingly became more supportive of the policy.

GLAD achieved another victory in the region when the Connecticut Supreme Court ruled in favor of same-sex marriage in 2008 in the case of *Kerrigan v. Commissioner of Public Health*. It was the first high court in New England to view sexual orientation as requiring heightened scrutiny. The Connecticut court relied on the first court in the country to do so, the California Supreme Court, earlier in 2008 (discussed below). Eventually, through litigation, legislation, or popular initiative, all of New England allowed same-sex marriage by 2013. The GLAD litigation provided great leverage to activists throughout the region and contributed to the proliferation of marriage equality policies, in addition to its direct effects.

Litigation Spreads with Mixed Results

Goodridge spawned a new wave of coordinated litigation by groups like Lambda Legal and the ACLU. A suit in New Jersey resulted in a Vermont-style judicial mandate and civil union policy. As was discussed, the Supreme Court of California mandated same-sex marriage in that state in an aggressive decision in *In re Marriage Cases*. This decision was overturned a few months later by Proposition 8, but the court found sexual orientation to be a suspect classification and applied strict scrutiny to invalidate California's ban on same-sex marriage. The court referenced its legacy as a civil rights innovator, particularly noting its decision in *Perez v. Sharp* (1948) striking down the state's ban on interracial marriage.

While the decisions starting with *Baker* were generally decided with emerging majority or plurality public support for the legal recognition of same-sex relationships, a decision by the Iowa Supreme Court, orchestrated by Lambda Legal, in 2009 was distinctly at odds with public opinion in the state. The group calculated that the judiciary would be receptive to their argument and that they could politically manage any potential backlash, given that constitutional amendments first need to go through the legislature or a constitutional convention—not simply as a result of signature gathering. The unanimous court applied heightened scrutiny on the basis of sexual orientation in its decision in *Varnum v. Brien* (2009). The justices knew that their decision was contrary to public sentiment in the state, but they emphasized their role in protecting minorities from majority oppression. The following year, three of the justices lost retention elections (nonpartisan elections in which there is no opponent, only a choice by voters to retain the judge for another fixed term), the first time Supreme Court justices had not been retained since the 1960s. However, partial control of the legislature by the Democrats, and the state party's strong support for the decision, prevented an amendment from being placed before the voters.

Forum shopping by marriage equality litigators did not always go as planned. In several progressive states, high courts refused to mandate same-sex marriage, including Washington State, New York, and Maryland. Many of the votes were close, but the majorities in these cases deferred to state arguments about procreation. However, all of these states subsequently legalized same-sex marriage through the political process.

The Turn to Federal Courts, The Proposition 8 Trial, and *U.S. v. Windsor*

After decades of generally avoiding the federal courts because of their conservatism and the legacy of *Baker v. Nelson*, litigation activists brought coordinated litigation aimed at striking down DOMA, starting in 2009. Assisting these efforts, the Obama administration, while first defending DOMA in the early years of the administration, reversed course and stopped defending the law, asserting that sexual orientation–based discrimination should trigger heightened scrutiny. The defense of the law was then taken over by the House of Representatives through an entity known as the Bipartisan Legal Advisory Group, or BLAG. Litigation commenced by GLAD, Lambda Legal, and the ACLU in the more liberal First, Second, and Ninth Circuits received favorable decisions from federal judges.

Controversy erupted over a plan by the lawyers who had argued on opposite sides in the famous case of *Bush v. Gore* (2000), Ted Olson (for George W. Bush) and David Boies (for Al Gore). These lawyers had not been directly involved in previous marriage equality litigation, but some California-based activists thought that their legal "star power" would assist in the strategy of overturning Proposition 8. Most marriage equality legal activists opposed the suit, favoring the strategy to first attack DOMA. Despite the criticism, Boies and Olson challenged the constitutionality of Proposition. 8 in federal court. Ultimately, both streams of litigation would be heard by the Supreme Court in 2013, when the court issued a decision to strike down part of DOMA, while issuing a more limited ruling that had the effect of invalidating Proposition 8. However, the court left standing other state amendments.

On the way to the Supreme Court, the second, and most visible, trial over same-sex marriage took place in the San Francisco federal courtroom of Judge Vaughn Walker in 2010. The trial concerning the legal challenge to Proposition 8 was covered heavily in the media and did not go well for the law's defenders. Their experts were few, and the Olsen and Boies' experts presented a strong case that marriage has evolved substantially over time and that same-sex parents were equal to opposite-sex parents. On the basis of this evidence, Walker found Proposition 8 to be unconstitutional. On appeal, the Ninth Circuit also invalidated Proposition 8, although on narrower grounds.

As stated above, the Supreme Court granted review of the Proposition 8 case (*Hollingsworth v. Perry*) along with another case challenging DOMA. Edith Windsor and Thea Spayer had been together for thirty years by the time that they married in Canada in 2007. (Same-sex marriage became legal throughout Canada in 2005.) Upon her death in 2009, Spayer willed her estate to Windsor, but the latter was charged with a federal tax bill of over $350,000. Had the federal government recognized their marriage, she would have owed nothing. She won in the district and appellate courts, with both levels finding part of DOMA to be unconstitutional.

In *United States v. Windsor*, the Supreme Court invalidated section 3 of DOMA, the section forbidding federal recognition of same-sex marriages. Now writing his third significant lesbian and gay rights opinion, Justice Kennedy found the law to be a violation of equal protection and due process provisions of the Constitution. He held that DOMA was purely a moral state-ment on homosexuality and lacked a legitimate policy purpose, thus echoing his decision in *Romer*. Following his decision in *Lawrence*, he also spoke repeatedly of the dignity of same-sex couples and emphasized the unequal treatment created by DOMA for families and their children. As he stated,

DOMA singles out a class of persons deemed by a State entitled to recogni-tion and protection to enhance their own liberty. It imposes a disability on the class by refusing to acknowledge a status the State finds to be dignified and proper. DOMA instructs all federal officials, and indeed all persons with whom same-sex couples interact, including their own children, that their marriage is less worthy than the marriages of others. The federal statute is invalid, for no legitimate purpose overcomes the purpose and effect to disparage and to injure those whom the State, by its marriage laws, sought to protect in personhood and dignity.[28]

He did not apply heightened or strict scrutiny, nor did he directly overrule *Baker*, thus leaving the jurisprudence a bit confused and up to lower courts to sort out in future litigation. Kennedy was joined in the opinion by the court's more liberal members: Ruth Bader Ginsburg, Stephen Breyer, Sonia Sotomayor, and Elena Kagan.

Again in dissent, Justice Scalia criticized the lack of clear standards in Kennedy's opinion but argued that the dignity language used by Kennedy could easily be invoked to invalidate state bans on same-sex marriage. He also, like his previous dissents, argued that morality alone was sufficient to allow a law to stand. He accused Kennedy of painting the members of Congress who enacted DOMA as "enemies of the human race," for opposing same-sex marriage.[29] His primary argument, however, was that the case should have been dismissed for a lack of standing, asserting that BLAG could not stand in for the executive branch.

This is exactly what a narrow majority of the court did in *Hollingsworth v. Perry.* Chief Justice John Roberts held that the citizen proponents of Proposition 8 lacked standing under federal jurisprudence, even though the California courts granted standing to such groups. These citizens stepped in to defend the law after California officials refused to defend the law in court. The effect of this ruling was to revert back to Judge Walker's decision, thus invalidating Proposition 8 only, not other state amendments. Four justices, Kennedy, Breyer, Sotomayor, and Samuel Alito (an interesting ideological mix), would have granted standing, given California's strong emphasis on citizen initiatives. As a result of the court's decision, same-sex marriage again became legal in California.

The two decisions were viewed by marriage equality advocates as the best possible scenario: federal benefits would now be attached to same-sex marriages, the court used positive language to describe same-sex couples, and a negative decision on the constitutionality of all state bans on same-sex marriage was avoided. Through the prism of the strategic model, it seems clear that the court was more willing to confront Congress than it was the numerous states with constitutional prohibitions on same-sex marriage. However, activists soon took Scalia's advice and used *Windsor* to begin attacking these amendments in a wave of litigation, and federal judges have consistently invalidated amendments, relying heavily on Kennedy's opinion. A return of the issue to the Supreme Court in order to directly address the constitutionality of state bans on relationship recognition appeared likely.

In *Obergefell v. Hodges* (2015), the same majority in *Windsor* applied the essential logic of that ruling in striking down state bans on same-sex marriage, thus finally nationalizing same-sex marriage. Justice Kennedy was again the author of the opinion, and he found the state bans to run afoul of the due process clause's fundamental right to marry and the equal protection clause. The decision also overruled *Baker v. Nelson.* After a long and winding path of litigation and political activism, marriage equality activists achieved their ultimate goal, much sooner than many had anticipated.

CONCLUSION

While not uniformly supportive of the rights of sexual minorities, courts have been key allies in the broader movement. They have been an effective counter-weight to majoritarian sentiments enacted into law and policy, and LGB rights activists have effectively used the language of rights and equality. While it took some time, the federal judiciary has become a more consistent ally of the movement, along with the many innovative state high courts that have been allies for decades, particularly in sodomy law and marriage equality litigation. While courts cannot wave a magic wand to achieve social change, their decisions can challenge and greatly unsettle the political status quo and provide marginalized groups with leverage and clout in the political system, particularly when activists carefully select the right time and place for litigation.

KEY TERMS, CONCEPTS, AND CASES

American Law Institute (ALI)
Amicus curiae brief
Attitudinal model
Backlash theory
Cause lawyers
Courts and social change
Forum shopping
Fundamental rights
Heightened scrutiny
Judicial activism
Litigation strategy
Legal consciousness
Legal framing
Legal model
Legal realism
Millian approach to privacy
Mini-ERA
Negative precedent
One-shotters
Rational basis review
Repeat players
Right to privacy
Sodomy laws
Standing/mootness doctrines
Stare decisis

Strategic model
Strict scrutiny
Summary judgment
Wolfenden Commission
Baehr v. Lewin (1993)
Baker v. Nelson (1972)
Baker v. State of Vermont (1999)
Boutilier v. INS (1967)
Boy Scouts of America v. Dale (2000)
Braschi v. Stahl Associates (1989)
Brown v. Board of Education (1954)
Doe v. Commonwealth's Attorney (1976)
Goodridge v. Department of Public Health (2003)
Griswold v. Connecticut (1965)
Hollingsworth v. Perry (2013)
Hurley v. Irish-American Gay, Lesbian, and Bisexual Group of Boston (1995)
In re Marriage Cases (2008)
Kameny v. Brucker (1961)
Kerrigan v. Commissioner of Public Health (2008)
Lawrence v. Texas (2003)

Obergefell v. Hodges (2015)   *Stoumen v. Reilley* (1951)
ONE v. Olesen (1958)   *United States v. Windsor* (2013)
Perez v. Sharp (1948)   *Vallerga v. Department of Alcoholic*
Romer v. Evans (1996)   *Beverage Control* (1959)
Roth v. U.S. (1957)   *Varnum v. Brien* (2009)

QUESTIONS FOR DISCUSSION

1. Have courts always been allies to the lesbian and gay rights movement?
2. What is the role of courts in achieving social change? Have courts contributed to progress for the lesbian and gay rights movement, or have they only responded to changes in the political arena?
3. What are the elements of an effective litigation strategy?
4. How much should sexual minorities rely on litigation for future progress? Has the time come to pursue a more exclusively grassroots and legislative strategy?

NOTES

1. Marc Galanter, "Why the 'Haves' Come Out Ahead: Speculations on the Limits of Legal Change," *Law & Society Review*, 9:1 (1974), 95–160.

2. John D'Emilio, *Sexual Politics, Sexual Communities: The Making of a Homosexual Minority in the United States, 1940–1970* (Chicago: The University of Chicago Press, 1983), 70.

3. James T. Sears, *Behind the Mask of Mattachine: The Hall Call Chronicles and the Early Movement for Homosexual Emancipation* (New York: Harrington Park Press, 2006), 164.

4. William N. Eskridge, Jr., *Gaylaw: Challenging the Apartheid of the Closet* (Cambridge, MA: Harvard University Press, 1999), 93.

5. *Stoumen v. Reilly*, 234 P.2d 969 (Cal. 1951), 971.

6. *Vallerga v. Department of Alcoholic Beverage Control*, 347 P.2d 909 (Cal. 1959), 913.

7. Eskridge, 94–5.

8. *Lynch Builders Restaurant v. O'Connell*, 103 N.E.2d 531 (NY, 1952).

9. Eskridge, 112–13.

10. Joyce Murdoch and Deb Price, *Courting Justice: Gay Men and Lesbians v. The Supreme Court* (New York: Basic Books, 2001), 30.

11. *Roth v. United States*, 354 U.S. 476 (1957), 484.

12. Pierceson, *Courts, Liberalism, and Rights*, 65.

13. See Marc Stein, *Sexual Injustice: Supreme Court Decisions from* Griswold *to* Roe (Chapel Hill: The University of North Carolina Press, 2010).

14. Quoted in Murdoch and Price, 57.

15. 387 U.S. 118 (1967), 130.

16. Murdoch and Price, 134.
17. *Romer v. Evans*, 517 U.S. 620 (1996), 633.
18. *Bowers v. Hardwick*, 478 U.S. 186 (1986), 190.
19. *Bowers*, 197.
20. *Bowers*, 205.
21. The tactics of the lawyers are drawn from Dale Carpenter, *Flagrant Conduct: The Story of* Lawrence v. Texas (New York: Norton, 2012).
22. *Lawrence v. Texas*, 539 U.S. 558 (2003), 578.
23. *Lawrence*, 562.
24. *Lawrence*, 602.
25. Carlos Ball, *From the Closet to the Courtroom: Five LGBT Lawsuits That Have Changed Our Nation* (Boston: Beacon Press, 2010), 55.
26. *Brause v. Bureau of Vital Statistics*, 1998 WL 88743 (Alaska Super. Ct. February 27, 1998).
27. *Baker v. State of Vermont*, 744 A.2d 864 (Vt. 1999), 889.
28. 133 S.Ct. 2675 (2013), 2695–696.
29. 133 S.Ct. 2675 (2013), 2709.

BIBLIOGRAPHY AND FURTHER READING

Ellen Ann Andersen, *Out of the Closets and into the Courts: Legal Opportunity Structure and Gay Rights Litigation* (Ann Arbor: University of Michigan Press, 2004).
Carlos Ball, *From the Closet to the Courtroom: Five LGBT Lawsuits That Have Changed Our Nation* (Boston: Beacon Press, 2010).
Dale Carpenter, *Flagrant Conduct: The Story of* Lawrence v. Texas (New York: Norton, 2012).
William N. Eskridge, Jr., *Gaylaw: Challenging the Apartheid of the Closet* (Cambridge, MA: Harvard University Press, 1999).
———, *Dishonorable Passions: Sodomy Laws in America, 1861-2003* (New York: Viking, 2008).
Evan Gerstmann, *The Constitutional Underclass: Gays, Lesbians, and the Failure of Class-Based Equal Protection* (Chicago: University of Chicago Press, 1999).
Lisa Keen and Suzanne B. Goldberg, *Strangers to the Law: Gay People on Trial* (Ann Arbor: The University Press of Michigan, 1998).
Michael J. Klarman, *From the Closet to the Altar: Courts, Backlash, and the Struggle for Same-Sex Marriage* (New York: Oxford University Press, 2013).
Susan Gluck Mezey, *Queers in Court: Gay Rights Law and Public Policy* (Lanham, MD: Rowman & Littlefield, 2009).
Joyce Murdoch and Deb Price, *Courting Justice: Gay Men and Lesbians v. The Supreme Court* (New York: Basic Books, 2001).
Jason Pierceson, *Courts, Liberalism, and Rights: Gay Law and Politics in the United States and Canada* (Philadelphia: Temple University Press, 2005).
———, *Same-Sex Marriage in the United States: The Road to the Supreme Court and Beyond* (Lanham, MD: Rowman & Littlefield, 2014).

David A. J. Richards, *The Case for Gay Rights: From* Bowers *to* Lawrence *and Beyond* (Lawrence: University Press of Kansas, 2005).

———, *The Sodomy Cases:* Bowers v. Hardwick *and* Lawrence v. Texas (Lawrence: University Press of Kansas, 2009).

Gerald N. Rosenberg, *The Hollow Hope: Can Courts Bring About Social Change?*, 2nd ed. (Chicago: University of Chicago Press, 2008).

Marc Stein, *Sexual Injustice: Supreme Court Decisions from* Griswold *to* Roe (Chapel Hill: The University of North Carolina Press, 2010).

Chapter 6

Public Policies

This chapter examines a range of contemporary public policies relating to sexual minorities. Transgender policies are more fully explored in chapter 7. Beyond the themes of diversity and urbanism, litigation and rights claiming, weaker religiosity/conservative resistance, and partisanship that tend to facilitate advances in LGBT policy, the concept of policy diffusion helps to explain how LGBT-related policy has advanced. Button, Rienzo, and Wald describe diffusion as occurring when "local decision makers look to officials in other nearby communities for guides to action in many policy areas. Uncertainty and the fear of unanticipated consequences tend to limit policy change and reform. Once a policy has been adopted by a large number of communities or by a dominant nearby city, however, it is increasingly recognized as a legitimate public responsibility."[1] Because of U.S. federalism, states and localities have jurisdiction over many policy areas relating to sexual minorities. States and localities have truly been the "laboratories of democracy" described by Louis Brandeis, but they have also been the sites of tremendous opposition. Other policy areas have been a mix of federal and state action. However, the federal government has only recently become a hospitable forum for LGBT policymaking. This overview is not meant to be an exhaustive examination of relevant policies, merely an introduction to important policy areas.

ANTIDISCRIMINATION LAWS

The Employment Nondiscrimination Act

One of the main goals of the early sexual minority rights movement was the inclusion of sexual orientation, and eventually gender identity, into state and federal antidiscrimination laws. The model for this type of policy is the federal Civil Rights Act of 1964. This law prohibits discrimination based on race, sex, religion, and national origin in employment and public accommodations, such as restaurants, hotels, and movie theaters. The first such law was enacted by Congress in 1866 to protect newly freed slaves and free African Americans in the marketplace, but the Supreme Court invalidated the law on the grounds that Congress's authority only extended to prohibiting discrimination by government, not private businesses. By the 1960s, largely in response to the Civil Rights Movement, the Court changed its interpretation and allowed such laws under Congress's constitutional power to regulate commerce. States have always possessed more power to regulate private entities under their general regulatory powers, historically called the police power.

In 1974, Congresswoman and feminist Bella Abzug of New York introduced the Equality Act in Congress. The law would have broadly outlawed discrimination in employment, housing, and public accommodations on the basis of sexual orientation, in addition to sex and marital status. Eventually, this strategy merged into efforts to add sexual orientation to the Civil Rights Act of 1964. When Abzug left Congress a few years later, Ed Koch took over leadership of the issue. However, efforts to enact this policy stalled for several decades. Opposition from the Religious Right, a lack of allies in Congress (even among Democrats), the HIV/AIDS crisis, and the early-1990s debate over lesbians and gays in the military undermined, or distracted from lobbying and activist efforts. By the 1990s, draft legislation was called the Employment Nondiscrimination Act (ENDA), a separate act focusing on the workplace, but not public accommodations more generally. This was seen as the most politically attainable piece of antidiscrimination policy, as polls indicated the highest level of public support for outlawing workplace discrimination. The election of a pro–gay rights president, Bill Clinton, along with Democratic majorities in Congress, led to renewed activism for the law by 1994 and 1995. In 1996, facing a hostile Republican majority in the House, members of Congress and activists developed a strategy to link ENDA with the proposed DOMA. The idea was to argue for the enactment of ENDA as a consolation for DOMA, which was expected to pass by large margins. However, this failed when the Senate voted 50–49 against the bill.[2]

The election of Democrats back to the majority in both houses of Congress in 2006 led to the next serious reengagement with ENDA. By this time, activists had successfully worked to include gender identity protections, along with sexual orientation. However, supporters in Washington, DC, including openly gay Democratic Congressman Barney Frank and the Human Rights Campaign, calculated that the inclusion of gender identity would lead to defeat for the bill. The revised bill passed the House, but it failed to pass the Senate. The bill also faced resistance from President George W. Bush. He stated his intention to veto the bill, arguing that the bill would infringe on religious freedom and state's rights, among other arguments. A gender identity–inclusive bill passed the Democratic-controlled Senate in 2013 by a vote of 64–32 (with 10 Republican votes), but never received a vote in the Republican-controlled House, thus continuing the Congressional stalemate. Speaker John Boehner asserted, in his defense of refusing to bring the bill up for a vote, that protections were already in place and that the law would lead to frivolous lawsuits. Of course, these suits would not be frivolous for those with legitimate discrimination claims. Politically, this argument is used against lawsuits political actors do not like, not only those that are truly lacking in legal merit, the more accurate use of the term.

In 2014, after seeing the stalled process in Congress, Commissioner Chai Feldblum of the Equal Employment Opportunity Commission (EEOC) began arguing that sexual orientation discrimination could be addressed by the EEOC under the sex discrimination provision of the 1964 Civil Rights Act, Title VII, under the theory that discrimination on the basis of sexual orientation is grounded in sex, or gender role, stereotyping. Indeed, in 2012, the EEOC ruled that this provision could be used to bring claims under federal law for transgender discrimination. However, the EEOC's interpretations are not binding on federal courts, and judges in these courts will likely want more clear statutory authority (such as ENDA) to rule in favor of the victims of discrimination. However, the position of the EEOC can be influential in expanding the interpretation of federal law. For instance, the EEOC's definition of sexual harassment under the sex provision of the Title VII was eventually adopted by the Supreme Court.

As written and passed by the Senate, ENDA includes clear language to make illegal sexual orientation and gender identity discrimination in the workplace. However, the law is more limited than the Civil Rights Act of 1964. As stated above, it does not apply to public accommodations or housing. Also, the religious exemptions are stronger than those in the 1964 law. Title VII allows for religious organizations to discriminate on the basis of religion, and only religion, in the carrying out of its religious mission. This is referred to as the "ministerial exception," in that it most directly applies to religious officials, such as priests or rabbis. This is generally not interpreted as applying to nonreligious employees in an organization, like social workers, janitors, food service workers, etc. However, ENDA allows religious organizations to broadly discriminate on the basis of sexual orientation and gender identity. As the text of the Senate-passed bill states, "This Act shall not apply to a corporation, association, educational institution or institution of learning, or society that is exempt from the religious discrimination provisions of title VII of the Civil Rights Act of 1964."[3] Thus, these organizations would be fully exempt from the law, not just for directly religious positions. The bill also clearly forbids any affirmative action policies for sexual minorities, as well as preventing any discrimination claims under the theory of "disparate impact," or claims that unintentionally discriminatory employment policies can still be actionable if they disproportionately affect a group in a negative fashion. Koch added that these provisions in the late 1970s as opposition to affirmative action for sexual minorities was an argument used against the broader nondiscrimination policy. Clearly, the bill is less protective than other civil rights laws. In the wake of the Supreme Court decision in *Burwell v. Hobby Lobby* (2014) in which the court found a religious exemption for the Affordable Care Act's birth control coverage mandate for private corporations, most LGBT rights groups withdrew support for ENDA. Only the Human Rights Campaign continued to support the bill out of pragmatism, but the organization called for an expanded antidiscrimination framework and a narrower religious exemption, citing the need to return to Bella Abzug's "visionary ideal."[4] Increasingly, advocacy groups abandoned the employment-protection-only tactic and called for the broader Civil Rights Act approach.

The withdrawal of support for ENDA and Republican resistance in the House make the future prospects of federal statutory protections appear bleak in the short term. Given this state of affairs, in July 2014 President Obama issued an executive order prohibiting discrimination on the basis of sexual orientation and gender identity by federal contractors, including colleges and universities receiving federal funds. He also added gender identity to Bill Clinton's 1998 order prohibiting discrimination on the basis of sexual orientation by the federal government. Religious groups lobbied heavily for a broad exemption from the order, inspired by the *Hobby Lobby* decision, but the Obama administration declined to add such an exemption.

State and Local Laws

Contrary to the struggle to enact an antidiscrimination law in Congress, states and localities have enacted scores of laws since the 1970s, but more than half of states lack statewide legal protections for sexual minorities. College towns and cities with significant LGBT populations led the way in the 1970s, reflecting the increased awareness, shared sense of identity, and mobilization of college students and staff in college towns and the most lesbian and gay-friendly cities. For example, East Lansing, Michigan (home to Michigan State University) was the first locality to adopt a policy of nondiscrimination for public employees in 1972 (a more expansive ordinance was enacted in 1973), followed by San Francisco the same year. At first, conservative opponents were not mobilized against these policies, as they were very new.

However, they soon mobilized to oppose these laws, and they were successful in repealing many of them, most famously the Dade County ordinance in 1997, led by the Bryant campaign. By the 1980s and 1990s, the policies proliferated through policy diffusion in other cities and progressive towns, many of them suburbs in large urban areas, using the laws of the primary city as a model. Wisconsin became the first state to enact a statewide law in 1982. These policies then spread to more progressive states. By the 1990s, it became increasingly common for these laws to also include prohibitions on gender identity discrimination, or activists lobbied for the addition of such protections to civil rights laws. Minnesota was the first state to include these protections in 1993. These laws vary in levels of protection, with not all of them touching on public accommodations and housing, and many with religious exemptions.

The following 21 states have sexual orientation or sexual orientation and gender identity antidiscrimination laws, with the initial year of enactment noted in parentheses: Wisconsin (1982), Massachusetts (1989), Connecticut (1991), Hawaii (1991), California (1992), New Jersey (1992), Vermont (1992), Minnesota (1993), Rhode Island (1995), New Hampshire (1997), Nevada (1999), Maryland (2001), New York (2002), New Mexico (2003), Illinois (2005), Maine (2005), Washington (2006), Colorado (2007), Iowa (2007), Oregon (2007), and Delaware (2009).[5] These are the most progressive states in the country, and the clustering of states in the Northeast, Upper Midwest, and the West mirror the clustering of states initially enacting relationship equality policies through litigation or legislation. Protections are absent in all of the South and the Great Plains, as well as more conservative Midwestern states (Indiana, Michigan, Missouri, and Ohio). Activist mobilization, combined with Democratic Party control of state government, explains most of the positive outcomes. Conservative opposition, anchored in the Republican Party, is still entrenched, despite public support for legal protections for sexual minorities.

These laws are generally enforced through a local or state civil rights or human rights commission. Those who feel that they have been discriminated against may file a claim with the commission. The commission then investigates the matter and decides if the claim has factual merit and is actionable under the antidiscrimination ordinance or statute. Penalties are typically fines levied against the discriminating entity, or other remedial sanctions. Decisions by commissions generally are appealable in court. For example, Elaine Photography was accused by a same-sex couple of discrimination under New Mexico's law after the photographer refused to photograph their commitment ceremony. (This occurred prior to the legalization of same-sex marriage in the state.) The state commission found that Elaine Photography discriminated on the basis of sexual orientation, and fined the business. This action was upheld by all levels of courts in New Mexico, and the U.S. Supreme Court denied the appeal in 2014, thus leaving the commission's decision in place. In state court, Elaine Photography argued that the discrimination was justified, given the business' freedom of speech and religion. The courts refused to allow for this type of exemption, generally arguing that to do so would undermine the entire antidiscrimination framework, not just for sexual minorities, but for other marginalized groups. Increasingly, however, opponents of rights for sexual minorities are invoking the threat to religious liberty in legal and political settings, especially as direct appeals to conservative and theological morality have lost political and legal clout.

These laws also have an indirect effect, in that they often create an incentive for government and business to provide a more welcoming environment for sexual minorities, particularly as a way to avoid complaints and litigation. The laws themselves also serve as an endorsement of the equal status of sexual minorities and have created more societal acceptance. It is now seen as good business practice to have companies against discrimination against sexual orientation and gender identity/expression and to create welcoming and supportive workplaces. According to the Human Rights Campaign, 88 percent of Fortune 500 companies have policies based on sexual orientation, and 57 percent based on gender identity.[6]

Public Opinion

The lack of state and federal progress stands in stark contrast to strong public support for antidiscrimination policies for sexual minorities. Gallup has been polling about employment discrimination protections based on sexual orientation since 1976. In that year, 56 percent of respondents supported protections. By 1989, this had grown to 71 percent. By 2008, public support for these protections was nearly unanimous: 89 percent.[7] Given these numbers, it is likely that majority support exists is every state, but twenty-nine states have yet to enact these policies. Support is also probably lower for housing and public accommodations, but likely still a national majority. Congress' failure to act is contrary to the views of 89 percent, or more, of the public. This is a clear example of the fact that public opinion alone does not determine policy outcomes.

HATE CRIME POLICIES

Hate crime laws generally add a penalty to an already existing crime (murder, assault, criminal damage to property, etc.) if the crime was motivated by hatred or bias toward a group. They do not create new crimes. They do not criminalize speech alone. Hate speech laws are often found in other countries, but they are nonexistent in the United States, due to the strong protections for free speech under the First Amendment. The idea behind hate crime laws is twofold: to deter bias-motivated crimes and to send a symbolic message that bias crimes are not accepted in society. They provide status and societal and legal protection to groups covered by the laws. Generally, hate crimes penalize criminal actions based on race, gender, religion, disability, sexual orientation, and gender identity. However, sexual orientation and gender identity were added in later rounds of policy creation. While the overall number of hate crimes is declining, sexual orientation and gender identity–based crimes have held steady, or increased. In the sexual and gender identity minority community, gay men and transgender individuals are disproportionately the victims of hate crimes, and crimes against them are often more physically violent.[8] As sexual and gender minorities have become more visible and politically active, violence has followed. Many of these crimes go unreported.

These protections have been more controversial, given that opponents of including sexual orientation and gender identity to hate crime policies object to the official sanctioning and protection of sexual and gender minorities. More broadly, opponents of hate crime laws assert that they are an inappropriate intervention by government into the thoughts of individuals. They, according to this view, create the "thought police." This critique is mostly found in libertarian circles. For instance, the gay author and blogger Andrew Sullivan forcefully opposes hate crime laws. He thinks they jeopardize free thought and expression. As he states, "The boundaries between hate and prejudice and between prejudice and opinion and between opinion and truth are so complicated and blurred that any attempt to construct legal and political fire walls is a doomed and illiberal venture."[9] Many religious opponents of the LGBT rights falsely assert that hate crime laws will make illegal religious condemnations of sexual diversity. Of course, the First Amendment protects these views and expressions.

As usual, the first hate crime policies protecting sexual minorities were created at the state level. While all states except Arkansas, Georgia, Indiana, South Carolina, and Wyoming have hate crime laws, protections for sexual orientation were added in states mostly after 2000, with the exception of Washington, D.C. (1989), Minnesota (1993), Washington state (1993), and California (1999). Most progressive states eventually adopted these policies, but even some conservative states adopted these laws in the 2000s, but they did not include gender identity protection: Arizona, Florida, Kansas, Kentucky, Missouri (with gender identity protections), Louisiana, Nebraska, Tennessee, and Texas.[10] This differs from the more unified conservative state resistance to antidiscrimination and relationship equality policies.

At the federal level, advocates won a victory with the passage of the Matthew Shepard and James Byrd, Jr., Hate Crimes Prevention Act of 2009, after a several-decades-long campaign for a federal hate crime law protective of sexual orientation and gender identity. A race-, national origin-, and religion-based law was enacted by Congress in 1968. The 2009 law was the result of a gradualist and coalition strategy, combined with the increased visibility of hate crimes, most notably the attack on Matthew Shepard in 1998. Matthew was lured outside of Laramie, Wyoming by his attackers because of his sexual orientation, severely beaten with the butt of a pistol, tied to a fence, and left to die. He was found alive but eventually died of his injuries. The law was also proposed as a more comprehensive reform to the federal hate crimes framework, thus also including increased protections and enforcement for already existing categories, such as race. Indeed, the horrific killing of James Byrd in Texas, also in 1998, was further impetus for the 2009 law. Byrd was dragged to death, chained to a truck, by white supremacists.

The first step to adding sexual minorities to federal hate crime policy came in 1989 when the Democratically controlled Congress passed the Hate Crimes Statistics Act. It was signed into law by Republican president George H. W. Bush. The law allowed for federal tracking of hate crimes on the basis of sexual orientation, in addition to race, ethnicity, and religion. The federal government was now on the record as viewing violence against sexual minorities as a significant problem. Congress furthered this policy, allowing for real legal redress for crimes based on sexual orientation occurring on federal property, with the Hate Crimes Sentencing Enhancement Act, signed into law by Democratic president Bill Clinton in 1993. Activists pushed for a broader law, and the bill that eventually became Matthew Shepard and James Byrd, Jr., Hate Crimes Prevention Act was introduced in Congress in 1997. Despite strong support and advocacy from President Clinton, the bill died in the House after being approved by the Senate in 1999. During the first six years of the George W. Bush administration, the legislative process stalled with Republicans in control of one or both houses of Congress. The election of Democratic majorities in both chambers in 2006 eventually resulted in the bill being approved by both houses, but President Bush threatened a veto of the larger defense spending bill, to which the hate crime bill was attached. It is standard practice in Congress to attach controversial amendments (or riders) to more-likely-to-pass bills. In this case, the tactic failed. The hate crime bill was removed. It would require a Democratic president (Barack Obama) and a Democratic Congress to finally enact the law in 2009. Throughout the process, LGBT groups worked closely with other civil rights groups, reflected in the fact that the law was named for victims of violence on the basis of sexual orientation and race. Opinion polls also reflected strong support for the policy. But opponents were able to leverage their connection with the Republican Party to keep the policy from being enacted for over a decade.

EDUCATION

The rights of LGBT students and their allies, particularly in educational settings, has recently become a significant policy area, after decades of inattention. Historically, schools have been hostile environments for sexual minorities, reflecting societal homophobia but with a special twist—the false cultural assumption that sexual minorities "recruit" children. Thus, for decades, school officials have resisted any positive discussion of sexual diversity and have allowed physical and emotional harassment of LGBT students, or those perceived to be LGBT or who transgress gender norms, fearful of "endorsing" sexual diversity, or out of their own homophobia. Reinforcing this dynamic, outside of higher education, schools are governed by local school boards, and local electoral politics plays a strong role in the creation and enforcement of school policies. Until recently, this local politics was a constraining force on policies supporting LGBT students and their allies, except in the most progressive of jurisdictions. Like many policy areas explored in this chapter, courts, especially federal courts, have significantly shaped policy. The First Amendment's free speech protections and the Equal Protection Clause of the Fourteenth Amendment have proven useful for the protection of LGBT rights in educational settings.

The first court victories came in the college and university setting. The Stonewall Riots inspired increased activism on college campuses. Overall, campus activism related to various social movements was at a peak in the late 1960s and early 1970s. Lesbian and gay students and their allies wished to form campus organizations for advocacy and support. However, university officials often denied these requests or tried to interfere with the normal functioning of the groups. The University of New Hampshire approved the Gay Students Organization in 1973, but the university suspended the group's ability to hold events as a result of negative publicity stemming from a GSO dance. The First Circuit Court of Appeals found the university's actions to be a violation of the First Amendment. The court found the group to be one that espoused views that were central to the First Amendment's protection of political speech about a controversial topic. Other federal appellate courts overturned the denial of recognition of lesbian and gay student groups at the Universities of Virginia and Missouri and Georgetown University, as well as other universities.[11]

The First Amendment has also protected LGBT students in secondary schools. In the landmark decision of *Tinker v. Des Moines Independent School District* (1969),[12] the Supreme Court ruled that high school students possessed freedom of speech rights in school, balanced by the need for order and discipline. In other words, students do not lose First Amendment protections when they walk through the schoolhouse door. In that case, the court ruled that a ban on students wearing black armbands to protest the Vietnam War violated the students' rights. The legacy of *Tinker* has protected the rights of LGBT students. In particular, the main principle of the case has been used as a tool to challenge the denial of gay-straights alliances (GSAs) in schools. A statute originally designed to guarantee that religious student groups could meet on public school property has also protected the rights of students in GSAs. The 1984 Equal Access Act states, "It shall be unlawful for any public secondary school which receives Federal financial assistance and which has a limited open forum to deny equal access or a fair opportunity to, or discriminate against, any students who wish to conduct a meeting within that limited open forum on the basis of the religious, political, philosophical, or other content of the speech at such meetings."[13] Federal judges have consistently ruled that public schools may not ban GSAs if all student groups are not banned. Of course, much depends on the willingness of students to start such groups. They are becoming much more common, but the local politics of an area may still place constraints on their creation. In such a decentralized policy arena like education, the law is not always followed.

Reflecting the homophobia of the larger society, students who are LGBT, or even perceived to be or generally transgress gender norms, have faced high levels of verbal and physical harassment from peers and school officials. Many school officials ignored, or continue to ignore, this problem out of their own homophobia and heterosexism, or the notion that bullying and harassment is a rite of passage. As a result of societal homophobia and the climate in schools, LGBT students contemplate and commit suicide at startlingly higher rates than their peers. As Stuart Beigel states, "Studies continue to show that LGBTs feel disproportionately unsafe in school and that the mistreatment they face interferes with their ability to succeed. Gay and gender-nonconforming students often stop attending classes regularly, and many drop out, run away from home, or attempt suicide."[14]

A groundbreaking case from the Seventh Circuit Court of Appeals, *Nabozny v. Podlensky* (1996) significantly shifted the legal dynamic for schools concerning bullying and harassment.[15] Jamie Nabozny endured years of verbal and physical harassment in the Ashland, Wisconsin public schools, but school officials did nothing to prevent the harassment or sanction the perpetrators. In fact, school officials often blamed Jamie for the harassment. Because of the severity of the harassment, he was eventually diagnosed with posttraumatic stress disorder and depression. He eventually left school and moved to Minneapolis, after which he sued the school district, first with the assistance of a local lawyer, then Lambda Legal. The organization had been looking for a test case dealing with schools and youth, but staff members had been hesitant about taking such cases earlier, given the controversial nature of youth sexuality. After a loss in district court, the Seventh Circuit ruled that the school had violated Jamie's Fourteenth Amendment rights, both based on sex and sexual orientation. The court held that had Jamie been a female student, the school would have taken action, but school officials ignored the harassment of a gay male student. Jamie and the school district eventually settled the case, but the Seventh Circuit decision gave Jamie much more leverage in the process. Before the decision, the district had been unwilling to settle. The publicity surrounding the case caused school districts to be more proactive about creating and enforcing antiharassment policies, often strongly encouraged by their insurance companies who would pay out damages from potential lawsuits like Jamie's. As Carlos A. Ball summarized the impact of the decision, "By the mid-1990s, most educators in the country were prepared to respond aggressively to instance of racial and sexual harassment. Many of them, however, deemed harassment on the basis of sexual orientation to be of lesser importance. . . . The *Nabozny* litigation made it clear that such differential treatment was unconstitutional."[16]

In addition to this litigation, activists had been advocating for and creating LGBT-inclusive antidiscrimination and harassment policies since the 1980s. These efforts began in teacher unions and through the organization, Gay, Lesbian and Straight Teachers Education Network (GLSEN). However, these have proliferated mostly in the Northeast, the Upper Midwest, and the West Coast. Conversely, some states in the South and interior West (Alabama, Arizona, Louisiana, Mississippi, Oklahoma, South Carolina, Texas, and Utah) have laws prohibiting school officials from discussing LGBT-related issues.[17] Given the decentralized and local character of school policy, discrimination persists in many forms, but the legal and policy framework exists to support LGBT youth, supported by the U.S. Constitution's most powerful provisions.

BANS ON "CONVERSION" OR "REPARATIVE" THERAPY

As chapter 2 outlines, the medical/psychological community was a central part of the oppression of sexual minorities until 1973. After the delisting of homosexuality as a disorder in the DSM, the mainstream medical/scientific community began to view sexual diversity as a natural part of human sexuality, not something to be "cured." Today, the major professional medical, psychological, counseling, and social work associations oppose any attempts to change sexual orientation through medical intervention or therapy and counseling. According to these organizations, these therapies are unnecessary, ineffective, and often harmful.[18] However, in faith-based counseling, therapies designed to "change" sexual orientation are still common. For instance, when Congresswoman Michelle Bachmann began a campaign for the Republican presidential nomination in 2011, it was widely reported that a faith-based counseling practice that she owned with her husband, Marcus Bachmann, offered this therapy. While denying that conversion therapy was administered against an individual's consent, Marcus Bachmann declared sympathy with conversion approaches on a radio show. "I think you clearly say 'what is the understanding of God's word on homosexuality.' We have to understand barbarians need to be educated. They need to be disciplined and just because someone feels it or thinks it doesn't mean we're supposed to go down that road."[19] This therapy is linked to an "ex-gay" movement, long centered around the organizations, the National Association for Research & Therapy of Homosexuality (NARTH) and Exodus International. However, by 2013, the movement began to unravel after one of its leaders, Alan Chambers, renounced efforts to change sexual orientation.

In progressive states, a movement to prohibit "conversion" therapy for minors began with a law approved in California in 2012. New Jersey followed in 2013, where Republican governor Chris Christie signed the bill into law. The California law applies to medical professionals and counselors and therapists licensed by the state. Those who violate the law are potentially subjected to sanctions of "unprofessional conduct." Thus, the law is grounded in the state's public health regulatory authority. Specifically, the law outlaws "any practices by mental health providers that seek to change an individual's sexual orientation. This includes efforts to change behaviors or gender expressions, or to eliminate or reduce sexual or romantic attractions or feelings toward individuals of the same sex."[20] Bills have stalled in other states, including Minnesota and New York. In response to this emerging policy movement, conservative opponents of rights for sexual minorities adopted a proconversion therapy plank, along with a general condemnation of homosexuality, of the 2014 Texas Republican Party platform. The platform reads:

> Homosexuality is a chosen behavior that is contrary to the fundamental unchanging truths that have been ordained by God in the Bible, recognized by our nation's founders, and shared by the majority of Texans. Homosexuality must not be presented as an acceptable alternative lifestyle, in public policy, nor should family be redefined to include homosexual couples. We believe there should be no granting of special legal entitlements or creation of special status for homosexual behavior, regardless of state of origin. Additionally, we oppose any criminal or civil penalties against those who oppose homosexuality out of faith, conviction, or belief in traditional values. . . . We recognize the legitimacy and efficacy of counseling, which offers reparative therapy and treatment for those patients seeking healing and wholeness from their homosexual lifestyle. No laws or executive orders shall be imposed to limit or restrict access to this type of therapy.[21]

Clearly, this is a new front in the ongoing battle between LGBT rights advocates and conservative opponents. Opponents have lobbied against these proposals, worked through Republican Party mechanism, and have gone to court challenging the laws once approved. Religious conservatives, led by Liberty Counsel, have challenged these laws in court, primarily claiming that they are unconstitutional restrictions on free speech. In the most significant court decision to date, the Ninth Circuit Court of Appeals unanimously upheld the California law as an appropriate exercise of the state's police power, and the U.S. Supreme Court allowed the decision to stand.[22]

MILITARY SERVICE

After decades of grassroots activism and litigation, a Democratic Congress and President Obama repealed the ban on openly gay, lesbian, and bisexual military service members in late 2010, effective in 2011. This was a change from the 1993 "Don't Ask, Don't Tell," policy, also enacted by a Democratic Congress and a Democratic president, Bill Clinton. In theory, LGB members of the military could serve, as long as they remained closeted, under this policy. However, investigations and expulsions continued for members who stayed quiet about their sexuality. That policy was a "softening" of a 1982 Department of Defense (DoD) policy categorically and uniformly banning sexual minorities from military service. Prior to this, dismissal for homosexuality/bisexuality could occur, but it was not mandatory, leaving a lot of discretion for military leaders. In fact, during times of war, expulsions declined, as the need for service members was greater. They increased during peacetime.

The military began to create formal policies during World War II as a result of the massive amounts of military personnel during that war, and the fact that many of them were lesbians, gay men, and bisexuals all in much closer contact with one another, making sexual minorities more visible, and thus potentially threatening, to military officials. As the historian Margot Canaday has demonstrated, lesbians faced the brunt of the military's World War II panic about homosexuality, especially given that the war constituted the first significant mobilization of women into the military. Women who chose military service were seen as not "normal" women, not playing traditional gender and sexual roles. As Canaday states, "The exclusion of women believed to be lesbians was, in short, closely related to the inclusion of women in the service in general."[23] This led to much more invasive investigations of women than men in the military during World War II, as women in the military were inherently suspect, in terms of sexuality. In addition, sexual orientation–based discharges made service members ineligible for benefits under the GI Bill of Rights, a massive federal program that provided benefits to veterans.[24]

Beyond homophobia and heterosexism, the military ban policies were generally grounded in vague arguments about "military cohesion and readiness." The 1982 DoD policy declared that "homosexuality is incompatible with military service," and that the presence of LGB individuals in the military "adversely affects the ability of the military Services to maintain discipline, good order, and morale."[25] There was little or no empirical basis for this claim, exemplified by the experience of the U.S. allies who lifted their bans with no negative consequences in the decades following the DoD directive. Eventually, the lack of an empirical basis for this claim led DoD leaders to support changing the policy by 2010, but the claim was consistently made to policymakers and the public as the ban was challenged in court and the public arena.

Legal challenges to the ban began in the 1970s with Leonard Matlovich's federal legal challenge to his dismissal by the Navy. For the next twenty years, federal courts grappled with the constitutional issues presented by lawyers for dismissed service members. Lawyers argued that a lack of uniform standards (before 1982) and decentralized and haphazard enforcement by commanders created a procedural due process problem. Indeed, this argument led to success in the Matlovich litigation. Lawyers also argued that the ban violated privacy rights (substantive due process), free speech protections, and discriminated on the basis of sexual orientation, thus violating the federal equal protection clause. While a few courts ruled in favor of dismissed service members, the general approach of the federal judiciary was to defer to the military. In a variety of cases and constitutional claims, the judiciary has deferred to military policy, despite constitutional problems, given the hierarchal and disciplinary elements of the military. In other words, members of the military do not have the same level of constitutional protects as nonmilitary persons. In addition, throughout the time of this litigation, sodomy laws existed in the military and in states, and the Supreme Court found them to be consistent with the Constitution. Also, sexual orientation fell under the highly deferential rational basis review, and this resulted in consistent deference to the military policy. The lack of legal raw material for a successful litigation strategy ultimately resulted in a political path to reform.

Under the 1982 policy, discharges became more consistent and numerous, averaging 1500 per year.[26] Eliminating this policy became a focus of the LGBT rights movement by the early 1990s. The movement had gained some influence in the Democratic Party by this time, and presidential candidate Bill Clinton pledged to change the policy in the 1992 campaign. However, this was not a main priority of the administration after Clinton's election, and Clinton faced significant opposition to lifting the ban on military service from the military, primarily from Joint Chiefs of Staff Chairman Colin Powell, and from Congress, primarily from Democratic senator Sam Nunn who was chair of the Senate Armed Services Committee. This resistance, and a lack of focus and organization on the part of the Clinton administration led to the compromise policy of "Don't Ask, Don't Tell (DADT)," enacted by Congress in 1994. Under the policy, service members could be discharged for actual or solicited same-sex sexual activity, declaring their homosexuality or bisexuality, or trying to marry someone of the same gender. After the policy was enacted, discharges continued at high levels. Court challenges to the new policy were met with familiar deference to the military and Congress. In reality, the situation had changed very little for LGB service members.

The election of Democrat Barack Obama in 2008, along with Democratic majorities in Congress, spurred activists to engage in another campaign to lift the ban. During the election campaign, Obama committed to eliminating the policy, but he did not take immediate action when he took office. Activists applied strong pressure, including strong action from the group GetEqual, members of which were arrested for chaining themselves to the White House gates in March of 2010. One of the main faces of this activism was dismissed service member Lieutenant Dan Choi. In 2010, the Obama administration engaged the issue, and, now, the military leadership supported repeal of the ban. Late in 2010, despite several filibusters in the Senate led by Republican Senator John McCain, Congress passed a statute to repeal DADT, and the policy was fully repealed in September 2011 after a process in the military set forth by the statute. Strong majorities of Republicans in Congress voted against repeal. In addition to activist pressure and support from within the military and in Congress, public opinion was strongly in favor of lifting the ban on open military service, with over 70 percent of respondents supporting repeal in some polls and clear majorities in others.[27]

HIV/AIDS POLICY

The movement for sexual minorities was greatly affected by the HIV/AIDS epidemic starting in the 1980s. HIV is the virus that can cause Acquired Immune Deficiency Syndrome (AIDS). While the virus is blind to sexual orientation, the gay male community was the epicenter of the epidemic in the United States. In other parts of the world, the epidemic is a disease with mostly heterosexual victims, and, over time, it has spread to the heterosexual community in the United States. Given how the HIV virus is transmitted (through bodily fluids such as blood and semen), the epidemic also was pronounced among those who needed blood transfusions and intravenous drug users. After early resistance, largely stemming from homophobia, policy began to change to combat the epidemic and protect victims of the disease, while other policies have been more problematic, especially laws criminalizing the transmission of the virus.

Unfortunately, the appearance of the disease in the gay male community came at a bad time politically. The Religious Right backlash against the lesbian and gay rights movement was in full force. They viewed the disease as retribution for the "sin" of homosexuality. White House advisor for Nixon and Reagan and eventual Republican presidential candidate Patrick Buchanan declared in 1983, "The poor homosexuals. They have declared war on nature and now nature is exacting an awful retribution." Religious Right leader Jerry Falwell called AIDS "the judgment of God."[28] To this day, social conservatives continue to point to AIDS as a reason to criminalize homosexuality and not recognize LGBT rights. The Religious Right was a key element of President Ronald Reagan's election in 1980, and he ran on a platform of social conservatism and fiscal austerity. As a result, his administration was slow to react, particularly in terms of federal funds for research on the disease, a delayed policy response clearly fueled by homophobia. Homophobia also limited action in the urban centers where the epidemic was most pronounced initially, like New York. The mayor of the city, Ed Koch, was a closeted gay man who feared being outed and losing political support by working too directly with the city's gay community.

As a result of this weak response from the government, activists began to build their own institutions to deliver support and resources to victims of AIDS. The Gay Men's Health Crisis in New York was such an organization, but it was focused more on delivering services, less on politics and activism. As policy progress continued to stall, groups like ACT UP (the AIDS Coalition to Unleash Power) formed to create awareness and put pressure on political actors. Their strategy was modeled on the more radical elements of the 1960s and 1970s social movements—confrontation and direct action as outsiders, but the organization also worked within the system. The group was quite media savvy, and drew a lot of attention to the issue, particularly the lack of research funding and the slow approval of potentially useful drugs by the Food and Drug Administration. Beyond government, they targeted the Catholic Church for its opposition to public policies such as government-sponsored condom distribution. Their most famous slogan was "Silence=Death." Through these organizations, the LGBT rights movement was building an infrastructure for future activism. Thus, the AIDS crisis was a source of increased activism and mobilization for the movement.

Eventually, a more robust policy response emerged, despite sustained and vigorous opposition from social conservatives, led by Republican senator Jesse Helms. By the early 1990s, federal funding for research increased significantly, pushed by a few well-placed members of Congress and their staffs. In 1990, Congress enacted, and President George H. W. Bush signed, the Ryan White Comprehensive AIDS Resources Emergency Act. According to political scientist Mark Carl Rom, the law passed because of the efforts of a broad coalition of activists and public health organizations, the "de-gaying" of the issue (Ryan White was a young hemophiliac who contracted the virus through a blood transfusion), and by spreading funds across the country in many Congressional districts. The law provides for direct federal payments to social service organizations to administer support for persons with HIV and AIDS, and is still a central part of HIV/AIDS policy.[29]

Today, as a result of increased attention and public and private resources, HIV is a manageable condition, if properly treated. In fact, antiretroviral treatments (ART) for HIV have become so effective that viral loads can become undetectable in persons with the virus. Pre-exposure Prophylaxis (PrEP) medications are over 90 percent effective in preventing transmission of the virus. However, tremendous stigma still remains for individuals with HIV.

Indeed, persons with HIV are criminalized through thirty-three state laws making illegal, usually as a felony, the knowing exposure of the virus to other persons, even in consensual sexual relations, sometimes even if a condom is used. To be criminally liable, there need not be actual transmission of the virus, under most statutes. Individuals convicted usually are required to register as sex offenders. Rather than viewing the issue as a public health matter where each individual should be responsible for protecting themselves from exposure to the virus, persons with the virus are made solely and criminally responsible. These laws were created in the early years of the AIDS crisis and the hysteria surrounding the disease. The first statute appeared 1986. Remarkably, the Ryan White Act required states receiving funding to possess either general or HIV-specific laws prohibiting the transmission of HIV. However, the laws are ineffective at stopping the spread of the virus, and they prevent people from seeking testing and treatment out of fear of potential prosecution. In addition, most laws were enacted before antiretroviral treatments were able to greatly reduce the risk of transmission. Activists and organizations are working to reform or eliminate HIV criminalization laws, but prosecutions continue, often influenced by the stigma that persists in the minds of prosecutors and jurors. In 2014, the U.S. Justice Department recommended that states eliminate these laws, except for the following circumstances: "First, states may wish to retain criminal liability when a person who knows he/she is HIV positive commits a (non-HIV specific) sex crime where there is a risk of transmission (e.g., rape or other sexual assault). The second circumstance is where the individual knows he/she is HIV positive and the evidence clearly demonstrates that individual's intent was to transmit the virus and that the behavior engaged in had a significant risk of transmission, whether or not transmission actually occurred."[30]

FAMILY LAW AND PARENTING

The issue of the rights of lesbian, gay, and bisexual parents developed first as more individuals came out of the closet in the 1970s, often filing for divorce in different-sex marriages and asking for custody of their children. Soon thereafter, same-sex couples (largely lesbians at first) began to have children through artificial insemination or through adoption. Courts and legislatures were faced with new family arrangements, and they responded with mixed results. Given that family law is the jurisdiction of states, a patchwork of policy responses developed. Judges have played a significant role, given the discretion given to judges in family law cases. Judges are expected to rule in the "best interest of the child" in each case, a very deferential and subjective standard. Thus, the policy response has depended on the willingness of judges to update the law in response to changes in family forms, their own homophobia or more progressive stance, and sometimes the reaction of legislators and voters to these changes.

The response to child custody claims by sexual minorities was generally quite hostile from courts, legislators, and the public in the 1970s and 1980s. Lesbian, gay, and bisexual parents were automatically deemed to be morally unfit, especially if they were engaged in an intimate relationship with someone of the same gender. Judges routinely cited the presence of sodomy laws on the statute books as *prima facie* evidence of the unfitness of LGB parents. Judges also cited the (incorrect) claim that LGB parents would "convert" straight children. This automatic denial of custody was referred to as the "per se" rule. This approach was reflected in the high-profile case from Virginia of *Bottoms v. Bottoms* (1995). In that case, the state Supreme Court agreed with the trial judge's assessment that Sharon Bottoms's lesbian relationship was sufficient to allow for her son's grandmother to successfully sue for custody. Over time, however, judges largely abandoned the per se rule in favor of the "nexus" approach. Under this test, judges must evaluate whether a parent's conduct poses real harm to the child. Of course, this is still a subjective standard, but homosexuality/bisexuality is not automatically grounds for a denial of custody, except for the most homophobic of judges.

The conscious creation of families with children by sexual minorities created a need for second-parent adoption, or the equivalent of stepparents in different-sex marriages, especially before same-sex relationships were legally recognized by states through civil unions, domestic partnerships, and marriage equality. Increasingly, partners of biological parents wished to form legal bonds with the children in their family. Without the formal connection, these individuals were legal strangers (in education and health care, for instance) to the children they lived with and cared for. Traditionally under family law, only married spouses were eligible to become legal co-parents.

In the 1990s, supreme courts in Wisconsin and Vermont ruled in opposite directions on the question. The Wisconsin court refused to allow a lesbian to adopt her partner's biological child in *In Interest of Angel Lace M.* (1994), even though Angel's biological father did not object to the termination of his rights as a parent. The court narrowly interpreted the adoption statute, unwilling to take an innovative role in the state's family law. The Vermont Supreme Court was willing to innovate and granted a same-sex second-parent adoption, despite the lack of a clear statutory provision in *In re Adoption of B.L.V.B.* (1993). Instead, the court used the "best interest of the child" standard to expansively interpret state adoption law. (Just a few years later, the court would rule that the state's lack of recognition of same-sex relationships was unconstitutional.) While the overall trend was to follow the path of the Vermont court, many courts and judges refused to change policy without statutory changes.

As of 2014, second-parent adoption for same-sex couples is legal (by statute, court decision, or the legal recognition of same-sex relationships) in twenty-four states: California, Colorado, Connecticut, Delaware, Washington, D.C., Hawaii, Idaho, Illinois, Indiana, Iowa, Maine, Maryland, Massachusetts, Minnesota, Nevada, New Hampshire, New Jersey, New Mexico, New York, Oregon, Pennsylvania, Rhode Island, Vermont, and Washington. The legal recognition of "de facto" parents is another important family policy for sexual minorities. Individuals who have lived with a child or children and operated as a caretaker, but without full legal custody or adoption, have been granted parental rights by courts and by statute. According to the National Center for Lesbian Rights, "Only a small number of states have said that a non-legal parent has no ability to seek custody or visitation with the child of his or her former partner, even when he or she has been an equally contributing caretaker of the child."[31]

Beginning in 1977 with Florida, some states have enacted policies explicitly banning sexual minorities from adopting children or serving as foster parents. After several constitutional challenges, a state appellate court invalidated the ban in 2010.[32]

New Hampshire enacted a ban in 1987, but it was repealed in 1999. Mississippi enacted an adoption ban in 2000. In the same year, Utah enacted a law prohibiting adoption by married same-sex couples. The Michigan attorney general declared a ban in 2004. Also that year, Oklahoma enacted a ban on adoptions from other states by same-sex couples who moved to Oklahoma, but federal courts invalidated the law. In 2008, voters in Arkansas approved a ban on adoption and foster parenting by all unmarried couples. However, this was struck down by the Arkansas Supreme Court in 2011. Thus, outright bans on parenting by sexual minorities are relatively rare and are looked upon skeptically by state and federal courts. Overall, the concept of LGB parents, while facing resistance in some quarters, has been much more accepted in U.S. policy than in the European context, where same-sex relationships were recognized earlier, but this recognition often lacked parenting rights. Some of this difference can be attributed to the fact that much of the progress on family policy has been driven by courts, often out of the direct view of the public.[33]

RELATIONSHIP EQUALITY

The litigation campaign for marriage equality is chronicled in chapter 5, but this section will focus on the development of policies protecting and affirming same-sex couples. These policies have taken different names and forms: domestic partnerships, civil unions, and same-sex marriage or marriage equality. This reflects the fact that advocates for relationship equality have taken a gradualist strategy, focusing on the most favorable jurisdictions and lobbying for the most politically palatable forms of relationship recognition and protection, hoping to expand these policies as the political and legal terrain became more favorable, and as opposition to relationship equality weakened. Domestic partnerships began as a limited set of protections (typically insurance benefits, hospital visitation rights, and some joint-property rights) extended to same-sex couples by local jurisdictions. These initially applied to government workers in that jurisdiction, but the concept eventually spread to cover all same-sex couples living in a jurisdiction. Policies were also expanded to offer more protections and benefits. For instance, California's domestic partnership policy was gradually expanded over the course of the 1990s and 2000s to mirror the protections and benefits of the state's marriage policy, despite the state's prohibition on same-sex marriage. Civil unions began in Vermont in 2000 after the state high court mandated some form of equal treatment for same-sex couples. These policies proliferated in more progressive states as a precursor to full marriage equality. However, these policies and statuses lacked federal recognition and protection, and they were generally not portable from one state to another. While advocates saw them as an important stepping-stone to full equality, critics painted them as "separate but equal" statuses. Virtually all states that started with domestic partnerships or civil unions eventually enacted marriage equality through the legislative/popular initiative process or as a result of court mandates. States that did not "upgrade" (Colorado, Oregon, and Wisconsin) also possessed constitutional amendments forbidding the recognition of same-sex marriage.

While marriage is an important religious rite in many faiths, marriage is not exclusively a religious institution. Marriage brings hundreds of legal protections and benefits in state law and over one thousand federal rights and benefits. Marriage is deeply embedded in public policy in the United States. Married couples are privileged in the law in ways that unmarried couples (not to mention single people) are not, and public policy in the United States has generally resisted granting these rights and protections to unmarried couples. The tax-free transferring of property, tax benefits, immigration rights, Social Security benefits, Veteran's benefits, health insurance benefits, and family protections are just a few of the myriad of rights and benefits triggered by marriage.

History and the Emergence of Domestic Partnerships

While the issue of equal treatment for same-sex relationships was not central to the early LGBT rights movement, neither was it ignored as a political and legal matter. Before Stonewall, the issue was periodically discussed in the pages of lesbian and gay publications, and many same-sex couples lived together and thought of themselves as married, but without legal protections and public benefits. Gay-friendly clergy began performing same-sex marriages in the 1960s and 1970s. As is explored in chapter 5, after Stonewall, couples who were denied marriage licenses went to court. Indeed, all throughout the 1970s, same-sex couples applied for marriage licenses. So many were applying in California, for instance, that the legislative was asked to clarify the state's marriage statute to apply only to one man and one woman. Interestingly, the revision was signed by Governor Jerry Brown in his first term as governor. Over thirty years later, Brown would become a strong supporter of same-sex marriage as California attorney general and again as governor. His refusal in both offices to defend Proposition 8 in federal court led to the invalidation of the law and the permanent legalization of same-sex marriage in California in 2013.

A serious, but in retrospect ill-fated, attempt to legalize same-sex marriage in Washington, D.C. took place in 1975. D.C. had recently been granted home rule authority by Congress, and the city council considered a range of legal reforms. Councilman Arrington Dixon proposed a family law ordinance that would have been gender-neutral, thus opening the door for two persons of the same gender to be married. Lesbian and gay rights activists saw the opportunity and mobilized in support of the law, including Frank Kameny. Indeed, Kameny viewed same-sex marriage as an important part of the broader movement, and he worked with a same-sex couple in Maryland who wanted to apply for a marriage license in order to generate media attention about the issue. After religious leaders voiced opposition to Dixon's bill, the gender-neutral proposal was dropped. It is also likely that Congress would have overturned the law, as it can do with the vote of only one chamber. D.C. would continue to be a relationship equality innovator. It was the site of unsuccessful litigation to enact same-sex marriage in the early 1990s, the city council enacted a domestic partnership law in 1992, and it enacted a marriage equality law in 2009.

Also in 1975, the county clerk in Boulder, Colorado, Clela Rorex, began granting marriage licenses to same-sex couples before she was ordered to stop. This eventually led to a U.S. Supreme Court case, *Adams v. Howerton* (1982), in which the Court denied a citizenship application for the noncitizen member of a Rorex-married couple. (This would have been granted had the couple been opposite-sex.) Thus, some activists and many everyday citizens conceived of legal marriage equality post-Stonewall, and took action to achieve it.

However, this occurred at the same time that conservative opposition to LGBT rights was emerging. By the late 1970s, marriage equality activism declined, replaced by the more gradualist domestic partnership approach. The first domestic partnership policy was enacted in Berkeley, California (a college town) in 1984 after lobbying and efforts to elect supportive members to the city council, followed by Los Angeles, Madison, Seattle, and West Hollywood. Cities and college towns continued to enact these policies for decades. However, these efforts seldom transcended city politics. Unlike other countries in Northern Europe and in Canada, policies recognizing increasing cohabitation among same-sex and opposite-sex couples outside of marriage did not take hold at the state or federal levels. Strong and organized religious conservatism led to the privileging of marriage as the status of entry into governmental benefits. For instance, when California revised its marriage law in 1977, some Democratic legislators from urban areas argued for a domestic partnership alternative for same-sex couples, but this idea received little support in the legislature. When a domestic partnership law was approved by the Board of Supervisors in San Francisco, influenced by events across the bay in Berkeley, the city's Catholic Bishop publicly argued that the law would "further erode the moral foundation of civilized society." The next day, Democratic mayor Diane Feinstein, vetoed the proposed ordinance.[34] A law was eventually enacted by voters in 1990 after a lot of political wrangling and grassroots organizing.

The Turn to Marriage Equality

The diffusion of domestic partnership policies in the 1980s combined with other factors led to the reemergence of relationship equality as a prime focus of the movement by the late 1980s and the 1990s. The AIDS crisis demonstrated the legal vulnerability of same-sex relationships, as partners of dead and dying victims were legally superseded by other family members concerning medical decisions and the allocation of property. Many individuals not only lost their loved ones, oftentimes not being able to visit them in the hospital, but they also lost their homes because the property was not in their name and ownership transferred to a more legally recognized relative. Also, a significant increase in parenting by lesbians and gay men illustrated the fragility of the legal bonds to children outside of marriage.

However, movement leaders either objected to marriage equality as a goal because of its connection to patriarchy and its regulation of sexual behavior or thought that a legal and political movement for marriage equality was doomed to be unsuccessful, given the political and legal climate of the country. After all, sodomy laws had been upheld by the Supreme Court in 1986. Yet, as they had done in the 1970s, same-sex couples applied for marriage licenses, were denied, and went to court. This triggered the activity in Hawaii and around the country discussed chapter 5 and below.

For about a decade, the movement for marriage equality was dominated by litigation strategies, supported by grassroots efforts. Increasingly, however, legislative paths were successfully engaged. The first state to enact same-sex marriage legislatively was Maine in 2009, but the law was repealed by voters. This was followed the same year by legislation in Vermont, Washington, D.C., New Hampshire (2010), New York (2011), Washington State (2012), Maryland (2012), Rhode Island (2013), Illinois (2013), and Hawaii (2014). Reflecting gradualism, many of these were "upgrades" from civil unions. The California legislature also tried to upgrade from domestic partnerships, twice passing legislation that was vetoed both times by Republican Governor Arnold Schwarzenegger. Also reflecting a new phase of same-sex marriage policy, voters authorized, through a referendum, same-sex marriage in Maine in 2012, and voters approved the legislation, through the "citizen veto" process, in Washington and Maryland that same year.

The opposition to relationship equality reflects the more generally heteronormative opposition to LGBT rights, but it also includes arguments about marriage as a religious and social institution. Opponents claim that the legalization of same-sex marriage is an infringement on the religious freedom of those who oppose it, and they argue that secular marriage policy should reflect majoritarian religious views of marriage. More secular opponents of same-sex marriage argue that heterosexual marriage is a fundamentally important social institution and fear societal costs associated with the legalization of same-sex marriage. This is an extension of anxiety about changes to marriage, such as increased cohabitation, the rise in single parenting, and increased divorce rates, that occurred over the course of the latter part of the twentieth century. These critics of same-sex marriage view it as part of the overall decline in the institution of marriage.

Political opposition to the recognition of, and protection for, same-sex relationships began in the 1970s as couples were married religiously and applied for marriage licenses. Many states, like California discussed above, revised their marriage laws to remove any ambiguity about who could get married, and to reinforce the heteronormative definition of the institution. A new phase of policy opposition began after the events in Hawaii in the early 1990s as the prospect of interstate recognition of same-sex marriage became, for the first time, a realistic prospect. States generally recognize marriages performed in other states as a result of the Full Faith and Credit Clause of the Constitution and legal principles of interstate policy recognition, but there are significant exceptions to the policy. In 1996, a Republican-controlled Congress, with many Democratic votes, attempted to reinforce these exceptions by enacting DOMA, signed into law by Democrat Bill Clinton. Section 2 of the law declares that states are exempt from recognizing same-sex marriages performed in other states, and section 3 forbids the recognition of same-sex marriages by the federal government. DOMA was an unusual federal intervention into a policy area, family law and marriage, traditionally the province of the states. Section 3 was struck down by the Supreme Court in *U.S. v. Windsor* (2013).

States also continued to revise their marriage statutes in response to the marriage equality litigation movement, but conservative opponents of same-sex marriage began to use the popular initiative processes common in many states to enshrine opposition to same-sex marriage, and often any form of relationship recognitions in the form of "mini-DOMAs" that also banned domestic partnerships and civil unions, in state constitutions. President George W. Bush supported a federal constitutional amendment banning same-sex marriage in his reelection campaign in 2004, but supporters in Congress lacked the supermajority needed for such an amendment. Between 1998 and 2012, voters in thirty states approved these constitutional bans, with twenty-one mini-DOMA amendments. Most of these states were in the South and the Great Plains where opposition to LGBT rights is strongest. An amendment failed at the ballot box in Minnesota in 2012, marking the end of this policy backlash. In the wake of the 2013 *Windsor* decision, lower federal courts began invalidating these amendments as a violation of the fundamental right to marry or as a violation of the Equal Protection Clause. The unified approach of judges from all ideological perspectives bodes well for the legal elimination of these policies, as well as providing encouragement for emerging grassroots efforts to repeal the amendments in some states.

In addition to the legal momentum, the political terrain shifted significantly. In 2012, President Barack Obama became the first sitting president to support marriage equality, declaring this support soon after Vice President Joe Biden did the same. This reflects a Democratic Party that is almost completely united in its support of marriage equality. Just a few years before, many Democrats were wary of supporting marriage equality, and many Democratic elected officials preferred political compromises such as civil unions. Some Republican elected officials began to endorse marriage equality, but the party remains overwhelmingly opposed. However, the organized opposition to marriage equality, riding high in 2004, was on the defensive, particularly after Obama's reelection in 2012 and the *Windsor* decision in 2013. By 2014, public opinion was quickly moving against them.

Public Opinion

The future prospects for the nationalization of same-sex marriage policy were bolstered by President Obama's support and the Supreme Court in *Windsor* but also by increasing, majority support for same-sex marriage in public opinion. When Gallup began asking about support for same-sex marriage in 1996, 27 percent of respondents were in favor. By 2004, this was 42 percent, and the 50 percent mark was passed in 2011, achieving a high of 55 percent in 2014.[35] This level of support is consistent with other national polls. The rise in support certainly made it easier for the Supreme Court to rationalize the policy in *Obergefell v. Hodges* in 2015.

CONCLUSION

The policy environment in the United States is highly complex, and this is no less true for policies for sexual minorities. Federalism, public opinion, partisanship, institutions, morality, and litigation are some of the relevant factors influencing policy outcomes, all in the context of homophobia and heterosexism. The relatively open system in the United States allows for both access and influence and contestation. While the overall direction appears to be headed in the direction of more favorable policies for sexual minorities, resistance and counter policymaking will likely continue from opponents.

KEY TERMS, CONCEPTS, AND CASES

ACT UP (the AIDS Coalition to Unleash Power)
Adams v. Howerton (1982)
Adoption/foster parenting bans
AIDS/HIV
Antidiscrimination laws
Antiretroviral treatments (ART)
"Best interest of the child" standard
Bottoms v. Bottoms (1995)
Burwell v. Hobby Lobby (2014)

Civil Rights Act of 1964
Civil unions
Cohabitation
"Conversion" or "reparative" therapy
De facto parents
Defense of Marriage Act (DOMA)
Dixon bill
Domestic partnerships
"Don't Ask, Don't Tell" policy
Elaine Photography case

Equal Access Act
Equal Employment Opportunity
    Commission (EEOC)
Employment Nondiscrimination Act
    (ENDA)
Federalism and LGBT policy
Gay Men's Health Crisis
Gay-straights alliances (GSAs)
Hate crime laws
History of military exclusion of
    sexual minorities
HIV criminalization laws
In Interest of Angel Lace M.
    (1994)
In re Adoption of B.L.V.B. (1993)
LGBT parenting
Legal and political challenges to the
    ban on military service
Local politics and education policy
Matthew Shepard and James Byrd,
    Jr., Hate Crimes Prevention Act
    of 2009

Mini-DOMAs
Ministerial exception
Nabozny v. Podlensky (1996)
Nexus approach
Obama 2014 executive order on
    federal contractor hiring
Per se rule
Pre-exposure Prophylaxis (PrEP)
Police power
Policy diffusion
Political parties and LGBT rights
    policy
Riders
Ryan White Comprehensive AIDS
    Resources Emergency Act
Same-sex marriage/marriage
    equality
Second-parent adoption
*Tinker v. Des Moines Independent
    School District* (1969)

QUESTIONS FOR DISCUSSION

1. Why is federalism such a central element in the creation of, or resistance to, public policies supportive of sexual minorities?
2. What are the policy needs of sexual minorities beyond the often-dominant policy of marriage equality?
3. Do you see the policy landscape fundamentally changing for sexual minorities in the coming years? Why or why not?

NOTES

1. James W. Button, Barbara A. Rienzo, and Kenneth D. Wald, *Private Lives, Public Conflicts: Battles over Gay Rights in American Communities* (Washington, DC: CQ Press, 1997), 73.

2. Susan Gluck Mezey, *Queers in Court: Gay Rights Law and Public Policy* (Lanham, MD: Rowman & Littlefield, 2007), 219.

3. S. 815: Employment Non-Discrimination Act of 2013, Section 6 (a).

4. Chad Griffin, "Why HRC Supports a Comprehensive LGBT Civil Rights Bill," *BuzzFeed*, July 9, 2014, http://www.buzzfeed.com/chadhgriffin/why-hrc-supports-a-comprehensive-lgbt-civil-rights-bill.

5. "State Nondiscrimination Laws in the U.S.," National LGBTQ Task Force, May 21, 2014, http://www.thetaskforce.org/static_html/downloads/reports/issue_maps/non_discrimination_5_14_color_new.pdfhttp://www.thetaskforce.org/static_html/downloads/reports/issue_maps/non_discrimination_5_14_color_new.pdf.

6. Human Rights Campaign, "LGBT Equality at the Fortune 500," http://www.hrc.org/resources/entry/lgbt-equality-at-the-fortune-500.

7. Gallup, "Gay and Lesbian Rights," http://www.gallup.com/poll/1651/Gay-Lesbian-Rights.aspx#3.

8. Brian Mustanski, "Are Violent Hate Crimes Against LGBT People on the Rise?" *Psychology Today*, "The Sexual Continuum," June 12, 2013, http://www.psychologytoday.com/blog/the-sexual-continuum/201306/are-violent-hate-crimes-against-lgbt-people-the-rise.

9. Andrew Sullivan, "What's So Bad About Hate," *New York Times Magazine*, September 26, 1999, http://www.nytimes.com/1999/09/26/magazine/what-s-so-bad-about-hate.html.

10. Human Rights Campaign, "State Hate Crimes Laws," June 19, 2013, http://hrc-assets.s3-website-us-east-1.amazonaws.com//files/assets/resources/hate_crimes_laws_022014.pdf.

11. *Gay Students Organization of the University of New Hampshire v. Bonner*, 509 F.2d 652 (1st Cir. 1974). The other cases were: *Gay Alliance of Students v. Matthews*, 544 F.2d 162 (4th Cir. 1976); *Gay Lib v. The University of Missouri*, 558 F.2d 848 (8th Cir. 1977); *Gay Rights Coalition of Georgetown University Law Center v. Georgetown University*, 536 A.2d 1 (D.C. App. 1987).

12. 393 U.S. 503 (1969).

13. 20 U.S.C. § 4071(a).

14. Stuart Biegel, *The Right to be Out: Sexual Orientation and Gender Identity in America's Public Schools* (Minneapolis: University of Minnesota Press, 2010), xvii.

15. 92 F.3d 446 (7th Cir. 1996).

16. Carlos A. Ball, *From the Closet to the Courtroom: Five LGBT Lawsuits That Have Changed Our Nation* (Boston: Beacon Press, 2010), 94.

17. German Lopez, "33 States Don't Protect LGBT Students in Anti-bullying Laws," *Vox*, August 11, 2014, http://www.vox.com/2014/8/11/5979789/school-bullying-lgbt-discrimination.

18. Human Rights Campaign (HRC), "The Lies and Dangers of Efforts to Change Sexual Orientation or Gender Identity," http://www.hrc.org/resources/entry/the-lies-and-dangers-of-reparative-therapy. The organizations identified by the HRC are: the American Academy of Pediatrics, the American Association for Marriage and Family Therapy, the American Counseling Association, the American Medical Association, the American Psychiatric Association, the American Psychoanalytic Association, the American Psychological Association, the American School Counselor Association, the National Association of Social Workers, and the Pan American Health Organization.

19. Jim Acosta and Erika Dimmler, "What's Going on at the Bachmann Clinic?" CNN.com, July 12, 2011, http://politicalticker.blogs.cnn.com/2011/07/12/whats-going-on-at-the-bachmann-clinic/.

20. Senate Bill No. 1172, Section 2, State of California, September 30, 2012.

21. Republican Party of Texas, "Report of Permanent Committee on Platform and Resolutions As Amended and Adopted by the 2014 State Convention of the Republican Party of Texas," http://s3.amazonaws.com/static.texastribune.org/media/documents/2014_Republican_Party_of_Texas_Platform.pdf.

22. *Pickup v. Brown*, 740 F.3d 1208 (9th Cir. Cal., 2013).

23. Margot Canaday, *The Straight State: Sexuality and Citizenship in Twentieth-Century America* (Princeton: Princeton University Press, 2009), 178.

24. Allan Bérubé, *Coming Out Under Fire: The History of Gay Men and Women in World War Two* (New York: Free Press, 1990); Canaday, *The Straight State.*

25. United States Department of Defense, Directive 1332.14.

26. Mezey, *Queers in Court*, 139.

27. See the polls from 2010 archived at PollingReport.com, http://www.pollingreport.com/civil2.htm.

28. Craig A. Rimmerman, *The Lesbian and Gay Movements: Assimilation or Liberation?* (Boulder: Westview Press, 2008), 37.

29. Mark Carl Rom, "Gays and AIDS: Democratizing Disease?," in *The Politics of Gay Rights*, Craig Rimmerman et al., eds. (Chicago: University of Chicago Press, 2000).

30. "Best Practices Guide to Reform HIV-Specific Criminal Laws to Align with Scientifically-Supported Factors," Civil Rights Division, U.S. Department of Justice, n.d., http://aids.gov/federal-resources/national-hiv-aids-strategy/doj-hiv-criminal-law-best-practices-guide.pdf., 4.

31. National Center for Lesbian Rights, "Legal Recognition of LGBT Families," May 2014, http://www.nclrights.org/wp-content/uploads/2013/07/Legal_Recognition_of_LGBT_Families.pdf. The quote is from page 6.

32. *Fla. Dept. of Children & Families v. X.X.G.*, 45 So.3d 79 (Fla. Ct. App. 2010).

33. This summary was significantly derived from Susan Gluck Mezey, *Gay Families and The Courts: The Quest for Equal Rights* (Lanham, MD: Rowman & Littlefield, 2009), 22–25.

34. Philip Hager, "S.F. Mayor Vetoes Disputed Law on Live-In Lovers," *Los Angeles Times*, December 10, 1982.

35. Gallup, "Same-Sex Marriage Support Reaches New High at 55%," May 21, 2014, http://www.gallup.com/poll/169640/sex-marriage-support-reaches-new-high.aspx.

BIBLIOGRAPHY

Carlos A. Ball, *From the Closet to the Courtroom: Five LGBT Lawsuits That Have Changed Our Nation* (Boston: Beacon Press, 2010).

———, *The Right to be Parents: LGBT Families and the Transformation of Parenthood* (New York: New York University Press, 2012).

Stuart Biegel, *The Right to Be Out: Sexual Orientation and Gender Identity in America's Public Schools* (Minneapolis: University of Minnesota Press, 2010).

Margot Canaday, *The Straight State: Sexuality and Citizenship in Twentieth-Century America* (Princeton: Princeton University Press, 2009).

Nathaniel Frank, *Unfriendly Fire: How the Gay Ban Undermines the Military and Weakens America* (New York: Thomas Dunne Books, 2009).

Susan Gluck Mezey, *Gay Families and the Courts: The Quest for Equal Rights* (Lanham, MD: Rowman & Littlefield, 2009).

Jason Pierceson, *Same-Sex Marriage in the United States: The Road to the Supreme Court and Beyond* (Lanham, MD: Rowman & Littlefield, 2014).

Nancy D. Polikoff, *Beyond (Straight and Gay) Marriage: Valuing All Families under the Law* (Boston: Beacon Press, 2008).

David Rayside, *Queer Inclusions, Continental Divisions: Public Recognition of Sexual Diversity in Canada and the United States* (Toronto: University of Toronto Press, 2008).

Craig A. Rimmerman, *The Lesbian and Gay Movements: Assimilation or Liberation?*, 2nd ed. (Boulder: Westview Press, 2014).

Randy Shilts, *And the Band Played On: Politics, People, and the AIDS Epidemic* (New York: St. Martin's Press, 1987).

Patricia D. Siplon, *AIDS and the Policy Struggle in the United States* (Washington, DC: Georgetown University Press, 2002).

Miriam Smith, *Political Institutions and Lesbian and Gay Rights in the United States and Canada* (New York: Routledge, 2008).

Chapter 7

The Transgender and Intersex Movements, Law, and Policy

This chapter explores elements of the movement for sexual and gender minority rights and equality that are sometimes overlooked or marginalized within the broader movement and whose distinct and complex histories and goals merit an exploration of commonalities and differences from the lesbian and gay rights movement. These identities are often most marginalized and least understood within the movement and by the larger political community. But they face a common opposition: a political and legal traditionalism that is intent upon enforcing a rigid gender/sex binary and heteronormativity. As LGBT rights lawyer and scholar Shannon Price Minter has noted, "Homophobia and transphobia are tightly intertwined, and because antigay bias so often takes the form of violence and discrimination against those who are seen as transgressing gender norms."[1]

THE TRANSGENDER MOVEMENT, LAW, AND POLICY

Terms and History

The transgender movement is complex, composed of a myriad of identities relating to gender identity and expression. Transgender, or trans, is an umbrella term used to refer to all of these identities. The often-conflicting relationship between individual feelings and desires and societal expectation about gender roles creates the modern transgender identity. Without society's demand that peoples' mannerisms, forms of dress, hairstyles, type and tone of speech, etc. match biological sex, there would be no tension and thus no need for the identity. While not a perfect framework, as will be discussed in the context of the intersex movement, it is useful to recall the distinction between biological sex (chromosomes, genitalia, sex organs, hormone levels, etc.) and gender (feminine and masculine standards developed and imposed by society). We should also note the difference between gender identity, which is one's internal understanding of gender, and gender expression, which is how one presents oneself to the world. Given the complexity of terminology of trans identities, the following list identifies some of the most prominent terms:

Transgender/trans: A term that refers to a person whose gender identity is not fully consistent with society's expectation of their sex assigned at birth. Often used as an umbrella term for all noncisgender identities.

Cisgender: A term that refers to a person whose gender identity and expression is consistent with their sex assigned at birth.

Transsexual: A term that specifically refers to a person who has undergone surgical intervention away from the gender assigned at birth or someone who strongly desires to do so.

Cross-dresser: A term that refers to a person who dresses in attire different from societal expectations for their sex assigned at birth. Replaces the dated term, "transvestite."

Drag Queen: Typically a gay male cross-dresser who may perform or entertain in drag.

Drag King: Typically a lesbian cross-dresser who may perform or entertain in drag.

Genderqueer: A person or approach desiring to challenge the gender binary by not utilizing either exclusively masculine or feminine gender expression.

Gender Nonconforming: Refers to an approach that does not fit with, or challenges, societally expected gender identity and expression.

Gender Dysphoria: A medical term in the DSM-5 that refers to the stress related to societal disapproval of gender variation.

Sex reassignment/gender-affirming surgery (SRS/GAS): Surgical treatment, beyond hormone therapy, intended to address gender dysphoria. There is variation in surgical intervention, largely captured by the distinction between top surgeries (cosmetic changes to the chest) and bottom surgeries (changes to the genitals).

Two-spirit: A term from Native American and First Nations culture referring to individuals with both masculine and feminine elements. Replaces the outdated and Western-imposed term, "berdache."

Transition: This term refers to the process of moving from the sex assigned at birth to one's gender identity through gender expression and/or hormone therapy and/or surgery. Not all transgender persons transition in the same way, with some transitioning through gender expression and presentation alone (hairstyles, dress, etc.), while others engage medical treatment to varying degrees.

A fundamental goal of the transgender rights movement is to let individuals determine for themselves, without hindrance from government or society (indeed, with the affirmation of both), their true gender and its expression in the way that best suits them. This requires an understanding on the part of citizens and policymakers of the complexity of gender and sex. The movement also provides an opportunity to challenge the gender binary and remove its coercive power.

Recall from chapter 2 that late-nineteenth-century theorizing about sexual diversity was heavily influenced by the gender binary. Sexual orientation and gender identity were often seen as two sides of the same coin—gay men were like women (feminine traits) and lesbians were like men (masculine traits), or "inverts." Indeed, a leading early thinker about what came to be known as transgender individuals was Magnus Hirschfeld. Hirschfeld coined the terms "transvestite" and "transsexual," and his institute was the first organization to begin to medically and surgically treat transgender individuals. However, Hirschfeld saw gender identity and sexual orientation as separate elements, unlike other sexologists of the time.[2] A student of Hirschfeld's, Harry Benjamin, became the leading authority on gender affirmation surgery in the United States.

The early theorists were likely reflecting the fact that early sexual and gender minority communities were quite different than contemporary communities in that they were organized more along gender bending than around sexual orientation. Historian George Chauncey has chronicled the role of the "fairy" in late-nineteenth and early-twentieth-century New York, or effeminate men who cross-dressed in safe spaces and places and/or emphasized feminine characteristics in their self-expression, including traditionally masculine clothing. As Chauncy describes, "Dressing entirely as a woman was hardly necessary to indicate that one was a fairy. In the right context, appropriating even a single feminine—or at least unconventional—style or article of clothing might signify a man's identity as a fairy."[3] These men often took a sexual role "ascribed to women" and engaged in sex with other men with little stigma for the person in the "man's" role.[4] In other words, gender roles, not sexual orientation, were the culturally valuable factor. This dynamic for women, as well as men, can be seen in urban areas, such as 1920s and 1930s Harlem during the Harlem Renaissance, with women acting and dressing in a masculine or "butch" manner, such as blues singer Gladys Bentley. Indeed, Harlem was the site of a vibrant culture of gay and bisexual men and women, with a strong element of gender role challenges. According to historian Lillian

Faderman, "In Harlem tolerance extended to such a degree that black lesbians in butch/femme couples married each other in large wedding ceremonies, replete with bridesmaids and attendants."[5] Chauncey describes Harlem during this time as more gender challenging than the more white Greenwich Village: "The Village's most flamboyant homosexuals wore long hair; Harlem's wore long dresses. The Village had cafés where poets read their verse and drag queens performed; Harlem had speakeasies where men danced together and drag queens were regular customers."[6]

This challenging of gender norms was met with a strong legal reaction in the form of laws criminalizing cross-dressing. Some of these laws were first enacted in the 1840s and 1850s, but many were enacted in the late-nineteenth and early-twentieth centuries. Under these laws, it was a crime to dress in a manner inconsistent with one's birth-assigned sex. While some of these laws were enacted to combat fraud, their overall purpose was to legally enforce gender norms. Cross-dressing was seen as a form of public lewdness, like nudity and public sex acts.[7] The gender binary was deeply embedded in society and backed up by the force of law and powerful social norms, often enforced by the implicit or explicit threat of violence. To this day, violence is directed at transgender individuals with greater frequency and ferocity than other sexual and gender minorities. Thus, like the lesbian and gay rights movement, but even more powerfully, there existed enormous constraints on the creation of a public and confident transgender rights movement. And this movement, while connected to the movement for sexual liberation, has been slower to form and still faces more powerful resistance in many areas of law and policy.

Developments in the mid-twentieth century assisted in the creation of a movement, but they also reinforced the medicalization of transgender identity and politics. Harry Benjamin had become a leading medical practitioner of hormone therapy and an advocate of gender-affirming surgery (he was not a surgeon but an endocrinologist), rejecting the common idea that transgenderism was a psychological condition. His influential book outlining his approach, *The Transsexual Phenomenon*, was published in 1966. Christine Jorgensen, caused a media stir in 1952 through a public declaration that she had undergone gender-affirming surgery in Denmark. According to historian Susan Stryker, "Jorgensen's fame was a watershed event in transgender history. It brought an unprecedented level of public awareness to transgender issues, and it helped define the terms that would structure identity politics in the decades ahead."[8]

Also in the 1950s and 1960s, transgender organizations and activism began to form, as did the homophile movement. At this time, the movements were largely separate, given the homophile movement's emphasis on dressing and acting "properly." But the movements also found connections in responding to the regulation of the state, especially in bars and other gathering places where LGB individuals often came together with T individuals, as was the case in the Stonewall Riots. The first of transgender organizations and publications to develop catered to the heterosexual male cross-dressing community. The leader of this organizing was Charles/Virginia Prince. Prince maintained a strict ban on gay men and transsexuals in organizations and the publication, *Transvestia*. His organizations were exclusively for heterosexual male cross-dressers. The magazine and Prince faced harassing prosecution due to its content, but its circulation was never banned, protected by the First Amendment. Despite Prince's limitation, Stryker views *Transvestia* as critical in shaping the movement: "The magazine significantly shifted the political meaning of transvestism [cross-dressing], moving it away from being the expression of criminalized sexual activity to being the common denominator of a new (and potentially political) identity-based minority movement."[9] It would take several decades for a more comprehensive trans movement to form and be accepted into the lesbian and gay rights movement. As transgender activist and writer Dallas Denny notes, "This [Prince's] policy effectively kept gay cross dressers and transsexuals out of one of the only two visible communities of gender-variant people. (The other group was the drag community.) Those who did remain tended to keep their issues of sexuality and gender identity to themselves or to act covertly on those feelings."[10] Thus, the movement was invisible, divided, and marginalized from the sexual minority movement—not a good recipe for building a movement.

A fleeting connection between the lesbian/gay and transgender movement occurred in Philadelphia in 1965 when the local homophile organization, the Janus Society, staged a sit-in at Dewey's restaurant after restaurant employees refused service to gay people and people wearing nonconforming clothing for the gender norms of the time. Stepping out of the rigid gender binary of the broader homophile movement, the society described its actions in the following manner: "All too often, there is a tendency to be concerned with the rights of homosexuals as long as they somehow appear to be heterosexual, whatever that is. The masculine woman and feminine men are often are looked down upon by the official policy of homophile organizations, but the Janus Society is concerned with the worth of an individual."[11]

Despite its relative invisibility, the transgender community was still on the radar of the authorities, and its regulation and harassment was sometimes met with resistance that had political implications. An incident similar to the one at Dewey's, but this time involving the police (at the request of the restaurant), took place the next year at Compton's Cafeteria in San Francisco. According to Stryker, the Compton's Cafeteria Riot of 1966 led to "direct action in the streets by transgender people [that] resulted in lasting institutional change" for the first time.[12] Transgender activists became involved in antipoverty activism, especially given that many transgender individuals were disproportionately affected by poverty due to societal marginalization and discrimination. A strategy of the Great Society antipoverty program was the empowerment of local organizations to create and administer programs to alleviate poverty, and there was a flowering of these organizations at the time.

On the East Coast, transgender individuals were leaders in the Stonewall Riots in 1969, but this role was soon forgotten in the organizing of the sexual liberation movement of the 1970s. Trans women found a less-than-welcoming home in the lesbian-feminist movement, and gay male culture and politics began to emphasize masculinity as a part of gay identity. As Denny states, "Some gay men and lesbians have argued that gender-variant people are embarrassments to the movement, holding it back, that transsexuals have no commonalities with the gay and lesbian community, or, conversely, that they are gay men and lesbians in denial, or are tools of the patriarchy."[13] This, of course, led to stagnation for the transgender movement, but a new phase of organizing, outside of, and challenging, the larger LGB movement emerged in the 1980s and 1990s. Eventually, lesbian and gay legal and political activist groups began to more actively include transgender issues, perspectives, and advocacy within their frameworks. For instance, in 2014, the National Gay and Lesbian Taskforce changed its name to The National LGBTQ Taskforce.

Political activism and consciousness raising has also changed the way in which the medical community views transgender persons. In the most recent DSM (DSM-5), "gender dysphoria" has replaced the diagnosis, "gender identity disorder." In a clear attempt to abandon the mental illness paradigm of transgenderism, the APA declares, "It is important to note that gender non-conformity is not in itself a mental disorder. The critical element of gender dysphoria is the presence of clinically significant distress associated with the condition. . . . Persons experiencing gender dysphoria need a diagnostic term that protects their access to care and won't be used against them in social, occupational, or legal areas."[14]

By 1996, activists had defined a clear, rights-based agenda, as reflected in the International Bill of Gender Rights (IBGR). The document lists ten fundamental and universal human rights:

1. The Right to Define Gender Identity
2. The Right to Free Expression of Gender Identity
3. The Right to Secure and Retain Employment and to Receive Just Compensation
4. The Right of Access to Gendered Spaces and Participation in Gendered Activity
5. The Right to Control and Change One's Own Body
6. The Right to Competent Medical and Professional Care

7. The Right to Freedom from Involuntary Diagnosis and Treatment
8. The Right to Sexual Expression
9. The Right to Form Committed, Loving Relationships and Enter into Marital Contracts
10. The Right to Conceive, Bear, or Adopt Children; the Right to Nurture and Have Custody of Children and to Exercise Parental Capacity[15]

As we will see, these rights may be conveyed and protected in a myriad of laws and policies, but the rights have not been yet fully realized in the United States. Some of these rights map onto already established or emerging rights for sexual minorities, but some require a different approach for transgender individuals.

In Focus: A Transgender Tipping Point?

Putting transgender actor Laverne Cox, from *Orange is the New Black*, on their cover, *Time* magazine declared a transgender tipping point in 2014. In 2015, Bruce Jenner confirmed with Dianne Sawyer that he was transgender and in the process of transitioning and that he had always struggled with his gender identity and soon came out as Caitlyn on the cover of *Vanity Fair*. The high-profile suicide of Leelah Alcorn, a transgender teen from Ohio, also received much media attention in 2015. Transgender author and activist Janet Mock maintained a high media profile. Certainly, the issue of transgender status and rights received a new level of media interest, but law and policy still lags far behind this mostly favorable coverage, as this chapter outlines. While this visibility signals a positive development in the movement, much work remains to be done, but the courage of activists at the forefront will certainly add to the momentum.

Public Policies and Legal Reform

Antidiscrimination Laws

Transgender and gender nonconforming individuals face significant discrimination in the workplace and other arenas. Forty-seven percent respondents in one extensive survey of transgender and gender nonconforming individuals reported being not hired for a job, fired from a job, or denied promotion because of their identity. Nearly all respondents (90 percent) reported workplace harassment or taking action to avoid harassment, such as hiding their gender identity or their gender transition.[16] As was discussed in chapter 5, the inclusion of gender identity and expression in antidiscrimination laws has been controversial, even within the lesbian and gay rights movement, and transgender protections have come later and with less uniformity. More recently, however, activists have worked for full inclusion of these protections in their general advocacy. Currently, eighteen states[17] and many more local jurisdictions prohibit discrimination based on gender identity. As with sexual orientation–based laws, these vary in terms of what is covered: employment, public accommodations, housing, etc. These laws are clustered in LGBT-friendlier regions: the Northeast, Upper Midwest, and the West. Only three states include sexual orientation but not gender identity. A majority of states, then, still do not provide these protections. However, in this realm, the federal government is more protective of transgender rights than LGB rights, with federal court and EEOC rulings that consider transgender discrimination to be a form of sex discrimination actionable under the Civil Rights Act of 1964, discussed below.

Political scientists Jami K. Taylor, Daniel C. Lewis, Matthew Jacobsmeier, and Brian DiSarro have found the diffusion of gender identity policies to be driven more by "spillover" from other states than from internal political considerations. These policies are more likely to be enacted along with sexual orientation protections. As they state, "Policymakers look to the experience of other states and find that constituents make little distinction between gay and transgender protections. If nearby states can pass these laws without electoral pushback, it is politically safe to pass it."[18] This does not bode well for regions lacking protection, especially in the short term. Indeed, the diffusion of policies appears to have slowed, having been enacted by most of the most progressive states. It will take a new round of engagement and activism to extend these protections to more conservative states, but gender traditionalism may be a significant barrier. However, increased federal protections may make state policies less necessary. More broadly, Taylor notes that law and policy concerning gender identity is fragmented and incoherent, largely due to the fact that the transgender community is comparatively small and its issues are not central to public policy conversations and considerations.[19] Indeed, even within the larger LGBT movements, the agenda of transgender advocates has been marginalized, but this has changed more recently, as has been discussed.

A common tactic by opponents of gender identity–based antidiscrimination protections is to exploit fears about restroom use, particularly the notion that transgender women are really men trying to gain access to women's restrooms to assault cisgender women. As Amy Stone describes this dynamic, "The Religious Right uses transgender smear tactics to attach the growing number of local and state nondiscrimination ordinances that include transgender protection, along with using them indiscriminately in other referendums and initiatives. In these smear tactics, transgender individuals become dangerous bogeymen, specters of the threat of gay rights."[20] As we will see, this also plays a strong role in debates over school policy.

Federal Antidiscrimination Protections

Recall from chapter 5 that the federal antidiscrimination law does not provide explicit protections for gender identity and that prospects for such a law are dim. However, interpretations of federal law have led to federal legal protections on the basis of gender identity. Title VII of the 1964 Civil Rights Act forbids employer discrimination on the basis of "sex." At the time that it was enacted, the notion that the provision would prohibit discrimination against transgender or gender nonconforming people was not considered. Indeed, the transgender rights movement was in its infancy at this time. By the 1970s, transgender individuals began to argue in federal court that the provision applied to them, but judges narrowly interpreted the statute. However, the case of *Price Waterhouse v. Hopkins* (1989) dramatically changed this dynamic and opened the door to a broader reading of the statute—one that could potentially protect transgender individuals claiming discrimination. In that case the U.S. Supreme Court ruled that accounting firm Price Waterhouse had potentially discriminated against Ann Hopkins in promotion considerations because she was too "masculine" and "aggressive." The firm had thus engaged in sex stereotyping. As the majority opinion stated, "In the specific context of sex stereotyping, an employer who acts on the basis of a belief that a woman cannot be aggressive, or that she must not be, has acted on the basis of gender."[21]

Because transgender and gender nonconforming individuals challenge gender stereotypes, this opened a new path for the law. Federal appellate courts applied the logic of the case directly to cases of transgender discrimination, and, in 2012, the EEOC ruled that Title VII protected against transgender discrimination.[22] While not a binding ruling on federal courts, it demonstrates that the federal civil rights bureaucracy is combatting anti-transgender discrimination. Federal statutory protection against transgender discrimination in health care also exists as a result of the Affordable Care Act, in that the Act prohibits sex discrimination by a health care entity that receives federal funding. As currently interpreted, the law does not consider the refusal to provide gender confirmation surgery to be a form of discrimination. Reflecting the pervasive nature of health care discrimination against transgender individuals, Lambda Legal filed the first federal lawsuit under the ACA in Illinois on behalf of a transgender woman who was denied hormone replacement therapy by a doctor in a rural part of the state.[23]

For decades, federal law did not consider surgical procedures to be mandated as a form of equal treatment for transgender people. A 1989 rule expressly forbade Medicaid to cover surgical treatments. However, in 2014, the Department of Health and Human Services invalidated this policy.[24] Also, given that programs such as Medicaid are federal/state partnerships, some progressive states (California, Oregon, Massachusetts, and Vermont) have begun to include a full range of coverage. Lawsuits have been filed in states not yet including all forms of treatment for gender dysphoria under Medicaid. In addition, some large companies and universities have begun to include surgical treatment in their student health plans, and the large health insurance company Aetna has begun offering this coverage in some of its plans for federal employees (encouraged, but not required, by the federal Office of Personnel Management to do so, along with other companies insuring federal employees), to be followed by coverage in private plans.[25] Thus, the policy is in flux but appears to be trending in favor of full coverage with the continued possibility of discrimination until the policy landscape is more uniform and clear.

Despite the elimination of the ban on military service by openly lesbian, gay, and bisexual people, transgender people are still banned, and discharged if discovered, from U.S. military service. There is no statutory ban; it is an internal military policy (Instruction 6130.03). The Obama administration has supported changing the policy, and the DoD began efforts to change the policy by 2016. The military is the only part of the federal government with a formal policy of discrimination toward transgender people.[26]

Combatting Violence

As discussed in chapter 5, transgender people, especially transgender women of color, face disproportionately high levels of sexual and physical violence. Recall from that chapter that many conservative states did not add gender identity when they added sexual orientation to hate crime laws. Federal hate crime law includes gender identity as a result of the Matthew Shepard and James Byrd, Jr., Hate Crimes Prevention Act of 2009. In addition, in 2013, Congress added language about gender identity and sexual orientation to the 1994 Violence Against Women Act (VAWA), allowing the protections and services provided by the law to be accessed by lesbians and bisexual and transgender women. The law provides funds for law enforcement and private agencies, such as domestic violence shelters, to combat domestic violence and serve its victims. Republicans objected to this expansion of the law, but the political cost of holding up authorization led to support from many Republicans. Given Republican control of the House at the time, that chamber was the main hindrance to reauthorization, but eighty-seven Republican members joined all Democrats in supporting expanded reauthorization after a nonexpanded Republican proposal failed.[27] Republicans publicly framed their opposition by resisting a provision allowing non-Native Americans to be prosecuted for violence toward Native American women on reservations, under tribal law. But ultraconservative Congressman Steve Stockman likely voiced the true feelings of many when he declared, "It's called a women's act, but then they have men dressed up as women, they count that. Change-gender, or whatever. How is that—how is that a woman?"[28] It was one of the few times that Speaker John Boehner did not follow the "Hastert rule," or the rule that the House Speaker only brings legislation to a vote that enjoys the support of a majority of Republicans.

Documents and the Right to Travel

The right to forms of identification (drivers licenses, passports, etc.) that reflect a person's chosen gender identity, rather than the identity assigned at birth, is an essential right for transgender persons. Making forms of identification accurate often involves changing the sex/gender listed on a birth certificate. As of 2013, twenty-five states explicitly allowed birth certificate amendments with documentation of surgical transition. Only Tennessee expressly forbids this, but the situation is murkier in the remaining states.[29] Without such a right, travel becomes difficult, if not impossible. Beyond travel, the absence of this right also opens the door to confusion and harassment by government officials and private actors, such as health care providers, complicating the transgender individual's relationship to the state and society in a wide variety of contexts. Interacting with government officials also creates the possibility of a transgender person being "outed" by that official. As Taylor notes, this makes gender identity much more public than sexual orientation: "Gay and lesbian people [generally] do not rely on the state to recognize their identity."[30] For example, transgender persons often face discrimination and harassment at motor vehicles agencies, including being called "it" and being forced to remove wigs and makeup before an ID photo was taken.[31]

Until recently, states and the federal government required proof of gender affirmation surgery or a court order to change documents and forms of identification. Advocates have compelled change in some jurisdictions, but barriers remain. In 2010, the State Department began to allow the updating of passports without surgery. The new policy requires a doctor's certification that a person has undergone some form of gender transition, but it largely leaves this up to the doctor to define.[32] To fully allow for transgender rights and equality, regulations in this area should become legally, medically, and economically less burdensome. For example, a proposal in New York City would expand the type of professionals certifying gender transitions, beyond only physicians, thus making the issue less about medicalization and more about individual choice and self-definition.[33]

Trans Youth and Education

As the transgender movement has grown and become more visible in politics and culture, more young people are coming out as transgender. Beyond strong antibullying and harassment policies, schools have been required to confront issues such as restroom use and participation in school activities, such as athletics, based on gender identity. Courts have addressed the issue and made policy in some states through their decisions, and legislatures in progressive states have begun to change policy, most notably California's AB 1266 enacted in 2013, the nation's first statewide transgender student rights law. But these policies have faced considerable transphobic backlash, especially relating to restrooms. Enforcing a strict gender binary, opponents have primarily grounded their opposition to transgender-inclusive policies in the public's fears associated with using the "wrong" restroom.

In 2014, the Maine Supreme Judicial Court, in the case of *Doe v. Regional School Unit 26,* ruled that a school district had engaged in discrimination by denying a transgender girl the right to use the girls' restroom, the first such state supreme decision in the country. The court relied on the sexual orientation provision of the state's Human Rights Act. The student had been allowed use of the girls' restroom until the grandfather of another student told his male grandchild to enter the girls' room with her. After the incident, the student was denied access to the girls' restroom.[34] The Colorado Division of Civil Rights ruled similarly in 2013 invoking the state's prohibition on sex and sexual orientation discrimination. The Massachusetts Department of Education issued rules prohibiting transgender discrimination in 2013, following the enactment of a transgender discrimination law.

California's law does not rely on legal or civil rights commission/state agency interpretation of sex- or sexual orientation/gender identity–based antidiscrimination laws but more clearly and directly protects transgender students from discrimination. The most critical section of the law states, "A pupil shall be permitted to participate in sex-segregated school programs and activities, including athletic teams and competitions, and use facilities consistent with his or her gender identity, irrespective of the gender listed on the pupil's records."[35] The law was authored by Democratic Assemblyman Tom Ammiano who was also a leader in relationship equality legislative efforts in the state. The law was opposed by the California Catholic Conference as well as religious and social conservatives in the state. No Republican voted for the legislation. Frank Schubert, the political consultant who was highly involved in the effort of enacting Proposition 8 also led and supported an ultimately unsuccessful effort to gather enough signatures to repeal the law.[36] According to Schubert, about two-thirds of the signatures gathered came directly from churches. In addition to arguments about the law violating the privacy rights of nontransgender students, especially in restrooms and locker rooms, opponents were focused on maintaining the gender binary. As Schubert declared, "All of this is damaging to society. They are using those children to advance an agenda to strip society of all gender norms and to move down a path where men and women are considered to be interchangeable, where gender is an irrelevant fact, something that's fungible and flexible."[37]

In October of 2014, the federal Department of Education, through its Office of Civil Rights, has also applied federal sex discrimination law, especially Title IX of the Educational Amendments of 1972, to transgender students and has required a school district in California to create inclusive and protective policies.[38] In that case, a transgender girl was subjected to extensive harassment without a proper response from school officials. This effectively places schools receiving federal funding under the authority of the Office of Civil Rights for future complaints of transgender discrimination, at least as long as the Department of Education is willing to apply this approach to interpreting Title IX. A change in administration could affect this.

Criminal Justice Policy

Transgender persons are arrested and incarcerated at rates much higher than their proportion of the overall population. This is especially true for transgender women of color.[39] Much of this can be traced to explicit bias in the criminal justice system by officials reflecting bias against transgender persons. Many of these women are profiled by the police as sex workers, or just generally harassed for their challenging of gender and racial norms.[40] A prominent example of this approach involves black transgender woman Monica Jones who was arrested in 2013 for "manifesting prostitution" for talking to people on the street in Phoenix, Arizona. At the time of her arrest, she was a student at Arizona State University and sex worker activist. Activists refer to this type of "crime" as "walking while trans."[41] Educating law enforcement officials about transgender issues and strong guidance from the Justice Department that transgender people clearly fall under sex discrimination protections could begin to eliminate this bias.

Transgender prison inmates face significant discrimination, harassment, and violence. To protect them from violence committed by other inmates, prison officials often segregate transgender prisoners in solitary confinement, thus making the inmates' incarceration even more marginalized and isolated. The need for this segregation would be lessened if inmates were assigned to facilities based upon their gender identity, but they are mostly assigned based on their birth-assigned sex. In addition, transgender inmates are often denied access to trans-related health care, even hormone therapy, not to mention surgical treatment that is often politically and legally more controversial.[42]

Increasingly, however, federal courts are intervening and mandating medical treatment under the Eight Amendment's prohibition on "cruel and unusual punishment." In recent decades, the federal courts have actively intervened in prison policy, and this can be viewed as yet another court intervention in this policy arena. Events from Wisconsin illustrate the political barriers to transgender politics and the role played by courts in protecting transgender rights. An inmate sued the state to require surgical treatment after hormone therapy had been provided by the state prison system for several years. In response to the suit, the Republican-controlled legislature enacted the Inmate Sex Change Prevention Act in 2005. The law banned funding for any type of treatment. A leading Republican legislator called the request for treatment "the most absurd thing I have ever heard of," adding, "The taxpayers should not be spending one dime for something like that."[43] The bill passed in the Assembly by a vote of 82–15 and by unanimous consent in the Senate.[44] However, the federal courts viewed the issue quite differently. A district court and the Seventh Circuit Court of Appeals found the law to be unconstitutional under the Eighth Amendment in the case, of *Fields v. Smith*.[45] In 2012, a federal district court in Massachusetts ruled that surgical treatment was required under the Eighth Amendment.[46]

THE INTERSEX MOVEMENT

The intersex movement posits that biological sex is a social construction, not just the social category of gender. The movement represents an even more radical challenge to the sex/gender binary, as even elements of the transgender movement envision two primary sexes, male and female. As was discussed in chapter 1, the term intersex refers to someone born with both male and female genitalia and/or reproductive organs, or sex organs and genitalia that do not conform to social norms and standards. In the past, and far too often today, surgical intervention was recommended by doctors to make intersex children "one sex or the other," and parents usually followed these recommendations without regard for the future development of the children and the choices about sex and gender they may eventually make. Obviously, this is another example of the medicalization of sexual and gender minorities. The medical term used to describe intersex individuals is disorders of sex development (DSD). About 1 in 2000 infants falls under this classification. This term has replaced the outdated term of hermaphrodite/ hermaphroditism. However, many intersex activists object to the use of the term "disorder." Central goals of the movement are: to bring awareness to the fact that sex is socially constructed; to advocate for policies that allow for intersex persons to control their own futures without unconsented surgical intervention; and the elimination of sex-specific designations in public policy and documents, such as birth certificates. Fundamentally, according to activists, the problem the movement is attempting to overcome is "the externally determined gender assignment, the practice of sexed standardization and mutilation, as well as medical authority of definition on sex."[47] The movement is not as well developed as the transgender movement, but this is gradually changing.

In fact, the intersex movement did not develop until the 1990s, in terms of group consciousness, activism, and mobilization. The 1950s was the start of systemic medical intervention with intersex infants, and doctors maintained control over their bodies until the movement against this role began decades later. Much of the activism in the movement is elite/expert driven, as there is not as much grassroots mobilization as in the LGBT movements. As Alice Dreger and April Herndon state, "There are online virtual communities of people with intersex, but large numbers of intersex people do not live together in brick-and-mortar communities, and only occasionally do they come together for meetings that are primarily about political consciousness-raising rather than about sharing information about a particular medical diagnosis."[48] Dreger is an influential nonintersex expert activist.

Like the transgender movement, allowing official documents to be easily amended is a policy goal of intersex activists, or, more controversially, the elimination of sex as a category on documents. As law professor Darren Rosemblum states,

> Marking "male" or "female" on a birth certificate sets children against a yardstick that will measure their conformity to these roles. For intersex children born without clearly male or female genitals, that conformity generates physical violence, with surgical alteration to conform infants' genitals to "M" or "F," without knowing if the baby will become a boy or a girl. The birth certificate functions to police and script the lives of both children and the parents.[49]

Some women's rights activists object to this policy approach out of a concern that the elimination of sex distinctions would make it more difficult for women to legally and politically challenge discrimination against women. Another option includes creating a third category on documents. For instance, Germany changed policy to allow for an X, rather than M or F, to recognize intersex designation on birth certificates. However, intersex advocates are concerned that this approach will continue marginalization by still privileging and normalizing male and female. Parents may still elect surgery to avoid the stigma of an X on the birth certificate.[50]

In the past, courts have not been hospitable forums for intersex litigation, but the courts have been reengaged more recently, with activists banking on the fact that judicial doctrine is now more favorable, as demonstrated by cases like *Lawrence v. Texas*. In 2013, the Southern Poverty Law Center and the intersex legal advocacy group Advocates for Informed Choice filed a lawsuit to challenge a decision by medical authorities to surgically treat an intersex child. The goal of the lawsuit, according to Advocates for Informed Choice, is "to end this inhumane practice."[51] This is clearly a legal strategy to end continuing surgical treatment of intersex infants, an unnecessary and medically and psychologically harmful treatment, according to activists and an increasing number of medical experts. One prong of the legal action is a South Carolina state court suit claiming medical malpractice on behalf of M.C., an intersex child who underwent surgery to feminize his genitals as a sixteen-month-old foster care child. M.C. came to identify as a boy as he grew older. The surgery was approved by doctors and state child welfare officials. The federal case makes claims that M.C.'s procedural and substantive due process rights were violated, because state officials did not provide a hearing before the decision was made and that, in terms of substantive due process, the surgery against M.C.'s consent was fundamentally unfair by violating M.C.'s "substantive due process rights to bodily integrity, privacy, procreation, and liberty." Federal district judge David C. Norton ruled that the case could proceed, a significant victory for the intersex rights advocates.[52] Unfortunately, he was overruled on appeal.

CONCLUSION

Often marginalized with in the larger LGBTI rights movement, in addition to the more significant cultural barriers stemming from a strong and more direct challenge to the gender binary, transgender and intersex individuals face a different legal, political, and policy landscape. The movements have been slower to form, and policies and laws have been slower to change, except for progress related to the linking of transgender discrimination to already established prohibitions on sex-based discrimination. Courts appear to be important allies for these movements, potentially offering some shelter from the negative consequences of being subjected to purely majoritarian politics.

KEY TERMS, CONCEPTS, PEOPLE, AND CASES

Benjamin, Harry
California's AB 1266
Cisgender
Compton's Cafeteria riot
Cross-dresser

Criminalization of cross-dressing
Dewey's sit-in
Disorders of sex development (DSD)
Doe v. Regional School District 26 (2014)

Drag king/queen
EEOC ruling
Eighth Amendment and prison policy
Fields v. Smith (2011)
Gender binary
Gender dysphoria
Gender identity/expression
Genderqueer
Gender nonconforming
Harlem Renaissance
Hirschfeld, Magnus
Identity document/right to travel
International Bill of Gender Rights
Intersex/intersex movement
Jorgensen, Christine
Litigation for intersex rights
Medicalization of sexual and gender
   minorities
Military ban on transgender service
   members

Policy diffusion/spillover
Price Waterhouse v. Hopkins (1989)
Prince, Charles/Virginia
Sex reassignment/gender-affirming
   surgery
Social construction of gender and sex
Stonewall riot
Title VII of the 1964 Civil Rights
   Act/Title IX of the Educational
   Amendments of 1972
Transgender
Transition
Transsexual
The Transsexual Phenomenon
Transvestia
Two-spirit
Violence against transgender people
Violence Against Women Act
Walking while trans

QUESTIONS FOR DISCUSSION

1. How are the transgender and intersex rights movements similar to, and different from, the movement for LGB rights?
2. Why do medical authorities still play a large role in the politics of transgender and intersex persons? What are the political and legal implications of this?
3. How is the gender binary more directly challenged by transgender and intersex persons? What are the implications of this?
4. Will the intersex and transgender rights movements soon lead to less rigid societal norms on gender roles and rigid definitions of biological sex?

NOTES

1. Shannon Price Minter, "Do Transsexuals Dream of Gay Rights? Getting Real about Transgender Inclusion," in *Transgender Rights*, Paisley Currah, et al., eds. (Minneapolis: University of Minnesota Press, 2006), 141–70: 142.

2. Leslie Feinberg, *Transgender Warriors: Making History from Joan of Arc to RuPaul* (Boston: Beacon Books, 1996), 95.

3. George Chauncey, *Gay New York: Gender, Urban Culture, and the Making of the Gay Male World, 1890–1940* (New York: Basic Books, 1994), 51.

4. Chauncey, *Gay New York*, 13.

5. Lillian Faderman, *Odd Girls and Twilight Lovers: A History of Lesbian Life in Twentieth-Century America* (New York: Penguin, 1991), 73.

6. Chauncey, *Gay New York*, 244.

7. William N. Eskridge, Jr., *Gaylaw: Challenging the Apartheid of the Closet* (Cambridge, MA: Harvard University Press, 1999), 27–28.

8. Susan Stryker, *Transgender History* (Berkeley: Seal Press, 2008), 47.

9. Stryker, *Transgender History*, 54.

10. Dallas Denny, "Transgender Communities of the United States in the Late Twentieth Century," in *Transgender Rights*, 171–91: 172.

11. This passage from the Janus Society newsletter is quoted in Marc Stein, *City of Sisterly and Brotherly Loves: Lesbian and Gay Philadelphia, 1945–1972* (Philadelphia: Temple University Press, 2004), 246.

12. Stryker, 64.

13. Denny, 174.

14. American Psychiatric Association, "Gender Dysphoria," http://www.dsm5.org/documents/gender%20dysphoria%20fact%20sheet.pdf.

15. Currah, *Transgender Rights*, 328–31.

16. Judith Grant, et al., *Injustice at Every Turn: A Report of the National Transgender Discrimination Survey* (Washington, DC: National Center for Transgender Equality and National Gay and Lesbian Task Force, 2011), 3.

17. California (1992, 2003), Colorado (2007), Connecticut (1991, 2011), Delaware (2009, 2013), Hawaii (1991, 2011), Illinois (2006), Iowa (2007), Maine (2005), Maryland (2001, 2014), Massachusetts (1989, 2012), Minnesota (1993), New Jersey (1992, 2007), New Mexico (2003), Nevada (1999, 2011), Oregon (2008), Rhode Island (1995, 2001), Vermont (1991, 2007) and Washington (2006). Washington, DC (1977, 2006) also protects on the basis of gender identity. New Hampshire, New York, and Wisconsin protect sexual orientation but not gender identity.

18. Jami K. Taylor, Daniel C. Lewis, Matthew Jacobsmeier, and Brian DiSarro, "Content and Complexity in Policy Reinvention and Diffusion: Gay and Transgender-Inclusive Laws Against Discrimination," *State Politics & Policy Quarterly*, 12:1 (2012), 75–98: 89.

19. Jami Taylor, "Transgender Identities and Public Policy in the United States: The Relevance for Public Administration," *Administration & Society*, 39:7 (November 2007), 833–56.

20. Amy L. Stone, *Gay Rights at the Ballot Box* (Minneapolis: University of Minnesota Press, 2012), 170.

21. *Price Waterhouse v. Hopkins*, 490 U.S. 228 (1989), 288.

22. *Macy v. Holder*, EEOC Appeal No. 0120120821 (2012).

23. Press release, "Lambda Legal Sues Doctor and Clinic for Denying Medical Care to Transgender Woman," Lambda Legal, April 16, 2014, http://www.lambdalegal.org/news/il_20140416_sues-doctor-clinic.

24. "Medicare and Transgender People," National Center for Transgender Equality, May 2014, http://transequality.org/PDFs/MedicareAndTransPeople.pdf.

25. Jason Millman, "One Health Insurer Just Took the Feds' Offer to End Transgender Discrimination. Who Else Will Follow?" *The Washington Post*, October 31, 2014, http://www.washingtonpost.com/blogs/wonkblog/wp/2014/10/31/one-health-insurer-just-took-the-feds-offer-to-end-transgender-discrimination-who-else-will-follow/.

26. Shannon Minter, "Lift Ban on Transgender Military Members," CNN.com, September 4, 2014, http://www.cnn.com/2014/09/03/opinion/minter-transgender-military-lady-valor/.

27. Tom Cohen, "House Passes Violence Against Women Act After GOP Version Defeated," CNN, February 28, 2013, http://www.cnn.com/2013/02/28/politics/violence-against-women/.

28. Betsey Woodruff, "Back in the Saddle," *National Review Online*, March 14, 2013, http://www.nationalreview.com/articles/342824/back-saddle-betsy-woodruff.

29. Jami K. Taylor, Barry Tadlock, and Sarah J. Poggione, "Birth Certificate Amendment Laws and Morality Politics," in *Transgender Rights and Politics: Groups, Issue Framing, & Policy Adoption*, Jami K. Taylor and Donald P. Haider-Markel, eds. (Ann Arbor: University Press of Michigan, 2014), 253.

30. Taylor, "Transgender Identities," 837.

31. Parker Marie Malloy, "Trans Women Harassed, Called 'It' by West Virginia DMV Employees," Advocate.com, July 7, 2014, http://www.advocate.com/politics/transgender/2014/07/07/trans-women-harassed-called-it-west-virginia-dmv-employees.

32. "Understanding the Passport Gender Change Policy," National Center for Transgender Equality, March 2014, http://transequality.org/Resources/passports_2014.pdf.

33. Matt Flegenheimer, "Easing the Law for New Yorkers Shifting Gender," *New York Times*, October 8, 2014, A1.

34. *Doe v. Regional School Unit 26*, 86 A.3d 600 (Me. 2014).

35. Assembly Bill No. 1266, http://leginfo.legislature.ca.gov/faces/billNavClient.xhtml?bill_id=201320140AB1266.

36. George Skelton, "Opponents Gear Up to Fight Transgender Law," latimes.com, October 20, 2014, http://www.latimes.com/local/la-me-cap-transgender-20131021-column.html.

37. Robin Abcarian, "Right wing frenzied over transgendered students choosing bathroom," latimes.com, December 10, 2013, www.latimes.com/local/lanow/la-me-ln-transgender-law-20131210-story.html.

38. Press release, "U.S. Department of Education's Office for Civil Rights Announces Resolution of Civil Rights Investigation of California's Downey Unified School District," U.S. Department of Education, October 14, 2014, http://www.ed.gov/news/press-releases/us-department-educations-office-civil-rights-announces-resolution-civil-rights-investigation-californias-downey-unified-school-district.

39. According to University of Richmond sociologist Eric Anthony Grollman, "While only 3% of the general population has ever been incarcerated, 16% of trans people have ever been sent to jail or prison. And, that figure is 41% for Black and Latina trans women." "Transgender People And The Criminal Justice System," http://egrollman.com/2014/06/30/trans-criminal-justice/.

40. Catherine Hanssens, et al., "A Roadmap for Change: Federal Policy Recommendations for Addressing the Criminalization of LGBT People and People Living with HIV," Columbia University Center for Gender & Sexuality Law, May 2014.

41. Sunnivie Brydum, "Arizona Activist Found Guilty of 'Walking While Trans,'" Advocate.com, April 15, 2014, http://www.advocate.com/politics/transgender/2014/04/15/arizona-activist-found-guilty-walking-while-trans.

42. Hanssens, "A Roadmap for Change."

43. Gina Barton, "Prisoner Sues State Over Gender Rights," JSOnline.com, January 23, 2005, http://www.jsonline.com.news/wisconsin.181956101.html.

44. 2005–2006 Wisconsin Legislature, Assembly Bill 184, https://docs.legis.wisconsin.gov/2005/proposals/ab184.

45. *Fields v. Smith*, 653 F.3d 550 (7th Cir. 2011).

46. *Kosilek v. Spencer*, 889 F. Supp. 2d 190 (D. Mass. 2012).

47. Emily Greenhouse, "A New Era for Intersex Rights," *The New Yorker*, December 30, 2013, http://www.newyorker.com/news/news-desk/a-new-era-for-intersex-rights.

48. Alice D. Dreger and April M. Herndon, "Progress and Politics in the Intersex Rights Movement: Feminist Theory in Action," *GLQ: A Journal of Lesbian and Gay Studies*, 15:2 (2009), 199–224: 208.

49. Darren Rosenblum, "For Starters, 'Unsex' the Birth Certificate," *New York Times*, October 24, 2014, http://www.nytimes.com/roomfordebate/2014/10/19/is-checking-the-sex-box-necessary/for-starters-unsex-the-birth-certificate.

50. Greenhouse, "A New Era for Intersex Rights."

51. "Project Integrity," Advocates for Informed Choice, http://aiclegal.org/programs/project-integrity/.

52. *M.C. v. Aaronson*, No. 2:13-cv-01303-DCN, United States District Court for the District of South Carolina, Charleston Division, August 29, 2013. The quote is used on page 4 of the decision by Judge Norton from the complaint in the case.

BIBLIOGRAPHY AND FURTHER READING

Paisley Currah, Richard M. Juang, and Shannon Price Minter, *Transgender Rights* (Minneapolis: University of Minnesota Press, 2006).

Laura Erickson-Scroth, ed., *Trans Bodies, Trans Selves: A Resource for the Transgender Community* (New York: Oxford University Press, 2014).

Leslie Feinberg, *Transgender Warriors: Making History from Joan of Arc to RuPaul* (Boston: Beacon Books, 1996).

Julie A. Greenberg, *Intersexuality and the Law: Why Sex Matters* (New York: NYU Press, 2012).

Susan Stryker, *Transgender History* (Berkeley: Seal Press, 2008).

Jami K. Taylor and Donald P. Haider-Markel, eds., *Transgender Rights and Politics: Groups, Issue Framing, & Policy Adoption* (Ann Arbor: University Press of Michigan, 2014).

Nicholas M. Teich, *Transgender 101: A Simple Guide to a Complex Issue* (New York: Columbia University Press, 2012).

Chapter 8

Global Developments

The previous chapters in this book examined the politics of sexual and gender minority rights in the United States, but, across the globe, this politics has been engaged, with some countries enacting policies more robust than those in the United States, while most other nations struggle with achieving rights and equality for these minorities. Indeed, there is no uniform pattern for sexual and gender minority rights. The story around the globe is one of both liberation with positive policy change and continued oppression, with some of this oppression accelerating. Why is this happening? While there is evidence that international institutions and human rights norms are assisting in the spread of liberalization toward sexual and gender minorities, internal politics still play a large role in determining a country's approach. Thus, the type of political and legal system, religion, public opinion, and historical development also play a role. For example, as Omar Encarnación argues, "The most favorable environment for gay rights is found in places where political freedoms, civil society, and the rule of law have taken root, especially in recent decades, as in Spain, South Africa, and Latin America. By contrast, gay rights are languishing where authoritarianism is on the rise and civil society is under attack, as in Russia, most of Africa, and virtually the entire Middle East."[1] The agenda of political leaders is also important. Increasingly, leaders in totalitarian regimes or weak democracies are deploying homophobia and opposition to rights expansion as a tool to consolidate their power.[2] In other words, homophobia is not necessarily deeply embedded in all currently hostile nations but is manipulated and exacerbated for political gain. Starting with the most supportive regions of the world, this chapter examines the progress and resistance to the liberation of sexual and gender minorities.

In this discussion, it is perhaps easy to fall into the highly misleading narrative of sophisticated, liberal democratic, LGBT-supportive West versus the underdeveloped and homophobic East. We need to avoid Western cultural triumphalism. While it is true that the rights of sexual minorities are best supported in liberal democracies (and most of these are currently in Western nations), the West only recently began to embrace sexual and gender minorities, and this embrace is still highly contested. We should not forget the ferocity of homophobia and heterosexism that pervaded most societies not that long ago, echoes of which persist. The U.S. Religious Right is more than happy to export this hostility as the tide turns against them domestically. As we will see, Religious Right activists have been involved in antisexual minority movements in parts of Africa and Russia.

EUROPE, CANADA, AUSTRALIA, AND NEW ZEALAND

Northern and Western Europe are home to some of the most supportive political cultures, public opinion, and policies for sexual and gender minorities. As was discussed in chapter 2, Germany was the original home of the modern gay rights movement. Denmark saw the formation of a gay rights organization in 1948, a couple of years before the creation of the Mattachine Society. Denmark was also the first country to recognize, and provide government benefits for, same-sex relationships in 1989. Same-sex marriage was first recognized in the world at the national level by The Netherlands in 2001. Eastern Europe, especially formerly Communist states, generally is less supportive, though some progress is being made in some countries. While not in Europe, Canada began to move at a similar pace, and with some similar dynamics, to Northern and Western Europe. Sodomy laws were eliminated in 1969, and marriage equality became policy throughout the country in 2005. A major difference is that while progress in Europe occurred mostly through electoral politics and policy change enacted by legislatures, change in Canada was significantly influenced by the courts, similar to the situation in the United States. Australia and New Zealand have followed the European model of a parliamentary route. The next section will not be an exhaustive survey of developments in all counties, but an overview of themes and highlights of the politics of sexuality and gender in Europe, Canada, Australia, and New Zealand.

Northern and Western Europe

Despite a promising start in Germany, the lesbian and gay rights movement found its most favorable setting in Scandinavia due to more secularization and social democratic (leftist) parties—factors that would lead to progress in Europe more generally. Indeed, after the Nazis destroyed the German movement, Germany was much slower to develop pro-LGBT policies than some of its neighbors. Europe's first gay rights organization outside of Germany, The Association/Circle of 1948, was founded in Denmark in 1948. The organization's founder, Axel Axgil, was motivated to found the organization by activity surrounding the United Nation's Universal Declaration of Human Rights of that year. In terms of Danish policy, same-sex sexual activity was decriminalized in 1933. By the 1960s, as cohabitation outside of marriage was becoming more common in Europe, political efforts to create legal frameworks for these relationships began, including same-sex relationships. It took several decades of discussion of debate, but registered partnerships for same-sex couples were enacted in 1989. Part of the timing was a reaction to the AIDS crisis, with some advocates arguing that formalizing same-sex relationships would dampen promiscuity. But it was mostly an affirmation of the value and dignity of same-sex couples by a progressive political system, supported by years of activism. According to political scientist Martin DuPuis, "Proponents' arguments centered around the principles of equality, freedom, and justice. . . . Legal equality implied an official, societal acknowledgment of the equal value of homosexual and heterosexual relationships."[3] Axgil and his partner of forty years were the first couple to be recognized under the policy. This policy quickly diffused to other countries in the region, including Norway (1993), Sweden (1995), and Iceland (1996). These countries also made discrimination on the basis of sexual orientation illegal in the 1980s and the 1990s. These nations "upgraded" to same-sex marriage in 2009 through 2012. More conservative Finland lagged behind, with registered partnerships in 2002 and marriage equality in 2014. This was all done without litigation, through party politics and through parliaments and parliamentary commissions, as is customary in civil law systems, as opposed to common law systems where judicial policymaking is more common. Interestingly, and predicting a European phenomenon, parenting rights were not included in initial legal frameworks and were added much later.

Despite eliminating sodomy laws in 1791 during the French Revolution and its reputation for sexual libertinism, France has only become a leader in LGBT policy quite recently. As historian Robert Beachy describes the decriminalization, "The New French Penal Code adopted by the National Assembly in 1791 simply ignored sodomy—inspired by the liberal principle that the state should not meddle in private affairs—making France the first European state to decriminalize same-sex eroticism."[4] French sexual libertinism has historically had a very heterosexist slant, but the left began to take up the cause of sexual minorities by the 1980s. The Socialist government enacted an antidiscrimination law during the decade, and a Socialist-led coalition enacted Civil PACS in 1999—the French version of registered partnerships. These provided many, but not all (especially parenting rights), of the rights of marriage but were open to same-sex and opposite-sex couples. French political culture frowns upon distinctions based upon identity in law and policy. As other countries in Northern and Western Europe moved in the direction of marriage equality in the 2000s, a more conservative government led by Nicolas Sarkozy, a staunch opponent of same-sex marriage, prevented policy change. In addition, the French courts have repeatedly refused to push the envelope on LGBT policy, invoking the civil law norm of deference to parliament. In 2013, the Socialist government of Francois Hollande enacted a same-sex marriage law, after making support for such a law part of his 2012 campaign for the presidency. Conservatives have held large demonstrations against the law, but public opinion supports marriage equality.

Despite being an economic leader in Europe, Germany has not been a leader on the question of LGBT rights, largely because of the influence of center-right Christian Democratic Union, a party that has played a large role in German politics since World War II. Paragraph 175 was repealed in East Germany in 1968 and in West Germany in 1969, but little progress occurred after that. A national antidiscrimination law was not enacted until 2006. A window of opportunity opened in 1998 with the election of the pro-LGBT rights coalition of the Social Democrats and Greens. They enacted the Life Partnership Act in 2001, and expanded this domestic partnership law in 2005. However, the Christian Democrats returned to power in 2005. The Constitutional Court has rebuffed activist demands to compel full marriage equality through litigation, but the court has ruled that some tax rights should be applied to same-sex couples.

In 2001, The Netherlands became the first country to legalize same-sex marriage nationwide. An antidiscrimination law was enacted in the early 1990s and a registered partnership law in 1998. Neighboring Belgium followed with same-sex marriage in 2003. In both countries, opportunities for activists opened up after Christian Democrats lost power and parties further to the left took over control of the governments. The election of a Socialist government in Spain led to same-sex marriage becoming legal in 2005. The Socialist Party in neighboring Portugal legalized same-sex marriage in 2010.

When marriage equality came to most of the United Kingdom in 2014, it came in spite of the country's homophobic history. Sodomy laws remained on the books until 1967, a decade after the Wolfenden Commission recommended that they be eliminated out of Millian concerns for personal privacy and "victimless" crimes. This did not end governmental homophobia, however. After 1967, the age of consent for same-sex intimacy was twenty-one, while it was sixteen for opposite-sex intimacy. This was not changed until 2004. In addition, The Conservative government of Margaret Thatcher, at the height of the antigay backlash of the AIDS crisis enacted Section 28, a law stating that local authorities "shall not intentionally promote homosexuality" by local government entities, including schools. Section 28 also helped to galvanize the lesbian and gay rights movement—a movement that successfully campaigned to have the opposition Labour Party include a nondiscrimination provision in its party platform in 1985. The Labour Party, elected to power in 1997 under Tony Blair was the vehicle to progress on LGBT rights. The party repealed Section 28 in 2003, and civil partnerships became law in 2005. The coalition government of Conservative David Cameron (the Liberal Democrats were his coalition partners) pushed through marriage equality by 2013, over the strong objections of many Conservatives Members of Parliament, but enough Liberal Democrats and Labour members were in favor to enact it. This law covered only England and Wales; Scotland enacted marriage equality in 2014; Northern Ireland had not enacted a policy as of early 2015. A successful referendum in heavily Catholic Ireland (a separation nation from the United Kingdom) on marriage equality occurred 2015. Decriminalization did not occur until 1993, but civil partnerships were created in 2010, reflecting a recent and rapid shift in the direction of protections for sexual minorities.

In Focus: Ireland and Marriage Equality

With a resounding 62 percent of the vote, same-sex marriage was approved in Ireland in 2015—the first nation to do so nationally through a direct referendum. Until quite recently, strongly Roman Catholic Ireland was seen as quite conservative on issues of sexuality. Abortion is still mostly illegal. The Catholic Church campaigned strongly against the measure, but Ireland appears to be going the way of other former Catholic strongholds like Spain, Portugal, and Argentina on issues of sexuality. Advocates hope to use this as a springboard to continue the spread of marriage equality in Europe, especially in Catholic countries like Italy.

Resistance in Eastern/Southern Europe

In Southern and Eastern Europe, a less favorable policy environment faces sexual minorities. Politics in these parts of Europe is generally less secularized, LGBT movements are much weaker, public opinion is less supportive, fewer leftist parties hold power consistently, and courts are generally are not allies. While antidiscrimination protections exist in some countries, and a handful of countries recognize same-sex couples through domestic partnership laws, only one country in the region recognized same-sex marriage, as of 2015. For instance, after some progress for LGBT rights through leftist parties in Hungary, the socially conservative Fidesz Party came to power in 2011 and enacted a ban on same-sex marriage in a new constitution. An exception to this state of affairs is Slovenia, the most progressive of the former Yugoslavian countries. In 2015, a center-left government enacted same-sex marriage.

In some quarters of Eastern Europe, direct attacks on the LGBT community through rhetoric from government officials and in policies have become more common in attempts by leaders to gain and consolidate power. LGBT rights are framed as a Western phenomenon that threatens national unity and national traditions. The attack on the LGBT community in Russia led by Vladimir Putin is the clearest example of this, but Putin's tactics have been utilized in other national contexts. In 2013, Putin signed the infamous "homosexual propaganda" law that essentially made it a crime to advocate for LGBT rights. Strong majorities oppose LGBT rights in Russia, and the short-term environment for LGBT activists and individuals looks bleak. The only bright spot is that same-sex sexual activity was decriminalized in 1993. U.S.-based anti-LGBT activists have applauded this approach, and have traveled to Russia and other countries to advocate these policies, including the president of the National Organization for Marriage, Brian Brown. In 2013, Brown gave a speech to the Duma urging legislators to ban sexual minorities from adopting children, and the legislature did so soon thereafter.[5]

Fourteen countries in Europe offer no legal protections or recognition for transgender individuals. With the exception of Ireland, most of these are in Central and Eastern Europe. Fifteen countries offer antidiscrimination protections based upon gender identity, and thirty-five allow gender to be changed on official documents. While surgical intervention has been required in most countries, an increasing number of countries are allowing this without surgery, and this trend should continue. The European Court of Human Rights has also expanded transgender rights in the European Union.[6]

Canada

Progress for the rights of sexual minorities in Canada was aided significantly by the creation of a new part of the Canadian Constitution, The Charter of Rights and Freedoms, in 1982 and a more assertive judiciary under the new constitutional arrangement. In particular, activists were aided by a provision of the charter, Section 15(1), that grants equality rights. After the decriminalization of sodomy by the United Kingdom in 1967, Liberal prime minister Pierre Trudeau pushed parliament to decriminalize sodomy in 1969. However, this did not lead to the federal government's embrace of sexual minorities. Indeed, Trudeau and his justice minister (and future prime minister)

Jean Chrétien rejected the inclusion of sexual orientation into the charter. In the text of the document, discrimination is prohibited on the basis of "race, national or ethnic origin, colour [sic], religion, sex, age or mental or physical disability."[7] However, in 1995, the Supreme Court of Canada declared that sexual orientation was an "analogous" category, and thereafter considered sexual orientation–based discrimination to fall under the jurisdiction of the charter and the courts that interpret it.[8]

However, by the 1980s and 1990s, activists began pursuing strategies for positive policy change, especially through the social democratic/leftist New Democratic Party and the provinces in which it governed. In 1977, Quebec enacted the nation's first provincewide antidiscrimination law, and the world's first such law beyond the municipal level. Ontario included sexual orientation in its human rights law in 1986, and other provinces followed. The most conservative province in Canada, Alberta, was forced to add sexual orientation to its antidiscrimination framework in 1998.[9] In addition, New Democrat governments began to recognize same-sex relationships similar to governmental recognition of cohabitating opposite-sex couples. Like many European countries, Canada created a legal framework for cohabitation. In 1999, the Supreme Court ruled that this framework must be applied to cohabitating same-sex couples under Section 15(1) in the case of *M. v. H.*[10] In addition to spurring policy change in the form of federal and provincial civil union laws, this decision triggered activism and litigation for marriage equality, and soon courts throughout Canada ruled that the nation's ban on same-sex marriage contravened the charter. In 2005, Canada became the fourth country in the world to legalize same-sex marriage at the national level after the initially reluctant Liberal Party put forth the legislation after consulting with the Supreme Court and receiving a favorable ruling. Opposition was strident and vocal, but Canada's Religious Right lacks the significant level of political clout maintained by its cousin in the United States. Conservative prime minister Stephen Harper held a vote to repeal the marriage law when his party came to power, but a majority in Parliament opposed the repeal.

In terms of transgender rights, some provinces explicitly forbid discrimination on the basis of gender identity and expression (Ontario, Manitoba, Nova Scotia, and Northwest Territories), while others interpret their laws to prohibit such discrimination. Legislation to add gender identity to the federal Human Rights Act stalled in the Senate after passing the House of Commons over the opposition of the Conservative government, but with the support of some Conservative members. Other Conservatives utilized typical, but highly inaccurate and transphobic, "bathroom fear" arguments. Provinces are also beginning to change their documents' policies to make it easier to change gender without surgery. In 2015, Ontario began housing prison inmates based on their chosen gender identity.

Australia and New Zealand

Despite strong public support for rights for sexual minorities, policy in Australia has lagged behind Western Europe and Canada. Sodomy laws were gradually eliminated at the state and territorial level between 1973 and 1997. Through cohabitation policies, de facto unions for same-sex couples with some rights are legal, but center-right governments in recent decades have thwarted progress. Indeed, the conservative government of John Howard enacted a ban on same-sex marriage in 2004. The election of the center-left Labor Party in 2007 opened up the policy process somewhat, but same-sex marriage legislation stalled from party leaders' fears of losing the support of rural voters. However, before losing power in 2013, Labor prime minister Julia Gillard enacted a sexual orientation, gender identity, and intersex status antidiscrimination law. A culture of parliamentary supremacy generally inhibits the ability of the courts to be strong allies to the movement in Australia. However, courts have ruled that a third gender may be recognized in law and policy.

More progress for sexual minorities has been made in New Zealand, despite sodomy laws having been repealed relatively late, in 1986. Sexual orientation was added to the national antidiscrimination law in 1993. Civil unions were legalized in 2004. Litigation to require same-sex marriage was rebuffed by the courts in the 1990s, but parliament enacted a same-sex marriage law in 2012. Since 2006, transgender discrimination has been forbidden by the government's interpretation that it is covered under the sex discrimination provision of the 1993 Human Rights Act.

LATIN AMERICA

When Argentina legalized same-sex marriage in 2010, many observers around the globe were taken by surprise that such an innovation occurred in Latin America, especially given its strongly Catholic and machismo reputation. However, this reputation obscures a rapidly changing policy landscape for sexual and gender minorities in Latin America. Same-sex relationships are recognized at the national or subnational levels in Argentina, Brazil, Colombia, Chile, Ecuador, Mexico, and Uruguay. Because of the adoption of European civil law, most countries colonized by Spain and Portugal lacked sodomy laws, but these laws do exist in areas of British influence in the Caribbean and Central America. This is not to say that homosexuality and challenges to the gender binary have been embraced in the region. In fact, sexual minorities have faced, and still face, enormous oppression and violence for challenging traditional sex and gender roles and practices, practices reinforced by the Catholic Church, and, increasingly, Evangelical Protestant Churches.

While Latin America includes many countries with a variety of institutional arrangements, political cultures, and developmental trajectories, some broad trends help to illuminate both progress and resistance for sexual and gender minorities. In many countries, presidents have a great deal of power and can drive the policy agenda. Related to strong executives, many nations have transitioned from military dictatorships to liberal democracies in recent decades. This transition, and the uncovering of human rights abuses, has led to a high level of rights consciousness and activist utilization of the new human rights framework. The perception that the Catholic Church was allied with totalitarian regimes, or did not do enough to oppose them, has led to a decline in the political clout of the Church, in addition to a more general secularization in some countries. The courts have been part of this increased attention to rights, despite strong norms and practices in the dominant civil law system stipulating that judges should only apply existing law to discrete cases but do not enjoy the freedom to set policy more broadly through their legal interpretations. However, some courts and judges have recently begun to challenge this deferential approach, and court decisions have played a significant role in expanding rights for sexual minorities in the region. For example, the Constitutional Court in Colombia has aggressively, and gradually, expanded recognition and protection of same-sex relationships, even mandating that the government legalize same-sex marriage, but the government has resisted. Courts also pushed a resistant political process toward the recognition of same-sex relationships in Brazil. In addition, while political parties on the right are still hostile to sexual minority rights, leftist parties have begun discarding their traditional homophobia and heterosexism reinforced by decades of Marxist skepticism of political agendas other than those that are class based. In other words, the left has been as hostile to LGBT right as the right in the past, but this is beginning to change. For example, Fidel Castro's regime was notoriously oppressive toward sexual minorities, but an LGBT rights movement is beginning to emerge in Cuba, in part through the advocacy of Raúl Castro's daughter, Mariela Castro. Public opinion on LGBT rights varies widely in Latin America, with lowest levels in the Caribbean and highest levels found in Argentina and Uruguay. Higher levels of education and economic development correlate with higher levels of support for LGBT rights in the region.[11]

The strength of LGBT social movements and organizations varies widely in Latin America. Countries such as Argentina, Chile, and Colombia have well-developed and sophisticated movements, while others, especially in more economically marginalized countries lack this crucial element for progress. As Shawn Schulenberg describes the situation in Panama, the problem "is the nascent and weak nature of the LGBT social movement organizations within Panama; with their lack of experience and very few resources at their disposal, they remain ill equipped to challenge the powerful heterosexism and homophobia in society required to change public opinion and gain access to elite allies within the government."[12]

There is also a different cultural context in Latin America than in the United States, Canada, or Europe. The creation of political identity surrounding sexuality is more constrained, as many young people live at home for a longer period of time (thus constraining an independent political identity) and same-sex sexuality is often expressed without a public, or political, identity as long as traditional gender roles are not openly challenged. Men who have sex with men, especially those who play an active role, are not always deemed to be gay or bisexual, nor do they self-identify as such. In short, there is not quite that same identity-based movement that exists in other countries, but this is gradually changing as the movement for sexual minority rights expands, and a more identity-based model is utilized by activists.[13]

The neighboring countries of Uruguay and Argentina were leaders in the recent wave of policies recognizing same-sex relationships. While activism had been building prior to 2005, Spain's legalization of same-sex marriage provided inspiration and a model for activists throughout Latin America. Indeed, the creation of civil unions in Mexico City was triggered by developments in Spain. Uruguay's 2007 civil union law was the first national law in the region and was facilitated by the election of a left-wing coalition of political parties in the national parliament. In 2013, this coalition included same-sex couples in the nation's marriage laws. Civil unions had been legalized at the subnational level in Argentina in 2002 and 2007, and a national same-sex marriage law was enacted in 2010. Activists had been divided over strategy—civil unions versus full marriage equality—but ultimately unified in favor of a marriage law. Test cases were also brought in the courts by couples applying for marriages licenses. Despite the fact that judges in Argentina are limited in their powers to set broad policy (their decisions only apply to the parties in that case and do not set a broader precedent), activists correctly calculated that the cases would place pressure on the political process. The law was also vigorously supported by President Cristina Fernández de Kirchner who referred to the opposition of Catholic Church as being grounded in the "times of the Crusades."

Also during this period (2008), civil unions were allowed under a new constitution in Ecuador, but the same document also declares that marriage is only between a man and a woman, at the request of the Catholic Church. Leftist president Rafael Correa was able to leverage his popularity to assist in the enactment of the civil union provision. Activists had also built strong connections with feminist and indigenous organizations and activists. These connections helped to add a provision outlawing discrimination on the basis of sexual orientation in the 1998 constitution.[14] After civil unions in 2006, same-sex marriage was legalized by leftist parties in Mexico City in 2010, and the Supreme Court declared that these marriages should be recognized by other states. Legal and political activism spread to a majority of states with courts as allies, but the process of making policy through the judiciary in Mexico's civil law can be slow. However a commentator has described this spread of activism and litigation as a "quiet marriage equality revolution."[15] An economic leader in South America, Chile has lagged behind other nations on policies protecting sexual minorities. The election of former Socialist president Michelle Bachelet in 2013 created an opening for change. Bachelet declared her support for same-sex marriage but worked to enact a civil union law supported by her predecessor. The law was enacted in 2015. Activists, however, were not content with this approach and initiated litigation with the Inter-American Court of Human Rights to force the government to recognize same-sex marriage. The strategy worked: Bachelet agreed to propose a same-sex marriage bill.

Transgender policy has not advanced as quickly in Latin America due to deeply embedded and rigid cultural norms about gender. Violence against transgender individuals is disproportionately high in Latin America, with Brazil and Mexico reflecting the highest number of murders in the world. Central and South America account for 79 percent of the reported killings of transgender persons worldwide from 2008 to 2014.[16] This likely stems from the gender traditionalism of the region combined with increased trans visibility and activism. Argentina has the most progressive transgender policy in the region. In 2012, a law was enacted allowing gender to be changed on official forms without proof of surgery or a judicial process. These more onerous processes are still required in Brazil, Bolivia, Chile, Colombia, Ecuador and Uruguay, countries where a document marker change is even possible. Argentina's law also mandates free hormone therapy and surgical treatment for transgender individuals who desire medical treatment, including minors.

AFRICA

The current situation for sexual and gender minorities is quite bleak, with the notable exception of South Africa. Several factors contribute to this state of affairs. First, there are few established democracies on the continent. Many countries are governed by authoritarian leaders. Consequently, civil society groups are weak and under attack, with authoritarian leaders using rhetorical and policy attacks on sexual and gender minorities as a tactic to maintain and increase power. These leaders have found allies in anti-LGBT activists in the West, especially the United States. In addition, sodomy laws are still in existence in most African nations—a legacy of colonial rule—with these laws first being imposed by European nations who controlled much of Africa well into the twentieth century. Part of colonialism also involved the exporting of Christianity to the continent, and contemporary African Christianity generally takes a highly traditional approach to sex and gender roles. This is also true of conservative versions of Islam that influence politics in northern and central Africa. A deep cultural bias against sexual and gender minorities is common throughout the continent, despite the fact that sexual diversity is a part of its history. As Olajide Akanji and Marc Epprecht state,

> The dominant trend in the historiography of homosexualities in Africa in the last two decades has been to show that homosexual acts are indigenous to Africa and were not necessarily regarded as problematic or scandalous in traditional cultures, but that views changed over time [to a more condemnatory stance]. . . . Meticulous as much of this scholarship is, it has not noticeably persuaded African leaders, who continue to trumpet an older, persistent, populist interpretation of history. In this interpretation, homosexual behaviour [sic] is "un-African," a foreign "disease" that was introduced to Africa by Arab slave traders, white settlers, or missionaries and is now spread principally by foreign tourists and sexual predators."[17]

In the near term, activists will be on the defensive in opposing negative policies stemming from the unfavorable cultural context while forming alliances with African and international organizations in an attempt to turn the tide. But this is likely a long-term project.

As of 2014, 37 countries criminalized same-sex intimacy, with three countries (Mauritania, Nigeria, and Sudan) imposing a potential penalty of death. Benin, Burkina Faso, Cape Verde, Congo, Chad, Cote D'Ivoire, Djibouti, Equatorial Guinea, Gabon, Guinea-Bissau, Madagascar, Mali, Niger, Republic of the Congo, Rwanda, Sao Tome & Principe, and South Africa are without specific prohibitions. A few countries outlaw employment discrimination based on sexual orientation: Botswana, Cape Verde, Mauritius, Mozambique, Seychelles, and South Africa.[18]

An example of a totalitarian leader using hostility toward sexual minorities as a tool to maintain and increase power is President Yahya Jammeh who seized power in a military coup in 1994. In 2008, he began a crusade against sexual minorities by declaring that he would behead them and gave them twenty-four hours to leave the country. While an international backlash caused him to backtrack a bit, he was not damaged politically within the country, and he reengaged the rhetorical and political attack in 2013 and 2014. There is no organized LGBT movement in the country.[19]

After a 2009 conference organized by American anti-LGBT Christian activists (including Scott Lively who blames gay men for the Holocaust), a Ugandan legislator, David Bahati, filed a bill in the Ugandan Parliament that applied the death penalty to sexual minorities and made it a crime to associate with, or advocate for, sexual minorities. Bahati has strong ties to a U.S. Evangelical Christian group, The Family. The organization sponsors the National Prayer Breakfast and has ties to totalitarian regimes in Africa.[20] Under intense international pressure, the penalty was reduced to life in prison. The bill became law after several years of consideration under the international pressure. The United States and other countries threatened to, or did, eliminate aid to Uganda. Activists turned to the courts for help, and the law was struck down on procedural grounds, but Bahati plans to resubmit the bill. Despite the international pressure, leaders like President Yoweri Museveni find tremendous appeal in scapegoating sexual minorities. Similar bills have proliferated to other countries in Africa.

South Africa's transition from an apartheid state to a multicultural democracy led to an exercise in constitution-building that was favorable for sexual minority rights. In fact, the 1996 constitution was the first constitution in the world to list sexual orientation as a category protected from discrimination. The Bill of Rights declares, "The state may not unfairly discriminate directly or indirectly against anyone on one or more grounds, including race, gender, sex, pregnancy, marital status, ethnic or social origin, colour, sexual orientation, age, disability, religion, conscience, belief, culture, language and birth."[21] (The document also prohibits such discrimination by individuals.) As Constitutional Court Justice Albie Sachs stated, "Our Constitution represents a radical rupture with a past based on intolerance and exclusion, and the movement forward to the acceptance of the need to develop a society based on equality and respect by all for all."[22] Using the new constitutional provision, the Constitutional Court invalidated the country's sodomy law in 1998. The courts, a forum thought by activists to be much more sympathetic to their claims than parliament, were receptive to arguments that the constitution required same-sex marriage. In 2005, the Constitutional Court mandated that parliament remedy the unequal treatment of same-sex couples. After some hesitancy from the governing African National Congress, the party enacted a same-sex marriage law. During the process, hearings were held throughout the country in which a great deal of heterosexism and homophobia were exhibited in citizen statements. However, in the end, this perspective was trumped by a positive constitutional framework and judges willing to expand constitutional protections for sexual minorities. In 2006, South Africa became the first country in Africa, and the fifth in the world, to legalize same-sex marriage.

THE MIDDLE EAST

Fundamentalist interpretations of Islam, prevalent totalitarian rule, and very weak LGBT social movements are some of the leading factors preventing the Middle East from seeing progress for sexual minorities. The significant exception to this state of affairs is liberal, democratic Israel. Same-sex intimacy potentially (in some cases only for men) brings the death penalty in Afghanistan, Iran, Qatar, Saudi Arabia, and Yemen. Significant prison sentences are possible in Kuwait, Gaza, Oman, Pakistan, Syria, and United Arab Emirates. There is no criminal penalty in Bahrain, Israel, Iraq, Jordan (and the West Bank), and Lebanon. Despite these bright spots on decriminalization, outside of Israel no other LGBT protective policies exist.

Outside of marriage equality, Israel has a strong set of policies protecting LGBT rights. It is also home to a large and open LGBT population, especially in the capital of Tel Aviv. A sodomy law that was a vestige of British rule was not enforced by the government after 1963 and was repealed in 1988. Four years later, an antidiscrimination law based on sexual orientation was enacted. Israel was also one of the earliest countries to allow openly LGB service members to serve in the military in 1993, and transgender individuals currently can serve under certain conditions. In 2015, the Supreme Court ruled that transgender individuals could change their legal gender designation without surgical intervention. While foreign same-sex marriages are recognized, religious authorities (Orthodox Jewish) control marriage within the country, and they are opposed. Israel recognized and gave some rights to same-sex cohabiting couples in 2004.

SOUTH AND EAST ASIA

Religious conservatism, gender traditionalism, weak grassroots movements, and political systems lacking a strong rights-based element, coupled with relatively weak judicial review, have made the rest of Asia difficult terrain for LGBT rights. Same-sex intimacy is still criminalized in many countries (Bangladesh, Bhutan, Brunei, Burma, India, Malaysia, Nepal, Singapore, Sri Lanka, Turkmenistan, and Uzbekistan). High courts in India (2013) and Singapore (2014) have upheld British rule–era sodomy laws on the grounds that only the nations' parliaments have the power to eliminate the laws. Even in advanced democracies such as Japan, South Korea, and Taiwan, there has been little policy progress. Same-sex relationships are not legally recognized in any country, as of 2014. However, movements are beginning to form and grow in the region, and significant progress could be seen in the coming years. Policy innovation on transgender rights has come from the region, however. A third gender category has been recognized in Bangladesh, India, Nepal, and Pakistan. This stems from South Asia's long history of a certain level of cultural acceptance for transgender individuals, or *hijras*. Despite the legal progress, tremendous stigma remains. Gender identity can be legally changed in several countries in the region, but typically only with surgical intervention. Taiwan lifted this requirement in 2014.

INTERNATIONAL ORGANIZATIONS AND MOVEMENTS

In addition to movements within nations, a global movement of activists and organizations is influencing policy for sexual and gender minorities. These activists often work through established international governing and legal institutions, such as the European Court of Human Rights and the Inter-American Court of Human Rights. A leading nongovernmental organization, or NGO, is the International Gay and Lesbian Human Rights Commission (IGLHRC). As Ryan Thoreson describes the organization,

> IGLHRC, founded in 1990 by an American activist in her mid-twenties, was among the first organizations devoted to transnational human rights work on behalf of gay and lesbian persons. By 2010, IGLHRC had grown considerably, with eighteen full-time staff in New York, Buenos Aires, Cape Town, and Manila, a budget of over $2 million, and influence extending from grassroots NGOs to the UN. Today, LGBT and same-sex practicing persons assert a visible presence in international agencies and the halls of the UN; regional mechanisms like the European Court of Human Rights, the Inter-American Court of Human Rights, and the African Commissions on Human and Peoples' Rights (ACHPR); and domestic human rights mechanisms and judiciaries on every continent.[23]

This international politics is limited by the lack of enforcement mechanisms of many international organizations and by a lack of consensus in international politics that LGBT rights are human rights. Critics also place this form of politics in the realm of Western, liberal, capitalist, universalizing globalization efforts that coercively attempt to change local cultural, political, and legal practices. Thus, the global expansion of LGBT rights is not immune from the larger debates about the wisdom and efficacy of globalization. Opponents of LGBT rights particularly frame their positions in antiglobalization terms.

In Europe a very strong network of activists and organizations exists, much of it the product of European integration efforts through the European Union. The nations that are most connected and integrated with this network have seen the most progress on LGBT rights.[24] As was discussed above, activists in Latin American have leveraged the power of the Inter-American Court of

Human Rights to further policy, largely because most Latin American countries recognize the organization's binding authority. In regions, such as Africa and Asia, where transnational institutions are not as powerful, their impact will be more advisory, but important nonetheless. In addition, after years of stalled progress (because of the antigay agenda of many power nations in the organization), the United Nations is beginning to more formally recognize LGBT rights. UN Secretary General Ban Ki-moon has emphasized the need to view LGBT rights as human rights. In 2015, an attempt by Russia to eliminate same-sex spousal benefits for UN employees was not successful. As political scientist Erik Voeten posits, "Russia is trying to reach out to potential allies who feel threatened by U.S. criticisms of their LGBT rights policies. Russian President Vladimir Putin and Ugandan President Yoweri Museveni have already bonded over this issue. . . . Russia seems to want to go a step beyond this by challenging more liberal ideas about human rights embedded in international institutions and perhaps positioning itself as a leader on this front."[25]

CONCLUSION

It would appear that for the next several decades, the uneven pattern of LGBT rights expansion will continue. Increased democratization will assist in the process, but leaders and activists in many nations will continue to be tempted by the ease of scapegoating sexual and gender minorities. This will be more difficult to do as the global LGBT rights movement develops, but this development will not be automatic. It will depend on the persistent efforts of organizations and activists and the expansion of the notion that the rights of sexual and gender minorities are indeed human rights, with appreciation for the unique path required in each country.

KEY TERMS AND CONCEPTS

Association/Circle of 1948
Authoritarianism and LGBT rights
Charter of Rights and Freedoms
    (Canada)
Civil law versus common law systems
Civil society
Cohabitation
Democratization and LGBT rights
Global efforts of U.S. anti-LGBT
    activists

"Homosexual propaganda" law
IGLHRC
Influence of leftist parties
International organizations/norms
NGO
Policy diffusion
Registered partnerships
Section 28
South African Constitution
Western cultural triumphalism

QUESTIONS FOR DISCUSSION

1. What factors facilitate/stall progress on sexual and gender minority rights in nations?
2. What is the role of international organizations in the global movement?
3. Will the global trend of regional variation continue in the coming years, or will there be more of a global convergence on LGBT rights?

NOTES

1. Omar G. Encarnación, "Gay Rights: Why Democracy Matters," *Journal of Democracy*, 25:3 (July 2014), 92.

2. See Michael L. Bosia and Meredith L. Weiss, "Political Homophobia in Comparative Perspective," in *Global Homophobia: States, Movements, and the Politics of Oppression*, Meredith L. Weiss and Michael L. Bosia, eds. (Urbana: University of Illinois Press, 2013), 1–29.

3. Martin D. DuPuis, "The Impact of Culture, Society, and History on the Legal Process: An Analysis of the Legal Status of Same-Sex Relationships in the United States and Denmark," *International Journal of Law and the Family*, 9 (1995), 86–118: 106; see also William N. Eskridge, Jr. and Darren Spedale, *Gay Marriage: For Better or Worse? What We've Learned from the Evidence* (New York: Oxford University Press, 2006) and Yuval Merin, *Equality for Same-Sex Couples: The Legal Recognition of Gay Partnerships in Europe and the United States* (Chicago: University of Chicago Press, 2002).

4. Robert Beachy, "The German Invention of Homosexuality," *The Journal of Modern History*, 82:4 (December 2010), 801–38: 807.

5. "The Export of Hate," The Human Rights Campaign, http://hrc-assets.s3-website-us-east-1.amazonaws.com//files/assets/resources/HRC_Export-of-Hate-final.pdf.

6. "Trans Rights Europe Map, 2014," Transgender Europe and ILGA Europe, http://www.tgeu.org/sites/default/files/Trans_Map_Index_2014.pdf; "Fact Sheet—Gender Identity Issues," European Court of Human Rights, March 2015, http://www.echr.coe.int/Documents/FS_Gender_identity_ENG.pdf.

7. The Charter of Rights and Freedoms, Section 15(1).

8. *Egan v. Canada*, [1995] 2 S.C.R. 513.

9. *Vriend v. Alberta*, [1998] 1 S.C.R. 493.

10. [1999] 2 S.C.R. 3.

11. See *Same-Sex Marriage in the Americas: Policy Innovation for Same-Sex Relationships*, Jason Pierceson, Adriana Piatti-Crocker, and Shawn Schulenberg, eds. (Lanham, MD: Lexington Books, 2010) and *Same-Sex Marriage in Latin America: Promise and Resistance*, Jason Pierceson, Adriana Piatti-Crocker, and Shawn Schulenberg, eds. (Lanham, MD: Lexington Books, 2013).

12. Shawn Schulenberg, "Same-Sex Partnership Rights in Central America: The Case of Panama," in *Same-Sex Marriage in Latin America: Promise and Resistance*, Jason Pierceson, Adriana Piatti-Crocker, and Shawn Schulenberg, eds. (Lanham, MD: Lexington Books, 2013), 73–74.

13. See Javier Corrales and Mario Pecheny, "The Comparative Politics of Sexuality in Latin America," in *The Politics of Sexuality in Latin America: A Reader on Lesbian, Gay, Bisexual, and Transgender Rights*, Javier Corrales and Mario Pecheny, eds. (Pittsburgh: University of Pittsburgh Press, 2010), 1–30.

14. Amy Lind, "Sexual Politics and Constitutional Reform in Ecuador: From Neoliberalism to the *Buen Vivir*," in *Global Homophobia: States, Movements, and the Politics of Oppression*, Meredith L. Weiss and Michael L. Bosia, eds. (Urbana: University of Illinois Press, 2013), 136–37.

15. J. Lester Feder, "Mexico's Quiet Marriage Equality Revolution," *BuzzFeed News*, February 26, 2015, http://www.buzzfeed.com/lesterfeder/mexicos-quiet-marriage-equality-revolution.

16. Press release, "Transgender Europe's Trans Murder Monitoring Project Reveals 226 Killings of Trans people in the Last 12 Months," Transgender Europe, October 30, 2014, http://www.transrespect-transphobia.org/uploads/downloads/2014/TDOR2014/TvT-TDOR2014PR-en.pdf.

17. Olajide Akanji and Marc Epprecht, "Human Rights Challenge in Africa: Sexual Minorities Rights and the African Charter on Human and Peoples' Rights," in *Sexual Diversity in Africa: Politics, Theory, and Citizenship*, S. N. Nyeck and Marc Epprecht, eds. (Montreal: McGill-Queen's University Press, 2013), 20.

18. Lucas Paoli Itaborahy and Jingshu Zhu, "State-Sponsored Homophobia," 9th ed. May 2014, International Lesbian Bay Bisexual Trans and Intersex Association.

19. Stella Nyanzi, "Rhetorical Analysis of President Jammeh's Threats to Behead Homosexual in the Gambia," in *Sexual Diversity in Africa: Politics, Theory, and Citizenship*, S. N. Nyeck and Marc Epprecht, eds. (Montreal: McGill-Queen's University Press, 2013), 67–87.

20. Jeff Sharlet, *The Family: The Secret Fundamentalism at the Heart of American Power* (New York: Harper, 2008).

21. Constitution of the Republic of South Africa, 1996, chapter 2, Section 9(3).

22. *Minister of Home Affairs and Another v. Fourie and Another*, [2005] ZACC 19, para. 59.

23. Ryan R. Thoreson, *Transnational LGBT Activism: Working for Sexual Rights Worldwide* (Minneapolis: University of Minnesota Press, 2014), 29.

24. Kelly Kollman, "European Institutions, Transnational Networks, and National Same-Sex Unions Policy: When Soft Law Hits Harder," *Contemporary Politics*, 15:1 (March 2009), 37–52.

25. Erik Voeten, "Why Russia Tried to Curb Same-Sex Partner Rights at the U.N. (And Why it Lost)," *Washington Post*, March 25, 2015, http://www.washingtonpost.com/blogs/monkey-cage/wp/2015/03/25/why-russia-tried-to-curb-same-sex-partner-rights-at-the-u-n-and-why-it-lost/.

BIBLIOGRAPHY AND FURTHER READING

Phillip Ayoub and David Paternotte, eds., *LGBT Activism and the Making of Europe: A Rainbow Europe?* (New York: Palgrave Macmillan, 2014).

Lynette J. Chua, *Mobilizing Gay Singapore: Rights and Resistance in an Authoritarian State* (Philadelphia: Temple University Press, 2014).

Marc Epprecht, *Sexuality and Social Justice in Africa: Rethinking Homophobia and Forging Resistance* (New York: Zed Books, 2013).

Marc Epprecht and S. N. Nyeck, *Sexual Diversity in Africa: Politics, Theory, Citizenship* (Montreal: McGill-Queen's University Press, 2013).

Jason Pierceson, Adriana Piatti-Crocker, and Shawn Schulenberg, eds., *Same-Sex Marriage in the Americas: Policy Innovation for Same-Sex Relationships* (Lanham, MD: Lexington Books, 2010).

———, *Same-Sex Marriage in Latin America: Promise and Resistance* (Lanham, MD: Lexington Books, 2013).

Ryan R. Thoreson, *Transnational LGBT Activism: Working for Sexual Rights Worldwide* (Minneapolis: University of Minnesota Press, 2014).

Meredith L. Weiss and Michael L. Bosia, eds., *Global Homophobia: States, Movements, and the Politics of Oppression* (Urbana: University of Illinois Press, 2013).

Index

About the Author

Jason Pierceson is associate professor of political science at the University of Illinois Springfield. His research interests include public law, political theory, and the politics of sexuality and gender. He is the author of *Courts, Liberalism, and Rights: Gay Law and Politics in the U.S. and Canada* and *Same-Sex Marriage in the United States: The Road to the Supreme Court and Beyond*. He is also the coeditor of *Moral Argument, Religion, and Same-Sex Marriage: Advancing the Public Good*; *Same-Sex Marriage in the Americas: Policy Innovation for Same-Sex Relationships*; and *Same-Sex Marriage in Latin America: Promise and Resistance*.